Metaphysics of Children's Literature

Bloomsbury Perspectives on Children's Literature

Bloomsbury Perspectives on Children's Literature seeks to expand the range and quality of research in children's literature through publishing innovative monographs by leading and rising scholars in the field. With an emphasis on cross and inter-disciplinary studies, this series takes literary approaches as a starting point, drawing on the particular capacity for children's literature to open out into other disciplines.

Series Editor:

Dr Lisa Sainsbury, Director of the National Centre for Research in Children's Literature, University of Roehampton, UK.

Editorial Board:

Professor M. O. Grenby (Newcastle University, UK), Dr Marah Gubar (Massachusetts Institute of Technology, USA), Dr Vanessa Joosen (University of Antwerp, Belgium).

Titles in the Series:

Adulthood in Children's Literature, Vanessa Joosen
The Courage to Imagine: The Child Hero in Children's Literature, Roni Natov
Ethics in British Children's Literature: Unexamined Life, Lisa Sainsbury
Fashioning Alice: The Career of Lewis Carroll's Icon, 1860–1901, Kiera Vaclavik
From Tongue to Text: A New Reading of Children's Poetry, Debbie Pullinger
Literature's Children: The Critical Child and the Art of Idealisation, Louise Joy
Rereading Childhood Books: A Poetics, Alison Waller

Forthcoming Titles:

Irish Children's Literature and the Poetics of Memory, Rebecca Long
Children's Literature and Material Culture, Jane Suzanne Carroll
Activist Authors and British Child Readers of Colour, Karen Sands-O'Connor
The Dark Matter of Children's "Fantastika" Literature, Chloé Germaine Buckley
British Children's Literature in Japanese Culture, Catherine Butler

Metaphysics of Children's Literature

Climbing Fuzzy Mountains

Lisa Sainsbury

BLOOMSBURY ACADEMIC
LONDON • NEW YORK • OXFORD • NEW DELHI • SYDNEY

BLOOMSBURY ACADEMIC
Bloomsbury Publishing Plc
50 Bedford Square, London, WC1B 3DP, UK
1385 Broadway, New York, NY 10018, USA
29 Earlsfort Terrace, Dublin 2, Ireland

BLOOMSBURY, BLOOMSBURY ACADEMIC and the Diana logo are
trademarks of Bloomsbury Publishing Plc

First published in Great Britain 2021
This paperback edition published in 2021

Copyright © Lisa Sainsbury, 2021

Lisa Sainsbury has asserted her right under the Copyright, Designs and
Patents Act, 1988, to be identified as Author of this work.

For legal purposes the Acknowledgements on p. x constitute an extension
of this copyright page.

Cover design: Eleanor Rose
Cover image © Lisa Sainsbury

All rights reserved. No part of this publication may be reproduced or
transmitted in any form or by any means, electronic or mechanical,
including photocopying, recording, or any information storage or retrieval
system, without prior permission in writing from the publishers.

Bloomsbury Publishing Plc does not have any control over, or responsibility for, any
third-party websites referred to or in this book. All internet addresses given in this
book were correct at the time of going to press. The author and publisher regret any
inconvenience caused if addresses have changed or sites have ceased to exist, but can
accept no responsibility for any such changes.

A catalogue record for this book is available from the British Library.

A catalog record for this book is available from the Library of Congress.

ISBN: HB: 978-1-3500-9368-3
PB: 978-1-3502-0473-7
ePDF: 978-1-3500-9369-0
eBook: 978-1-3500-9370-6

Series: Bloomsbury Perspectives on Children's Literature

Typeset by Newgen KnowledgeWorks Pvt. Ltd., Chennai, India

To find out more about our authors and books visit www.bloomsbury.com
and sign up for our newsletters.

For Chris

Well, here at last, dear friends, on the shores of the Sea comes the end of our fellowship in Middle-earth. Go in peace! I will not say: do not weep; for not all tears are an evil.

The Return of the King *(1955) by J. R. R. Tolkien*
The Lord of the Rings *(Tolkien [1968] 1994: 1007)*

Contents

List of Figures	ix
Acknowledgements	x

	Introduction: Climbing Fuzzy Mountains	1
	The astonishment of being	1
	Metaphysical groundwork	7
1	Ontological Exchange	15
	Like a ghost standing in front	15
	Childhood solitudes	20
	Of Clocks and skates	24
	Only the boots were different	36
	The last chandelier	43
2	Something Matters: Things about Nappies	55
	Foundational cataloguing	55
	Things round-about-us	65
	Other fancy stuff	73
	Gallery of false principles	83
3	Something Else Matters: Rhizomes and Animal Messes	93
	Birch tree reverie	93
	Immersed becomings: Heather is never only heather	99
	The butterfly effect	111
	Animal messes	117
4	Mapping the Nowhere	135
	Nowhere shut in	135
	Belonging not where	141
	Here-and-now	153
	Poles of inaccessibility	160
	Nowhere for miles and miles	175

5	Nothing Matters: Absent Imaginaries	187
	Ghosting	187
	Oscillating ontologies	200

Conclusion: Mountains of Metaphoric Refrain   213

Notes   217
References   231
Index   243

Figures

0.1	Fuzzy boundaries and the astonishment of being in the Lonely Mountains	6
1.1	Self–Other exchange	28
1.2	Self–Other exchange	28
2.1	Toys in wait	60
2.2	Thingness on the line	62
2.3	Emergent thingness	66
3.1	'Heather is never only heather'	100
3.2	Immersive snapdragon inhales a bumblebee in its puffed petals	105
3.3	A shoal swims through a fluid seascape of ontic immersion	106
3.4	Repetition of ferns breathes life into Fox's habitat	108
3.5	Horse immersed in the plant-life of grasses	110
3.6	Piggy's gaze through the window complicates the limits of existence	119
3.7	Raven refuses to be spoken for – Raven is Raven	123
4.1	A 'strange new creature' reflects Levinasian dwelling *with*-in	147
4.2	The thingness of objects is replete with nowhere	150
4.3	Ocean Chart from the 1876 edition of *The Hunting of the Snark*	166
4.4	The whereness of self-awareness	177
5.1	Ontological quandary	205

Acknowledgements

I did not attempt this journey alone – I am indebted to all those who have contributed to *Metaphysics* in various ways. I am grateful to the University of Roehampton for affording me a period of leave to complete the book, and in particular to staff of the Department of English and Creative Writing and the National Centre for Research in Children's Literature. A number of people have been helpful in granting permission to use material in the book, including Hannah Binymin, Jennie Brown, Neil Burden, Raegan Carmona, Lauri Hornik, Brigid Healy, Ron Hussey, Marva Jeremiah, Erja Lehtinen, Lily Malcom, Laura Milunic, Melissa Minty, Grace Nyaboko, Hanna Pajunen-Walsh, Anjelica Rush, Carrie Sharland, Mary Sullivan and Jessica Woollard. For their generosity and assistance with images and permissions, Marcy Campbell, Amy Griffiths, Corinna Luyken, Jackie Morris, Antoinette Portis and David Wiesner deserve special recognition.

    Many individuals have offered guidance, not least David Avital, Lucy Brown and the wonderful team at Bloomsbury who were committed to the project from its conception. Sincere thanks are due to those who shared in the evolution of *Metaphysics*, including Clémentine Beauvais, Matthew Grenby, Ian Haywood, Jeff Hilson, Nicki Humble, Peter Hunt, Jane Kingsley-Smith, Gillian Lathey, Clare McManus, Maria Nikolajeva, Laura Peters, Kim Reynolds, David Rudd and Mary Shannon. Thanks especially to Jane Carroll and Alison Waller for their invaluable counsel throughout. Heartfelt appreciation goes to my parents, family and friends for understanding – particularly when I could not be there. Millie Lamkin and Neal Richardson were tireless in their encouragement and reassurance – I could not have written this without them. Finally, I pay tribute to Noodles, my dear departed muse, who kept company with me.

Introduction: Climbing Fuzzy Mountains

By the afternoon they had climbed so high that they had reached the clouds, and the going was slippery and dangerous. Damp veils of mist swirled around them. They were dreadfully cold (Moomintroll thought longingly of his woolly trousers), and surrounded completely by an awful floating emptiness.

(Jansson [1946] 1967: 69)

The astonishment of being

When first Moomintroll and Sniff set out on a 'great expedition' (Jansson [1946] 1967: 37) to investigate 'strange goings on' (33) in their valley, they are not daunted by the prospect of climbing to the Observatory on the Lonely Mountains. In *Comet in Moominland* (1946) by Tove Jansson, the Muskrat philosopher – who knows that everything is unnecessary – sends the friends on a philosophical quest of sorts and they are excited to explore the 'Unknown', which stretches before them, 'wild and enticing' (39). Jansson's poetic landscape of childhood invests in the sort of 'cosmic gesture' that Gaston Bachelard locates in childhood in *The Poetics of Reverie* (1960), for the child who 'knows that the moon, that great blond bird, has its nest somewhere in the forest' (Bachelard [1960] 1971: 100). Such a cosmic gesture entails a formidable and unpredictable commitment though, and consequently, when Moomintroll and Sniff ascend into 'an awful floating emptiness', Sniff begins to feel sorry that he joined the expedition (Jansson [1946] 1967: 70). Attention to the crooked path travelled to the Lonely Mountains reveals the vagueness involved in relationships between language and our world;[1] the childly properties of this expedition and the (eventual) ascent it entails;[2] and the ontological potential of childhood reverie. In this excursion to the Lonely Mountains the metaphysical grounds of children's literature start to be exposed.

Childly anticipation of adventure tempers any anxiety that Moomintroll and Sniff might feel about dangers facing them in the Lonely Mountains and from which Moominmamma tries to protect them by stuffing rucksacks full of warm clothes (37). Moomintroll certainly expresses concern over the ominous signs prompting their journey, indulging in 'thoughtful' contemplation (27) and muttering: '"I don't like it. I don't like it at all"' (35). However, his disquiet is displaced – onto the adults around him, such as Moominmamma and the Muskrat – and deferred, so that 'Moomintroll was so excited he had almost lost his fear of the comet' (37). At this point, their expedition is imbued with *childhood potential*, which looks forward in anticipation to what might be. These anticipatory conditions are reminiscent of Bachelard's investment in flight and freedom and the 'potential childhood' configured (throughout life) in images of childhood reverie ([1960] 1971: 101). The images Bachelard has in mind draw on memories of childhood and yet the openness to reverie is instilled during childhood experience – thus, childhood itself is a site of reverie for Bachelard, so that adults *and* children are open to memories and dreams:

> Our memories bring us back to a simple river which reflects a sky leaning upon hills. But the hill gets bigger and the loop of the river broadens. The little becomes big. The world of childhood reverie is as big, bigger than the world offered to today's reverie.
>
> (102)

The oneiric wonder of childhood expressed in terms of rising through landscapes is manifest in Moomintroll's excited anticipation and embedded in the journey itself, which follows a similar pattern to the loops and undulations evoked by Bachelard. Jansson's expedition begins on a river, moving down waterfalls and ravines before climbing to the highest peak in the Lonely Mountains. This fluctuating pattern of ascent is also deployed by Peter Hollindale as a figurative challenge to models of childhood that assume 'a mental picture of childhood as a gradual, steady climb towards a plateau of achieved maturity' (Hollindale 1997: 37). Hollindale suggests that a more 'irregular journeying' is involved for child and adult, whereby the adult 'climb[s] back the way [they] came' or the child slides 'back down bits of scree' and that this irregularity finds expression in children's literature (38). Bachelard's appraisal of the adult's ability to 'return to the lair of reveries' ([1960] 1971: 102) is also articulated via Hollindale's concept of 'childness', although Hollindale insists on the *presentness* of the child in the exchange he traces between child and adult. Rather than considering this as a temporally static component of childness, it is helpful to consider presentness in

Heideggerian terms of *Da-sein*. Hollindale identifies childness as a distinguishing property of a text in children's literature (1997: 49), a property contingent on the child's presence, Da-sein (being-there), in order that the dynamic conditions of children's literature are satisfied. While childness elucidates the exchange between adult and child in children's books, the temporal conditions of this exchange are also crucial and Clémentine Beauvais's concept of *might* exposes the future-facing nature of childhood experience. In *The Mighty Child* (2015) Beauvais explores the power relations between the child and adult respectively in terms of might and authority: 'To be mighty is to have more time left, to be authoritative is to have more time past' (Beauvais 2015: 19). When the Muskrat is introduced as 'a wise man who knows about everything' (Jansson [1946] 1967: 26), he is established in Beauvais's position of authority gained through past experience, in contrast to Moomintroll's mighty potential to discover and achieve something important in the Lonely Mountains. Evidently then, the anticipatory pleasure articulated by Moomintroll and Sniff invests in the flight of childhood reverie and the power invested in the mighty child, while also invoking the irregular dynamism of childness.

Irregular dynamism might well describe the expedition to the Lonely Mountains as it evolves. After an early encounter with crocodiles, to which Moomintroll loses his protective woolly trousers, the prospect of the mountains grows more daunting: 'Day after day the world was shrouded in greyness' (Jansson [1946] 1967: 42), and 'in the distance greyish-yellow mountains climbed steeply towards the sky' (43). The Lonely Mountains take shape as a looming backdrop to their journey and, when the blue-and-purple range comes nearer, 'they were so high that sometimes their tops disappeared in the heavy rolling clouds' (52). Attempts to reach the mountains in a straightforward way are frustrated, as the raft heads down a waterfall and they 'seem to be going right down into the earth, instead of up to the top of the mountains' (57). Along the way, Moomintroll and Sniff meet Snufkin, an itinerant artist who accompanies them, and the Hemulen who rescues them from a subterranean tunnel inside the mountain. However, when they reach the vicinity of the Lonely Mountains, nobody is quite certain that they have actually arrived:

'Are we in the Lonely Mountains now?' asked Sniff.
'I've no idea', said the Hemulen, 'but there are plenty of interesting moths'.
'I think it *must* be the Lonely Mountains', said Snufkin, gazing at the
massive piles of rock, endless, desolate and silent, which towered on
every side. The air was chilly.

(60)

Although Snufkin claims a degree of expertise here, he cannot be certain that this is indeed the Lonely Mountains. As the 'irregular journey' towards the mountains has confirmed, the range shifts in scale according to proximity and their tops are often obscured. The massive rock piles of which the summits are made up also makes them difficult to identify – and of course this is a problem for any explorer intent on a particular objective. If a given destination comprises vague properties, how might it be identified?[3] This is the point at which Moomintroll and Sniff are confronted with the world in all its complexity – not in terms of its dangers, so much as its daunting mystery. The towering, endless rocks surrounding them in 'desolate silence' convey the overwhelming enormity of the world in which they exist. Indeed, much of the language accompanying their expedition exacerbates this sense of something murky and increasingly strange in the world about them; fog swirls in chasms and valleys and the 'dreaming heads' of the 'age-old mountains' are 'lost in mist' (63). The friends also encounter a black hole at the centre of the mountains, from which they narrowly escape in the Hemulen's butterfly net – and this can be considered something of an ontological hole. Jansson does not pause to explain what these geological entities are and the mysterious threat of their presence throws up unanswered questions, so it is not surprising that Moomintroll and his friends now feel apprehensive. Potentially, they have encountered a fuzzy mountain and the metaphysical propositions that account for it. Fuzzy mountains are difficult to deal with due to their inherent vagueness and, as will become clear, they have a specific relevance to Moomintroll's expedition and to children's literature more broadly.

Achille Varzi considers that 'Vagueness is a pervasive phenomenon of human thought and language and, plainly, the world of geography is not exempted from its grasp' (Varzi 2001: 9). This vagueness comes about because, for instance, there 'is no precise lower bound to the height of a mountain, hence no criterion demarcating the lowest mountain from the tallest hill' (9). Given that some philosophers consider this vagueness to be 'truly ontological', 'To say that there are no definite boundaries demarcating Mount Everest (for example) would then amount to treating Everest as a fuzzy object' (10). Varzi is dealing here with what Tim Crane and Katalin Farkas describe as *borderline* cases, whereby the identity of entities is difficult to establish – and hence Snufkin cannot be certain that they are in the Lonely Mountains. The analogy Crane and Farkas use to explain vagueness is particularly relevant in the context of childhood discourse: 'We cannot ... say exactly when someone ceases to be young. ... Vague predicates like "young", whose applicability turns on small changes, which do not make a difference in themselves, but gradually add up to a change that does', amount to borderline cases, whereby individuation cannot be clearly established (Crane and Farkas 2004: 147). It is precisely due to the challenges involved in establishing what we might mean by a literature for the young that concepts such as childness and might are so important for interrogating children's literature. Philosophers have taken various routes to deal with fuzzy objects, and a debate involving Willard Van Orman Quine, Gareth Evans and David Lewis proves useful for unpacking the looming metaphysical hole in *Comet in Moominland*.

Quine counters arguments for ontological fuzziness (in mountains or young people) on the grounds of the individuation of objects in space and time – although Crane and Farkas suggest that the logical conclusion of his enquiry would be to suggest that mountains and young people are not actually physical entities (147). Evans and Lewis then make a related step, which does not involve such ontologically drastic findings. They challenge the idea that 'the world itself might *be* vague' (Evans [1978] 2004: 209), contending that the world is full of determinate things. The things themselves cannot be vague, because 'whatever is in the world, the physical objects, is determinate. It is vague, however, *which of these determinate objects* is denoted by our words ... So vagueness is not a feature of the world, but a feature of the relation between language and the world' (Crane and Farkas 2004: 148). These knotty ontological debates around the identification of objects have fascinated and frustrated philosophers for decades. Moreover, these arguments rely on the sort of ambiguities in language – and its relationship to the experiential world – that poetic literature takes advantage of in order to grapple with ontological conundrums such as this.

Returning to Moomintroll's passage into vagueness on the Lonely Mountains, it is clear that linguistic expression – via adjectives, adverbs or figurative allusion – incrementally configures a sense of ontological wonder around entities in the world. Jansson's illustrations take this sense of wonder even further, as she unfolds the physical and atmospheric presence of the Lonely Mountains through a layering of images that move towards and around them (Figure 0.1).[4] The purpose of this poetic and visual language in *Comet in Moonland* is not to find a solution to philosophical problems – in the manner attempted by Quine and company – but to identify and engage with such conundrums through the conditions of children's literature. Moomintroll's expedition opens him to the profundity of being in the world; hence, when they reach the mountains in the clouds the party is beset by 'an awful floating emptiness' (Jansson [1946] 1967: 69). This is the sort of metaphoric woolliness – even in the absence of woolly trousers – that has divided philosophers in the twentieth century, but

Figure 0.1 Fuzzy boundaries and the astonishment of being in the Lonely Mountains (Jansson [1946] 1967: 64).

of course metaphor is a rich metaphysical resource for the poet.[5] This is the moment at which I leave Moomintroll on his lonely summit and move back to Bachelard whose poetics seeks to identify this sort of childly engagement with the world: 'There are moments in childhood when every child is the astonishing being, the being who realizes the *astonishment of being*' (Bachelard [1960] 1971: 116). Bachelard's project is to present 'an ontological philosophy of childhood which underlines the durable character of childhood' (20), and as part of this project he identifies the childly aspect of the *astonishment of being*. Bachelard explores poetry *of* childhood as part of his project, but children's books such as *Comet in Moominland* fall outside of his domain of enquiry. As this journey into Jansson's Lonely Mountains suggests though, children's books have an important contribution to make to an ontological philosophy of childhood through their metaphysical groundwork and an engagement with childness in the astonishment of being.

Metaphysical groundwork

In the irregular pathway I have traced between philosophies of ontological vagueness, *The Poetics of Reverie*, *Signs of Childness*, *The Mighty Child* and *Comet in Moominland* can be found to be underpinnings of *Metaphysics of Children's Literature*, in which I identify metaphysical structures of children's literature. I establish various ways in which children's books respond to some of the ultimate questions of reality in a manner that is unique to children's literature. Identification of these metaphysical structures allows for a deeper understanding of the conditions of children's literature, which provide young readers with a sense of the nature of reality and what it means to be in the world. The metaphysical structures explored in each chapter can be seen to shape children's literature at the level of form and convention; essentially, these structures lay down a metaphysical groundwork in children's books. *Metaphysics of Children's Literature* does not identify metaphysical children's literature as a quasi-genre, rather I am concerned with the metaphysical implications of children's literature at large. This means that books, which might be considered philosophical in terms of subject and approach – Antoine De Saint-Exupéry's *The Little Prince* (1943), Jostein Gaarder's *Sophie's World* (1991) or *Where Were You, Robert?* by Hans Magnus Enzensberger (1998) – are not a necessary concern of *Metaphysics*, though a number of these works weave into my discursive framework.

The corpus of *Metaphysics of Children's Literature* is built from an international field of picturebooks, novels, short stories and poetry, drawing on texts for children written in English (or translated into English), from 1945 to the present. The focus on Western literature not only reflects by own area of specialist knowledge but also acknowledges links between a regional literature and a Western philosophical tradition. This period of sociopolitical upheaval is especially fruitful for my investigation, since increasingly it gives rise to children's books shaped through an evolving metaphysical groundwork. The First and Second World Wars were catalysts for an interrogation of ideas that had shaped earlier children's literature and this is evident in a range of books for children from *The Borrowers* by Mary Norton (1952), to Jacqueline Woodson's *brown girl dreaming* (2014). While the primary focus is on children's literature post-1945, discussion is placed in the context of earlier cultural and philosophical developments where relevant. For example, I could not discuss the metaphysical conditions of nowhere in Chapter 4 without recourse to the early progress of utopian children's literature in the eighteenth century.

Metaphysics of Children's Literature has much to reveal about the workings of children's literature and contributes to a recent critical push towards theorizing children's literature on its own terms. Negotiating the conditions of power in books for young people has been key to recent developments in critical discourse, as demonstrated in *The Hidden Adult* (2008) by Perry Nodelman; *Power, Voice and Subjectivity in Literature for Young Readers* (2010) by Maria Nikolajeva; and *The Mighty Child* by Beauvais. In *Metaphysics of Children's Literature* I take further steps in this process, for example, identifying the play of power in ontological tensions thrown up between self and other in books for young people. The *ontological exchange* (introduced in Chapter 1) is an ontic structure that brings the child out of Bachelard's childhood solitude and into a moment of ontic rupture. During this exchange, being is negotiated (in part) at the level of power relations. Consequently, Nikolajeva's concept of *aetonormativity* and Beauvais's notion of the *mighty child* are crucial to the development of my own thinking, and these terms are employed throughout. Beauvais's mighty child is already drawn into my discussion of *Comet in Moominland*, but the conditions of Nikolajeva's *aetonormativity* also apply. Nikolajeva proposes the concept as an expression of the 'adult normativity that governs the way children's literature has been patterned' (2010: 8) and this aetonormativity is manifest in the pre-conditions of Moomintroll's journey to the Lonely Mountains. A network of adult voices – including Moominmamma and the Muskrat – prepare the way for the children's ontic encounters (even if the children can be seen to challenge the normative position through their mighty engagement with fuzzy mountains) and thus aetonormativity is the starting point from which the adventure proceeds.

I approach metaphysics as the area of philosophy that deals with general questions about the nature of reality (or the world); what sorts of things exist; what things in reality are like; or what it means to be a human or a non-human entity. Recognizing developments in a modern philosophical landscape, I distinguish metaphysics from epistemological concerns, which deal with general questions of knowledge. In this sense, I am not working from Aristotelian first principles, which bring together questions of being, causation and knowledge. Having said this, there is no doubt that questions of being overlap with questions of knowledge (as will become increasingly clear). When considering the relationship between appearance and reality, Crane and Farkas make a useful distinction, which helps to establish the sort of nuances involved in philosophical discussion:

> Our concern in metaphysics is with how things are, rather than with how we know them. However, the possibility of effecting a strict separation between these two questions is not an easy matter. For our access to the world, to how things are, is through the way it appears to us. And therefore we can ask the question of whether there is anything *beyond* appearances; whether the world is in fact independent of the way it appears to us. This is a genuine metaphysical question.
>
> (Crane and Farkas 2004: 61)

In children's literature studies it can be difficult to escape the question of knowledge, or of how knowledge is passed on to children through literature, so I have been mindful of the distinction made here – between how things are and how we know about them – in my exploration of the metaphysical groundwork in children's literature. Of course these boundaries can be crossed – and as Crane and Farkas point out, it is inevitable that they will be – but it is important that an awareness of distinctions remains in place.

The issue of whether there is anything beyond appearance is central to 'birch tree poem' in Woodson's *brown girl dreaming*, a poem that is also concerned with how we know things.[6] Indeed, its concerns and figurative images link the poem to questions at play in *Sophie's World*:

> There were birch trees – *bjørketreer* – all around the large garden, sheltering it partly, at least, from the worst squalls. It was because of those trees that the house had been renamed Bjerkely over a hundred years ago.
>
> (Gaarder [1991] 1996: 239)

Jostein Gaarder has fun here with an extended pun over two chapters – 'Berkeley' and 'Bjerkely' (234–50) – that overlays discussion of Bishop George Berkeley's subjective idealism (an extreme form of empiricism) with the revelation that Sophie, the book's focal character until this point, might only exist in the mind of an author writing about her. In *Three Dialogues* (1713) Berkeley pushes to extreme conclusions John Locke's notion of *secondary qualities* – which inhere in the mind rather than external entities – and calls into question material reality to the extent that 'We only exist in the mind of God' (Gaarder [1991] 1996: 236). The theological dimension to his metaphysics notwithstanding, from Berkley's perspective there can be no tree in Jacqueline's classroom: 'The idea or thing which you immediately perceive, neither sense nor reason inform you that it actually exists without the mind' (Berkeley 2004: 95). According to Berkeley, the house and garden in which Hilde Møller Knag reads about Sophie – and the trees after which her own home is named – no more exist than the ice storms conjured by Jacqueline's imagination after her sighting of a picture of a birch tree. Unsurprisingly, Sophie finds this position difficult to accept and it is not the conclusion reached in Woodson's poem either. For Sophie and Jacqueline, the presence of birch trees hangs on the modality of *might*. Indeed, a fictional realist would contend that if an entity can be conceived as possible – and we can say that it might exist – then it comes into being as a fictional object and has ontological status as a result.[7] Once again knowing and being is interlinked, as the possibility of knowing something can bring it into being.

I rehearse all this in order to demonstrate the importance of metaphysical questions underlying the acquisition of knowledge. Moreover, I want to point out the confluence of figurative language and inference between Woodson's verse novel and Gaarder's philosophical mystery as they draw out the being of birch trees. There is a sort of metaphysical/metaphorical transfer here, which allows for ideas to develop across literary genres and hints that such concerns can be tracked across a range of children's literature (and I am suggesting something more than an intertextual relationship, though it also works on this level). In his *Dictionary of English Etymology* (1966), C. T. Onions points to an etymological convergence between 'metaphysics' and 'metaphor', whereby misinterpretation in the etymological chain of development has shifted the meaning of both words. Reflecting on the infamous misappropriation of *metá* in Aristotle's *Metaphysics*, Onions observes that although the Greek *metá* 'does not normally imply "beyond" or "transcending" it came to be so interpreted in this word probably on the model of such a correspondence as *metaphor* and *transfer*'

(Onions 1966: 572–3). Onions is not suggesting that metaphor and metaphysics mean the same thing as a result of this common process of correspondence, but a relationship is implied in this etymological development. After all, metaphor and metaphysics share a root that has since yielded shoots and these shoots are related as they push from *metá* (Greek) to *trans* (Latin). There is complicity in metaphysical *transcendence* and metaphoric *transfer* and this etymological resemblance seems crucial in understanding the role of metaphoric transference in unfolding metaphysical questions – and certainly as they play out in works of art. These etymological roots are symptomatic of something more widespread in developments across philosophy and the arts. It seems to me that Bachelard is getting at this sort of correspondence in *The Poetics of Reverie*, when he argues that metaphysicians ignore poetry at a cost. In *The Sovereignty of Good* (1970) Iris Murdoch also confirms the crucial philosophical role played by figurative language, arguing that metaphors are 'fundamental forms of our awareness of our condition' (Murdoch [1970] 2001: 75). Moreover, the correspondences of metaphor and metaphysics in *Sophie's World* and *brown girl dreaming* draw on states of childness and mighty potential, which send out shoots across the field of children's literature.

Metaphysics of Children's Literature is essentially a book about something and nothing in children's books and its chapters are arranged around metaphysical structures I have identified in children's literature. These structures are not exhaustive, but they provide irrefutable evidence of the metaphysical remit and consequence of children's literature. These metaphysical structures allow for the interrogation of being and non-being with reference to the general conditions of reality through a process of metaphorical transference (into metaphysical transcendence). Chapter 1 introduces my concept of *ontological exchange*, which I establish as a fundamental metaphysical structure of children's literature. It reveals itself in a range of different ways across the field, but principally it can be described as an ontic encounter between self and other, whereby being is tested and made aware of its status as being. I determine a working model of ontological exchange through extended readings of two children's novels, before focussing on the mechanisms of exchange in a wider range of texts in my corpus. Chapter 1 focuses on what it means to be human, yet my discussion of ontological exchange anticipates the shift in subsequent chapters to consider: material objects; non-human being; the conditions of nowhere; and the importance of nothing in children's literature. Chapter 2 shifts attention from what it means to be human to a concern with the ontological properties of material objects in the world. I argue that baby books have an ontic function that is rarely recognized in childhood (and related literary) studies, which tend to focus on the developmental or epistemological conditions of this formative literature. I reveal that baby books provide a foundational context for ontological projects, which seek to explain the conditions of reality in relation to material objects and more abstract propositions. My findings in relation to the ontic remit of baby books allow me to probe the ontological conditions of things in the wider field of children's literature in the final section of this chapter, considering the role of artefacts and objects in museum and historical fiction.

Chapter 3 makes a move away from the thingness of material objects in order to uncover a system of metaphysical connectivity and becoming manifest in the flora and fauna of children's literature. My initial focus is on plants in children's books and the immersive presence of biological organisms that could exist in the external world (i.e. I do not include the talking trees or plants of fantasy worlds in this chapter). In the closing stages of this chapter I suggest that children's literature is able to respond to 'messes' made by animals (and other non-humans) in metaphysical systems that do not allow for them. Aspects of post-human entanglement relevant to the immersive metaphysics outlined in this chapter are also considered. Chapter 4 locates *nowhere* as a multifaceted ontic structure, entrenched in the conditions of children's literature. I distinguish nowhere as an entity of ontological significance in its own right, while also revealing ways that nowhere attests to the conditions of being human. Charting the regions of nowhere confirms the multiplicity of its manifestation in books for young readers and identifying its ontic breadth and depth requires historical underpinning throughout; the chronological boundaries of this chapter are fluid as a result. I demonstrate that the utopian shoots of nowhere are rhizomorphic in their reach, which I investigate in relation to: the fabular renditions of belonging and displacement; local political conditions of the here and now; and *nowhere in extremis* at *poles of inaccessibility*. In the closing section of this chapter, I move on to expose the *awareness of whereness* involved in mapping the mundanity of nowhere in children's books. Chapter 5 uncovers nothingness in the metaphysical groundwork of children's literature through the lens of two pervasive tropes: absent parents and imaginary friends. I reveal that conventional properties of children's books reach beyond genre, indicating a metaphysical commitment to nothing as an ontic structure of human experience. Absent parents frequently throw up a palpable absence with ontic value for the becoming-child and I draw on a variant range of parental absence to explore the metaphysical implications of this omnipresent void. Imaginary friendships have a particular psycho-emotional function in children's books, yet they also point to an ongoing concern with the ontological status of fictional objects and *qualia* in children's literature. Through an exploration of imaginary beings in prose and picturebook form, I disclose the metaphysical impact of the non-existent on human experiences of the external world.

1

Ontological Exchange

No on[e] can stay in himself; the humanity of man, subjectivity, is a responsibility for others, an extreme vulnerability. The return to self becomes interminable detour. Prior to consciousness and choice, before the creature collects himself in present and representation to make himself essence, man approaches man.

(Levinas [1972] 2006: 67)

She wasn't alone. The Tough Tom was crowded. All about her in that small place under the hill that led nowhere were footprints. They were the footprints of people, bare and shod. There were boots and shoes and clogs, heels, toes, shallow ones and deep ones, clear and sharp as if made altogether, trampling each other, hundreds pressed in the clay where only a dozen could stand. Mary was in a crowd that could never have been, thronging, as real as she was. Her feet made prints no fresher than theirs.

(Garner 1976: 52–3)

Like a ghost standing in front

Like silk on Mary's bobbin running through a fracture in the Engine Vein on Alderley Edge, an ontological thread wends its way through the veins of children's literature, linking a series of fractures that allow access to those still small enough 'to get past the fall' (Garner 1976: 56). These fractures demonstrate that it is testing to be human and they offer an enlightening point of entry into my exploration of the metaphysical regions of children's literature. In *The Stone Book* (1976)[1] by Alan Garner, Mary discovers a host of phantom footprints waiting for her at the end of 'the crack in the hill' (46) and they 'put a quietness on' her (54). In terms set out by Emmanuel Levinas in *Humanism of the Other* ([1972] 2006) Mary has discovered that 'no one can stay inside [her]self'. Her father made the same discovery, "'When I was about your size'" (56), for it is an experience shared and passed on from one generation to the next. In this moment of silent exchange Mary has communed with others by touching her hand to ancient rock and, as her father observes, '"once you've seen it, you're changed for the rest of your days"' (56). This is just one example of fracturing brought about by *ontological exchange*, which operates as a core metaphysical structure of children's literature. Ontological exchange manifests variously across the field (as I go on to demonstrate), but essentially it is an ontic meeting of self and other during which being is tested and made aware of its status as being.

Mary's ontological exchange in *The Stone Book* entails a rite of passage, involving entry to the Engine Vein – a seam in the rocks opened by mining excavation. Mary has entered the vein at her father's behest and when she reaches the walls of the 'Tough Tom', she feels a connection with ancestral spirits. Beside her father's mason mark and the image of a bull, she finds 'a white dimension hand' to which she lifts her own and finds that 'Both hands were the same size ... The hands fitted. Fingers and thumb and palm and a bull and Father's mark in the darkness under ground' (52). Touching her hand to an other hand produces a spectre of being – an oscillation of Sartrean being and non-being – which reveals to Mary her place in generations of other beings past and yet to be. Recognizing that the Engine Vein might be 'shovelled up' in years to come, Mary's father confirms the importance of exchange between past, present and future, adult and child, one being and an other: 'you'll have to tell your lad, even if you can't show him' (57). In her own moment of exchange in the Tough Tom, Mary is confronted with her existence relative to others who have passed through that place and she enters into a reflective period of contemplation – of 'quietness', as her father puts it. Mary experiences herself in relation to the dimension stone that only she could touch in this moment – only she could be there at this time – and her encounter in the Tough Tom allows her to accept from her father a stone book 'that had in it all the stories of the world and the flowers of the flood' (61).

Mary's experience is an expression of Heideggarian Da-sein (being there), yet childness also inheres in her ontological exchange, for it involves forward movement of being, reaching beyond generations that have visited previously. The childness of Mary's encounter allows adult and child to *exchange* experience of what it means to be – and for Mary this means moving into her future, having been (and being) inside the Engine Vein. Hollindale identifies exchange as a 'key word' in the development of his argument for childness and by bringing it into service I draw in childness to the remit of ontological exchange. Hollindale's notion of exchange also helps to demonstrate the dynamic and (at least) two-way nature of these ontological phenomena in children's books. However, this is not to say that the ontological exchange is always an affirmation of being. Woodson's verse-narrative memoir of coming into being, *brown girl dreaming* (2014), renders figuratively the widespread function of ontological exchange in children's literature, whereby being asserts or defends itself, against a threat from the other.

In common with *The Stone Book*, *brown girl dreaming* raises apparitions of the past through the mechanism of ontological exchange. In the single-stanza poem 'ghosts', the narrating persona (Jacqueline) is refused – 'still keeping you out' – by a phantom arising from the force of the other's prohibitive directives:

> In downtown Greenville,
> they painted over the WHITE ONLY signs,
> except on the bathroom doors,
> they didn't use a lot of paint
> so you can still see the words, right there
> like a ghost standing in front
> still keeping you out.
> (Woodson 2014: 92)

The persona is rendered spectral by association with the other, since effectively Jacqueline is erased by the ghostly words that deny her – they are still keeping her out. This particular self–other exchange emerges from a sociopolitical moment in the early days of the American civil rights movement[2] and deployment of second person renders the impact of segregation grammatically. A doubling of signification both distances the narrator from herself – where 'you' signifies 'me', yet is not me – and acknowledges the shared experience of a town (and country) haunted by prejudice that undermines selfhood – where 'you' signifies 'us' (on a sociopolitical level). Indeed, the young Jacqueline is implicated in a sort of metaphorical transfer or exchange between self and other as ghostly words rise up to deny her.[3] In his discussion of metaphor, signification and sense making, Levinas observes: 'There would seem to be a distinction between the reality given to receptivity and the signification it can acquire' ([1972] 2006: 9). Jacqueline's reception of the whitewashed words is caught *real-ly* in this moment, yet even before this instance of crisis it had acquired layers of meaning, which proliferate as signification grows in the direction of ontological conviction. Earlier on in 'the ghosts of the Nelsonville house', the Woodsons are introduced as 'one of the few Black families in this town', where if you 'Look closely. There I am / in the furrow of Jack's brow ... Beginning' (Woodson 2014: 10–12). Jacqueline's *being* is pronounced in her *beginning*, feeding into signification as she heads periodically into and out of ontological rupture.

The process of exchange is thus played out in what Levinas terms the '*beyond of the metaphor*' ([1972] 2006: 9). While relevant to this particular occurrence of crisis, the notion of exchange encompasses all moments of rupture identified in my corpus, since it captures the transfer of signification involved in the interchange between being and other. *The Stone Book* and *brown girl dreaming* speak generally and deeply to the experience of being human as expressed recurrently in contemporary books for children. Ghosts such as theirs emerge from the earliest pages of children's literature and here they stand in the twentieth and twenty-first centuries, ready to begin.[4] As *brown girl dreaming* confirms, metaphysical ghosts are not always the stuff of fantasy or fantastic realism and nor does the ontological exchange necessarily involve ghosts and apparitions (metaphoric or literal). Ontological exchange can take place between human children of a similar age, between adults and children or between entities of separate ontological categories, such as animals and children – though of course anthropomorphized animals typically stand in for human beings during the exchange.[5]

The Owl Who Was Afraid of the Dark (1968) by Jill Tomlinson is a book for younger readers, which throws up an accusatory and reciprocal ontological exchange across the human–animal divide. Tomlinson's chapter book is full of ontic phrasing, such as this from Mrs Barn Owl – 'You *are* what you *are*' (7) – who insists that her son's identity is contingent on *being in the dark*. The ideological agenda of conformity and assimilation at work throughout is elided by anthropomorphic sleight of hand. This agenda is supported by an ontic surface grammar, which reveals that the emphasis on *what it means to be* is politically and ontologically driven and demonstrates (if proof were needed) that metaphysical systems are not shaped in a sociocultural vacuum. The ontic remit of the book is underscored by an ontological exchange, wherein a little girl mistakes Plop (the young Barn Owl) for a 'woolly ball' ([1968] 1992: 45). After several countermoves in their exchange the girl declares that Plop cannot 'be a proper owl' and he responds that she 'can't be a proper girl' (45-6) – and properness indicates that being is contingent on relative values. Such arguments characterize a chapter book in which Plop discovers what it means to *be* an owl (human) in the world and the ontological exchange pivots on 'concrete relations with others' in Sartrean terms: 'The Other *looks* at me and as such he holds the secret of my being, he knows what I *am*' ([1943] 2003: 385). Jean-Paul Sartre identifies looking as a key agent in the process of exchange he describes in *Being and Nothingness* (1943), an action that is central to many of the ontic interactions at work in children's literature.

As might be becoming clear, examples of ontological exchange can be found in literature from different periods or cultures and in books for readers of various ages. Accordingly, *Tow-Truck Pluck* (1971) by Annie M. G. Schmidt and Fiep Westendorp or Woodson's *Each Kindness* (2012) implies a junior audience, while *The Cuckoo Sister* (1985) by Vivien Alcock or M. T. Anderson's *The Astonishing Life of Octavian Nothing* (2006) implies an adolescent readership. The tenor and structure of ontological exchange differ from one text to another, but a pattern of commonality allows them to be identified as part of a metaphysical structure central to children's literature. What each exchange has in common – and this is the stuff of Mary's ontological thread in *The Stone Book* – is the persistence of the self's drive to *be* as much as (or even more than) anyone else. Ontological discourse is animated by the question of being in relation to others and philosophers find diverse solutions as to how (or if) the self comes to *be in full possession of being*. For example, tensions in the existentialism of Sartre and the humanism of Levinas are fruitful in drawing out the operations of ontological exchange in books for children. It seems inevitable then that filtering through the ontological exchange I identify in children's literature are different approaches to how human beings exist in relation to others. Furthermore, children's literature is saturated with the 'problems of others' as Beauvais (2015: 103–43) puts it, while John Stephens observes that 'Picture books are produced for an audience beginning to grapple with self-other interactions, and this is a major theme and significance of the mode' (1992: 198–9). Therefore, the ubiquity of an ontological mechanism characterized by self–other interaction is not surprising, though the exchange should not only be seen in terms of self–other discourse.

Each ontological exchange recounts a moment (captured by so many writers for children) when solitary childhood is confronted with 'the lives of others which bring events into our life' (Bachelard [1960] 1971: 128). As they are presented in children's literature, such moments are by turn epiphanic, motivational, reassuring, reflective, uncomfortable, perplexing or disturbing and recognize that the process of being human in the world is complex. Even moments of epiphany in the manner of *The Stone Book* are usually unsettling; they 'put a quietness on' (1976: 54). As Beauvais remarks wryly in her discussion of others, 'Unfortunately, I have to share the world with you. We are here together and this *togetherness* is inescapable' (2015: 103). This suggests that a function of children's literature is to prepare the implied child reader for an inevitable moment of ontological rupture – common to human experience – whereby Bachelard's 'solitudes of childhood' (99) are disturbed. The important role played by reading about such moments of rupture can be inferred from Hollindale's observation that 'In reading, children can share an imagined child's solitude in a way that other media do not permit' (1997: 20). My focus is not on the child's reading experience, but the imagined child's solitude is frequently an aspect of ontological exchange. Solitude is one way in which ontological exchange brings into relief the notion of being itself, thereby revealing its fragility. Furthermore, isolation can emphasize how unnervingly close being is to Sartre's non-being: 'The permanent possibility of non-being, outside us and within, conditions our questions about being' (Sartre [1943] 2003: 29). Although Sartre soon problematizes this position in *Being and Nothingness*, he acknowledges the spectre of negation surrounding the notion of being. The urgency of 'explicitly retrieving' being conveyed throughout Martin Heidegger's *Being and Time* ([1927] 1996) is also encapsulated in ontological exchange. In these moments is reflected the horizon of understanding in which being sits. As Heidegger explains,

> The fact that we live already in an understanding of being and that the meaning of being is at the same time shrouded in darkness proves the fundamental necessity of repeating the question of the meaning of 'being'.
>
> ([1927] 1996: 3)

In Heidegger's terms, being is paradoxically beyond and within the grasp of understanding and thus always in need of retrieval. The ontological exchange expressed in children's literature can be seen as part of this process of retrieval and also reflects another cause of Sartrean anguish (in relation to the being's own status), which arises from the realization that being resists absolute comprehension. It does not seem far-fetched to suggest that the ubiquity of ontological exchange in children's literature reflects the constant human effort to understand the incomprehensible.

Childhood solitudes

As I have suggested, an important characteristic of ontological exchange is the transition it marks from being alone (the solitude of selfhood) to being with others. Playing around the ontological exchange are the remnants of Bachelard's childhood solitude, not yet in the intoxicating realms of memory but immediately thrown into past experience. Childhood solitudes become quickly buried – to be re-encountered via poetic reverie – though never entirely lost in Bachelard's terms: 'These solitudes of today return us to the original solitudes' ([1960] 1971: 99). Bachelard seemingly identifies the angst of rupture, typical of ontological exchange, as he observes: 'Childhood knows unhappiness through men. In solitude it can relax its aches' (99). One of the inherent truths of ontological exchange is that the loss of childhood solitude is difficult to bear, manage or comprehend – yet many books for children suggest that it is inevitable and even desirable. It is rare that literary children remain solitary, moving inexorably into relationships, however painful or difficult they might be. Indeed, a didactic and ideological impulse can be traced in the impetus to find companionship in childhood (though the negatively charged exchange challenges this position, as I go on to reveal). A child without friends is frequently considered a tragic figure, as suggested by the prevalence of imaginary friendships in children's books, which are often perceived as symptomatic of loneliness in need of comfort.[6] *Being together* is sought after by the urgency and pervasion of a narrative drive towards ontological exchange. Narrative frequently pushes for the banishment of solitude, as exemplified in books published across decades and cultures, including: *Karlson on the Roof* (1958) by Astrid Lindgren; *The Bunyip of Berkeley's Creek* (1973) by Jenny Wagner and Ron Brooks; *The Way Back Home* (2007) by Oliver Jeffers; or *The 1,000 Year-Old Boy* (2018) by Ross Welford. In these examples, to be alone is to be in crisis – Jeffers's boy is stuck on the moon, 'all alone and afraid' (2007: 10[7]) after his aeroplane runs out of petrol – and thus ontological exchange arises from necessity out of the human predicament.

    The unnamed boy of *The Way Back Home* previously appeared in *Lost and Found* (2005), Jeffers's earlier tale of solitude undone. The boy evokes the child–adult pilot of Saint-Exupéry's *The Little Prince*, for the condition of their solitudes communicates over the sixty years that separate them. Before crashing his own aeroplane and meeting the little prince, Saint-Exupéry's pilot has been living alone. The failure of grown-ups to understand his artwork has the pilot a 6-year-old in stasis, caught up in an extension of Bachelard's childhood solitude. Solitude is emphasized in the moments before the pilot's ultimate meeting with otherness: 'I was more isolated than a shipwrecked sailor on a raft in the middle of the ocean. Thus you can imagine my amazement, at sunrise, when I was awakened by an odd little voice' (Saint-Exupéry [1943] 1991: 7). The figurative passage out of isolation, in terms of a 'sunrise awakening', suggests the dawning of ontological awareness ('I was awakened') precipitated by the strangeness ('odd little voice') of the other.

Echoes of the dawning brought about by ontological exchange in *The Little Prince* can be traced in *The Way Back Home* when the boy's solitude is disrupted after a Martian crash-lands on the moon alongside him. The boy is plunged into darkness, 'his torch began to go out' (Jeffers 2007: 10), before an exchange with the other (Martian), which is conveyed as a moment of sightlessness: 'Both the boy and the Martian could hear noises in the dark and both feared the worst' (14). I will return to the mechanisms of this ontological exchange in due course – for now it is enough to observe that it precedes an enlightenment in which 'their eyes got used to the dark' and 'they both realised they'd met someone else in trouble. They weren't alone any more' (15) – and this shift to illumination is reflected in the illustrative background, as it moves from inky darkness on the verso to light blue on the recto.[8] Jeffers's picturebook can be considered an economical slice of Saint-Exupéry's philosophical narrative, suggesting that human being is contingent on a movement away from solitude towards a meeting with the other and that we cannot *be* fully until the exchange has been made. It captures for the youngest readers the sort of profound moment elucidated by Levinas in his meditation on humanism: 'The Desire for Others that we feel in the most common social experience is fundamental movement, pure transport, absolute orientation, sense' ([1972] 2006: 30). For Levinas, the coming together (out of solitude) with fellow beings is ontologically fundamental and I argue that the ontological momentum in children's literature holds with this.

Correlative ideas can be found in the poetry of Bachelard's solitude, which is open to Levinasian investment in metaphor as an essential path to discovering being. Bachelard perceives that 'Those original solitudes, the childhood solitudes leave indelible marks on certain souls. Their entire life is sensitized for poetic reverie, for a reverie which knows the price of solitude' (99). However, such is the ontological and sociocultural momentum to leave behind original solitudes, uncertain souls – those not destined for poetry – are likely to overlook or undervalue them. Certainly it is not common for children's books actively to embrace solitude on its own terms, though examples can be found.

Me, All Alone, at the End of the World (2005) by M. T. Anderson and Kevin Hawkes details the sensual and creative awareness of solitude when, 'I lived by myself at the End of the World' and 'The days were slow and fine' as 'I looked for treasure with old maps from fallen empires' ([2005] 2007: 3–4). This meditative picturebook finally rejects companionable pleasures, relocating its narrator to 'the Top of the World' (32) in order to find a utopian empty space where happiness is not dependent on fun and friendship.⁹ The closing lines suggest that this state of loneliness is not permanent but that experience of it will better equip humans for being in the world: 'I feel the soft loneliness of a world falling in shadow. For the time being, I am happy here, here by myself at the Top of the World, all alone' (32). The importance of reverie is confirmed, emphasizing Bachelard's notion that childhood prepares us well for reverie in later life: 'childhood is at the origin of the greatest landscapes. Our childhood solitudes have given us the primitive immensities' (102). Bachelard's 'commerce of grandeur' (102) is threatened by capitalist economies of 'FUN without END' (Anderson and Hawkes [2005] 2007: 27) and this picturebook makes a direct plea for the grandeur of solitude. It is concerned less with the challenges of being together with others than a Marxist project that detects dehumanization in economically motivated companionship. Whatever its political agenda, a picturebook devoted to solitude is rare, though children's literature broadly recognizes the importance of lone moments as Wordsworth's 'perilous ridge' echoes down the years from *The Prelude* (1850).[10]

Occasionally, solitude is presented as a state of being that must be left behind or enjoyed only in brief snatches and (more rarely) as something in short supply. For example, in Ivan Southall's *Josh* (1971) the eponymous young poet has been 'emotionally wrung out' by the inhabitants of Ryan Creek and finds himself momentarily alone: 'Peace and quiet. Glorious peace and quiet. Stretching out again on his chest in the beautiful sun, a great weight gone, beautiful relief, unwinding, something that might have been a poem again stirring down deep' ([1971] 1973: 84). The 'stirring' of poetry identifies Josh Plowman as one of Bachelard's 'certain souls' on whom childhood solitudes are strongly marked, but his experience of it is fleeting as he is plunged back into the maelstrom of other lives in Ryan Creek. I return to *Josh* and its take on ontological exchange at the end of this chapter, yet already there are hints of existential malaise that mark it out from *Me, All Alone* and *The Way Back Home*. Josh values solitude as a break from the overwhelming effort of dealing with the other and Southall confirms that being together is challenging. After all Levinas does not claim that the discovery of humanity will be easy, painless or necessarily enjoyable: 'The desire of the absolutely Other is not, like a need, extinguished in pleasure' ([1972] 2006: 44). For Levinas this desire cannot be fulfilled; the desire for the other is necessary and ongoing. Notwithstanding the love of solitude professed by Josh, the direction of energy in children's literature renders solitude a problem to be solved and it is frequently rejected outright, as in *The Way Back Home*.

Of Clocks and skates

Solitude is a central concern of *The Borrowers* (1952) by Mary Norton and *Tom's Midnight Garden* (1958) by Philippa Pearce, novels that first drew my attention to the prevalence of ontological exchange in children's literature. They speak to each other via their reciprocal staging of arguments about ontological status between young protagonists, offering clear examples of ontological exchange with wider relevance across the field. Generically the books are slightly different – miniature and time-slip literature respectively – but both are examples of domestic fantasy[11] in which isolated children are brought together by experiences that challenge their sense of the ordinary. Critics have observed that these novels deal thematically and figuratively with the developmental process of growing up. In *Narratives of Love and Loss* (1987) for example, Margaret and Michael Rustin offer psychoanalytic readings of both works and argue that 'issues of emotional development in children' are key ([1987] 2001: 2). They make a case for a 'poetic realism' (2) through which the books focus on the 'development of an inner identity independent of and sometimes hidden from parents' and on characters with a 'developing sense of personal self' (2–3). The Rustins' approach usefully unravels the literary manifestation of psyche and subjective experience in the emotional landscapes of childhood. However, a consideration of the mutual ways in which these texts deal with what it means to *be* at the level of existence reveals the ontic importance of coming out of solitude.

The Borrowers introduces a family of miniature beings who live under the floorboards of a 'strange old' country house (Norton [1952] 2003: 8). Arrietty Clock is a 13-year-old female borrower who lives a solitary childhood with her parents, Pod and Homily. Her only access to the world outside her home is a grating 'through which Arrietty could see the garden' and she spends hours watching birds that come into her restricted view (16–17). The Clock family are the last of their kind left in the house and survive by 'borrowing' food scraps and various material items from the human beings who live upstairs. This book – the first in a six-part series[12] – deals with the aftermath of the Clocks' engagement with a human boy who (while convalescing at his aunt's home) sees Pod borrowing a cup and saucer. Homily and Pod live in dread of 'being seen' by humans, though until the opening of this story they have not shared the reason for their terror with Arrietty. Fearing the consequences of Pod's sighting and Arrietty's own restlessness – '"it'll give her a bit of interest like and stop her hankering"' (69) – her parents decide to relate their history and to permit Arrietty to accompany Pod on his next borrowing trip. As can be inferred from

Homily's opening question when she begins her tale – '"You know about the two giants?"' (45) – Arrietty knows little of human beings (beyond that which she might have gleaned from her limited, precious library), but she is desperate for contact with lives other than her own. When Arrietty subsequently meets the human boy on her first outing with Pod – 'that dreadful, wonderful, never-to-be-forgotten day' (72) – she is primed for a confrontation with otherness and her response to the boy diverges from her parents' horrified distrust.

Ontological exchange in *The Borrowers* is anticipated from the outset (though this is not the case with all exchanges). A much-discussed[13] metafictive framing device has already introduced the Borrowers as creatures who *might* be real and the boy who *might* have seen them. Mrs May has *possibly* told the tale to the narrator when she was a child: 'It was Mrs May who first told me about them. No, not me. How could it have been me ... Kate, she should have been called' (1). Norton's use of modal auxiliaries raises general questions about narrative reliability, while also emphasizing that *possibility* is a particular concern of this novel. Dealing with things 'that can or may be',[14] possibility has etymological links to ontology in its concern with 'what things exist' (Effingham 2013: 1). Ostensibly the focus of possibility is on the Borrowers themselves and Kate soon asks: '"Are there such things ... As people, other people, living in a house who ... borrow things?"'(4). Immediately Borrowers are proposed as 'people' who have a claim on being at the very least and *possibly* a claim on humanity. Their otherness here actually pulls them closer to humanity – they are other *people* – rather than distancing them from it. Furthermore, in this proposition is early confirmation that *The Borrowers* is very much concerned with what it means to be human; indeed in its fascination with Borrowers is embedded the book's exploration of human being.

Ontological exchange is foreshadowed by Arrietty's response to the perspective on her home afforded by her first borrowing trip: 'Here she was on the other side of the grating – here she was at last, on the outside – looking in!' (86). Arrietty sees her home from the *other* side – a glimpse of her proximity to being human – and her experience of otherness is expressed in terms of Levinasian desire (longing for the other that is already bound with self). As she explores a corner of the garden, Arrietty's solitary childhood is reiterated and she reveals herself as a child prone to Bachelard's reverie: 'The air was filled with scent. "But nothing will play with you," she thought and saw the cracks and furrows of the primrose leaves held crystal beads of dew' (90). The beauty she sees around her heightens Arrietty's awareness of her own state in solitude and an extensive consideration of her surroundings slows down the narrative action to the pace of reverie. Arrietty is disturbed when the boy spots her and they engage in combative dialogue infused with fear, curiosity and loneliness – but each seems to recognize in the other something that has been missing. Each has some evidence of the other's existence, although this evidence has trusted to distant observation until now. 'Being seen' has been stressed throughout the novel and at the opening of their encounter Arrietty is aware of the boy's eye before any other part of him: 'It was an eye. Or it looked like an eye. Clear and bright like the colour of the sky. An eye like her own but enormous' (92). As Maurice Merleau-Ponty asserts in *Phenomenology of Perception* (1945) though, sight does not give access to a ready-made world – he refuses an empiricism that provides access to a world out there and waiting to be seen. Sight provides access to a 'visual field' and 'an opening to a system of visible beings through my position' ([1945] 2012: 224). For Merleau-Ponty (along with other sensations) 'vision is always limited', and 'there is always an horizon of unseen or even invisible things around my present vision' (224–5). Inevitably then, sight cannot provide Arrietty and the boy with fully formed access to the world; nevertheless, it does offer 'access to thought and reflection' on that which they see (225).

Seeing alone is not enough for them to conquer fear, solitude or curiosity, and initially they engage in a process of information exchange as they seek to understand the other on familiar grounds. For example, they establish each other's age in a performance of typical childly behaviour. However, agitation ensues as their questions approach the central concern of their unexpected meeting. It is the boy who cuts through this hesitation at the other's door, bringing about the exchange by challenging Arrietty's ontological status:

> He stood for a moment, as though embarrassed, and then he said: 'Can you fly?'
> 'No,' said Arrietty, surprised; 'can you?'
> His face became even redder. 'Of course not', he said angrily; 'I'm not a fairy!'
> 'Well, nor am I,' said Arrietty, 'nor is anybody. I don't believe in them.'
>
> (97–8)

This qualifies as ontological exchange, because it is an episode in which self and other are distinguished and whereby the ontological status of one or more of the participants is thrown into doubt (or relief). In this exchange the self 'I' interrogates the other 'you' in an attempt to ascertain the ontological status of the other with which s/he is confronted. The boy unbalances Arrietty with his question and she retorts with a counter-challenge. The result is a *reciprocal ontological exchange* as manifest in the echo of inquisitives – 'can you?' – and responses – 'I am not'/'nor am I'. Since the boy has no rational or experiential explanation for Arrietty's existence, he looks to the fantastic for answers. In *Fantasy: The Literature of Subversion* (1981) Rosemary Jackson suggests that fantasy means 'to make visible or manifest' ([1981] 1988: 13), which might allow the boy to see beyond the limitations of his own sight. Or perhaps it is the case that Arrietty is *super*human, her diminutive stature exaggerating her status as being. Arrietty refuses the boy's othering with calm reasoning though (embodying Merleau-Ponty's thoughtful reflection on sight), in which she embraces herself in an inclusive response: 'nor is anybody' – neither I, nor any other *person* believes in fairies. There are conflicting pulses of doubt here (I am not sure what I am yet) and certainty (I am certain that I exist) as Arrietty and the boy attempt to assert their own existence by distancing themselves from fanciful nonentities (such as fairies). The crux of the exchange establishes the actuality of their existence, rather than its nature – for now their conditions of being are uncertain, yet they are keen to assert that they exist. Ontological exchange takes on further urgency in the context of a tale of ethnic survival, since its narrative arc depends on the basic fact of the Borrowers' existence.

The exchange also confirms the microscopic function of miniature literature, illustrating Bachelard's observations in *The Poetics of Space* (1958) that 'Large issues from small' and that 'the miniscule, a narrow gate, opens up an entire world' ([1958] 1994: 154–5). Clues have been left throughout the novel that human being is an overriding concern and this is pushed to its logical conclusion when – after helping the Borrowers to borrow on a grand scale – the boy defiantly identifies as a Borrower: '"I am not a thief … I'm a Borrower"' (Norton [1952] 2003: 208). It is not the case that the boy has lost his humanity, rather that he has humanized the other and realized that the proximity of Borrowers supports his own sense of human being; in embracing the other and becoming a Borrower he *is* more than ever before. In this moment of exchange the Levinasian contract is delivered: 'The Other … arises behind all collection of being, as the one to whom I express what I express. I find myself facing the Other' (30).

Focalization and identification in terms of reader response are important considerations in the mechanisms of exchange between self and other in *The Borrowers* – and childness is an undercurrent of this exchange. If the boy is unequivocally human then it seems possible that the reader will identify with him as a fellow human being. The narrative frame has introduced him as brother to the narrator (or at least this is the conceit she has set up), so something of his background is known. An empathetic response to him might also be elicited by

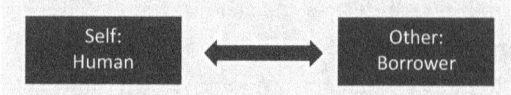

Figure 1.1 Self–Other exchange.

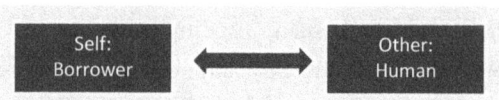

Figure 1.2 Self–Other exchange.

his status as convalescent and the revelation that his fate is to die in combat on the North-West Frontier (Norton [1952] 2003: 7). He is a human being imbued with a past and a future and we meet him in the present moment of ontological exchange as Norton plays with the *anachronies*[15] of her tale. If the exchange is a meeting of self and other then we might see it in terms of Figure 1.1.

This would suggest that the boy is 'self' to Arrietty's 'other' and that through the exchange the reader is to come to an understanding of Arrietty as other. However, this account of the identification process does not allow for the fact that the central narrative is focalized through Arrietty and that human beings are defamiliarized through the conventions of miniature literature. The reader perceives Arrietty's world from her perspective and is effectively miniaturized alongside her, so that when Arrietty feels threatened by the boy's looming presence in the garden the reader can relate to her experience. In this transaction, boy becomes other to Arrietty's self as expressed in Figure 1.2.

What we have here is an exchange whereby the human being is othered in relation to the Borrower, inviting further reflection on the state of human being through identification with the other. Detailing these potential positions of identification emphasizes the narrative's oscillation between humanization and dehumanization. Ontic dynamics function at the level of narrative structure as well as being worked through theme and story. Following this exchange the reader is well placed to consider humanity alongside Arrietty, as she asks big questions to match the enormity of humanity as a proposition from her point of view: '"whatever sort of a world would it be? Those great chairs ... I've seen them. Fancy if you had to make chairs that size for everyone? And their great houses ... their great beds ... the *food* they eat"' (100). Issues of ecology and economics are raised here, signalling an ecocritical and Marxist subtext alert to the consequences of human being on the environment and for human being in the line of production. From an ontological perspective though, the crucial point is that Arrietty is starting to consider the conditions of an other mode of existence in terms that she understands. The human being is measured against *things* used by Borrowers and this is the first time Arrietty has had cause to consider that human beings are entities of a different order from chairs, beds and food.[16] There is a Sartrean recognition here that *things* differ: 'The reality of that cup is that it is there and that it is *not me*' ([1943] 2003: 3).

Ontological exchange is confirmed as part of a wider ontological drive by Arrietty's mispronunciation: '"you're a Human Bean or whatever it's called"' (107), which effectively calls into question human being. Of course, ironic sleight of hand obscures Norton's intimate interest in the human condition and the fact that her Borrowers uncover more about humanity than do her human characters. As Jackson reveals of fantasy literature, 'Its introduction of the "unreal" is set against the category of the "real" – a category which the fantastic interrogates by its difference' (4). Arrietty is thereby able to interrogate reality from her situation of difference. Arrietty's relationship with the boy also challenges Mrs May's generalization in the narrative frame that Borrowers '"thought human beings were just invented to do the dirty work – great slaves put there for them to use"' (10). These assumptions are contested by Arrietty's meeting with the other, leading her to challenge her parents' position and to proclaim: '"I don't think human beans are all that bad"' (156). Pod insists that '"no good never really came to no one from any human bean"'(157), but a Levinasian contract with the other has been established via an ontological exchange that destabilizes Pod's point of view.

Levinas is absolutely aware of the human capacity for cruelty, acknowledging that recognition of the other can be painful: 'To suffer by the other is to take care of him, bear him, be in his place, consume oneself by him' ([1972] 2006: 64). Levinas (as does Norton) writes in the wake of 'the unburied dead of wars and death camps' and argues that a humanist perspective on the other is crucial if we are to open up a future for humankind beyond death: 'The crisis of humanism in our times undoubtedly originates in an experience of human inefficacy accentuated by the very abundance of our means of action and the scope of our ambitions' (45). Figuratively, something of this is expressed by Arrietty's instinctive refusal of humanity's enormity during ontological exchange. Levinas goes on to argue that a Heideggerian 'care for one's self' (45)[17] has overreached itself and disintegrates conceptually and psychologically without an embedded notion of the other. Levinasian ontology interrogates human being for itself and finds that the other is inscribed already in the self. The journey that must be made to discover this is likely to be painful and thus Arrietty 'shivered slightly in the boy's cold shadow' (Norton [1952] 2003: 109), a shadow that already and inevitably she carries within her.

The ontological project at work in *The Borrowers* extends beyond the moment of ontological exchange, as it is played out in various ways throughout the novel. Nonetheless, the exchange is a pivotal moment in which both children articulate the urgency of validating self in relation to others. It is a point to and from which the ontological drive of the book flows and its alignment with Levinasian ontology demonstrates a humanist concern for bringing together self and other that permeates post-war children's literature. When Levinas proclaims that 'youth is authenticity' he brings into play an idea of a youth that ruptures context and in its surplus of vulnerability takes 'charge of one's fellow man' ([1972] 2006: 69). Levinas suggests that there is a propensity for youth to open itself to the other through an essential recognition of what it means to be vulnerable, hence it is unsurprising that books for children emphasize this vulnerable openness to the other. It seems to me that children's books of this period make an ontological move that recognizes the drive to existential self-awareness, tempered by an inescapable responsibility for the other. As I will demonstrate, ontological exchange in *The Borrowers* is typical of a wider determination in children's literature to experience the world outside and to try out ways of making contact with the other.

In *The Borrowers* ontological exchange is anticipated in the conventions of a miniature literature that embeds negotiation of the other in its structure. However, it is not the case that ontological exchange is always so smoothly implanted in theme, structure and plot. In *Tom's Midnight Garden* ontological exchange permeates the poetry of a time-slip novel about childhood loss and disappointment that is also concerned with scientific, psychoanalytic and metaphysical theories of time, memory, change and duration. As Pearce has admitted,[18] there are 'flaws' in the exposition of time in her novel that (in part) draw on J. W. Dunne's dream-theory in *An Experiment with Time* (1927). I will briefly sketch the sort of flaws thrown up by the plot, before suggesting that they are an important aspect of the poetic and metaphysical conditions flowing from ontological exchange.

Let us take a pair of skates. In taking a pair of skates we open some vexing and distracting metaphysical dilemmas.[19] This pair of skates – presented as concrete object – is left by a girl (Hatty) in the late 1890s for a boy (Tom) from the 1950s, so that they can skate together in 1895: 'He saw the two brown-paper packages in the hole, drew them out and unwrapped them: they were a pair of skates, with boots still screwed and strapped to them' ([1958] 2008: 179). The fact of the skates' materiality in Tom's present seems to provide tangible evidence that he has been moving back in time to a point at which the Cambridgeshire Fens froze. One objection raised here might be that it is impossible for the same skates to be worn by two different people (Tom and Hatty) at the same time. This would rely on a rather mechanistic view of duration and *presentism*, explained here by Jeffrey Brower in his development and defence of Aristotle's *endurantism*:

> Ordinary objects persist. And on our ordinary conception of persistence, they do so by *enduring* – that is, by being *wholly* present at each of the times they exist … Many philosophers now reject our ordinary conception of persistence in favor of the doctrine of temporal parts. On the standard development of this doctrine, things persist not by enduring but by *perduring* – that is, by being *partially* present at each of the times they exist.
>
> (2010: 883)

Perduration – championed by Lewis in *On the Plurality of Worlds* (1986) – allows for the idea of temporal parts and the idea that things (skates) change in each instant of their existence. Imagine that the skates start to rust. Endurance allows that the same object be rust free and corroded at the same time, which Lewis argues is nonsensical (just as Tom and Hatty skating on the same skates seems impossible). For Lewis, the only solution is to accept the concept of perduration, through which the temporal parts of things account for change in the same object – thus things are only 'partially present at each of the times they exist'. This permits the skates to be rust-free in the first year of their existence and corroded in the next; we recognize them as the same skates because they have perdured. Under the conditions of perdurance, Tom and Hatty are able to skate on 'temporal parts'; the skates perdure under the floorboards in each separate moment from when Hatty put them there to when Tom finds them. The reason that Tom does not find countless skates – one pair for each moment of their existence – is that he only looks for them once (in one 'of the times they exist'). However, as necessary as it seems to explain this pivotal plot development, perduration works against the theoretical flow of time at work elsewhere in the book – in which past, present and future meld together in a Heideggerian within-time-ness – and this is why the skates might seem to jar as a narrative and poetic conceit.

Furthermore, it is later revealed that Tom and Hatty have come together in their midnight garden as a result of Hatty's powerful dreams and memories – essentially their garden is a dreamscape. So where does this leave the skates?

Having been established as concrete objects, their ontological status is destabilized by the revelation that Hatty (now Mrs Bartholomew) has been dreaming about her past. If Tom's request for Hatty to leave the skates for him was part of their shared dreamscape, it seems unlikely that they would exist in his waking life for him to take back in to the (dreamed of) garden. It could be that in his desperation to continue his midnight adventures Tom's grip on reality is receding and that he has dreamed his discovery of the skates. He wonders as much himself – 'When Tom woke ... almost he thought that he must have dreamt of the discovery' ([1958] 2008: 179) – and it is only a short step to suggest that Tom has experienced a false awakening (the possibility that Tom's dreams have fused with Hatty's is also hinted at later). Descartes confirms the metaphysical complexity of differentiating dream from reality: 'there is no criterion enabling us to distinguish our dreams from the waking state and from veridical sensations', going on to say that images of our waking experience do not exist in external objects and therefore we cannot prove that such objects exist ([1641] 2017: 79). Metaphysicians have long challenged this Cartesian dualism in its separation of mind and body, yet these concerns arise from the quandary presented by the skates. So much then for a pair of skates – permit me to rewind a little.

Tom's Midnight Garden is a tale of solitude, loss and disappointment that brings together Tom and Hatty, English children from different points in time in order (among other things) to make an ontological exchange. Tom is sent to stay with his Aunt Gwen and Uncle Alan after his brother Peter contracts measles, ruining plans to build a tree house in their garden. His dull, well-meaning relations are unused to children and struggle to entertain Tom in their gardenless flat. Tom is roused from bed soon after his arrival when the Grandfather clock downstairs strikes thirteen, a clock owned by the landlady Mrs Bartholomew, who once was and is Hatty. Tom finds a beautiful garden awaiting him and eventually discovers that his entrance to it is linked to the clock and that the garden is a manifestation of the past life of the house and its owner, as well as his own frustrations and desires. In the garden Tom meets Hatty, an orphan who resides in the grudging care of her aunt and male cousins. Even though Tom visits the garden sequentially every night – and the tale is told from his point of view – the seasons of the garden change from one visit to the next and he meets Hatty at different points in her childhood. Tom and Hatty become playmates and start to wonder about the conditions of their encounters. As they struggle to make sense of their place in this slip of time, eventually they clash in a heated ontological exchange:

In a wild defence of herself, Hatty still goaded him: 'Your hand didn't go through my wrist; my wrist went through your hand! You're a ghost, with a cruel, ghostly hand!'

'Do you hear me?' Tom shouted. 'You're a ghost, and I've proved it! You're dead and gone and a ghost!'

([1958] 2008: 107)

In common with *The Borrowers* this is a *reciprocal ontological exchange*, during which Tom and Hatty are confronted simultaneously with doubts about their own existence. The exchange is reciprocal because the challenge to self is met with a direct challenge from the other. There is a tonal shift here though, from indignation in *The Borrowers* to furious anger in this exchange, whereby each child pronounces the other a ghost. This is literally a life or death argument involving palpable anguish as Tom and Hatty try to convince the other that they still exist; Hatty's defence of *herself* is 'wild' and Tom shouts in a display of rage. As is evident from their reciprocal reactions, the children have taken their own status as living beings for granted, while harbouring doubts about the actuality of the *other*. It is worth noting that the reader follows closely Tom's experiences in the novel as focal character and consequently is privy to his earlier questions about Hatty: 'Hatty's image haunted the room for Tom ... and so it was, perhaps, that he began, at first idly, then seriously, to consider whether she herself were not, in some unusual way, a ghost' (101–2). It is possible then that the reader may share Tom's uncertainty about Hatty's status and fantasized alongside him about her death: 'Hatty had lived here, long, long, ago ... here she had lived, here died' (102). Hence it is likely that the reader will be brought up in this moment of exchange, as Hatty calls into question Tom's ontological status.

This is not Hatty and Tom's first encounter of course, suggesting that a simultaneous attraction to and horror of the other – expressed through a series of unexplained events, such as Tom's ability to pass through a closed door – has built to this moment of crisis. Both have suffered degrees of loneliness, resulting in a mutual longing for the other in Levinasian terms, but there is something else here. Their argument reveals curiosity about non-being and death that transforms into Sartrean anguish when they realize that self-negation could be possible. Sartre explains that 'anguish is distinguished from fear in that fear is fear of beings in the world whereas anguish is anguish before myself. Vertigo is anguish to the extent that I am afraid not of falling over the precipice, but of throwing myself over' ([1943] 2003: 53). Understood in these terms, Hatty and Tom are afraid for/of themselves and not of/for each other; they feel anguish because their confrontation has revealed something negative – in the Sartrean sense of nothingness in the face of being – about their own ontological status.

This exchange gets to the heart of the skate problem, which (to recap) throws into relief the contradictory metaphysical presentation of time in the novel and the ontological slippage involved in dreaming/waking states of consciousness – the skates do not fit and two pairs of skates should not be together. The skates underscore the novel's fascination with tension and disjuncture, which is echoed in the children's relationship. Essentially the exchange occurs because Tom and Hatty are not together – have not embraced the other – and the ontological exchange has drawn attention to this refusal of otherness. The truth of the exchange lies in the beyond of the book's sustained metaphor about existential anguish and the book is preoccupied with this. As the exchange reveals, Hatty and Tom have long known (or at least sensed) that they cannot be experiencing synchronous childhood. Hatty's childhood has long gone and from this perspective the Hatty met by midnight is not a living being. Tom has not yet been born, so in this sense he too is a non-being. She is nothing. He is nothing. And yet the skates suggest that they are both alive – which apparently cannot be. The cannot-be-ness of ontological exchange – and a long-sweeping skate across the Fens on impossible skates – is crucial to the book's poetic truth and the metaphysical possibilities thrown up. The children cannot be together in this moment of exchange and *yet they are* – the implied reader is as convinced of this as are the children themselves, because their presence alongside the other is central to the book's poetry. It is not a comfortable coming together though and while they might seem to be friends there is always a lack of proximity in their companionship. Tom fades away from Hatty during the skate – 'his blades left no cut or bruise upon the surface of the ice' (190) and she describes him as 'unreal-looking' (198) – and Tom has failed to see that Hatty is growing out of the garden. Indeed, ontological exchange reveals that broadly this is not a book about friendship.

Pearce's novel gives full attention to conveying metaphorically Bachelard's notion of solitude ruptured and to the existential anguish (impossibility) of being nothing. Tom and Hatty each long for a playmate, yet in their childhood garden they struggle with the conditions of ontological exchange required of them. If there is to be anything approximating friendship between Tom and Hatty, it comes much later in the twilight of the final chapter when Tom recognizes Hatty in Mrs Bartholomew. As can be seen in the immediate aftermath of the earlier ontological exchange, there are hints of the humanist investment in otherness located in *The Borrowers*. In this emotional moment of exchange Hatty's tears might seem to render her alive to Tom in the Levinasian sense of carrying the other with him: 'He put his arm around her: "All right, then, Hatty! You're not a ghost – I take it all back – all of it. Only don't cry!"' (107). This reading is not quite convincing though, since Tom's concern for Hatty's suffering is short-lived. Tom quickly exhibits a Sartrean resistance to anything but being *for-itself* as he 'continued secretly to consider the possibility of her being a ghost' because 'if Hatty weren't a ghost, then perhaps that meant he was' (109). In Sartrean terms eventually Tom and Hatty must accept that being is the project of the self and that they cannot expect others to help them with this – that is, being with others (playing in the garden) is not enough to assuage existential anguish.

The final chapter, however, points to uneasiness with an existentialist position – albeit tentative – that could leave Mrs Bartholomew to die alone and Tom bereft if played to its full symbolic potential. At this point of explication and closure, *Tom's Midnight Garden* moves beyond Sartre towards what looks like a Levinasian embrace of the other. Yet there is something of an impasse (another skate moment) in terms of metaphysical resolution; the book is not quite convinced about the ontological position it ends up taking. When Tom leaves the garden and embraces Mrs Bartholomew (Hatty) as an old woman there is some recognition that being for others is an inevitable part of being for yourself, but this episode is not as intense or urgent as the earlier ontological exchange. Their hug is observed at a remove, while Aunt Gwen describes the interaction in retrospect: '"He ran up to her, and they hugged each other as if they had known each other for years and years"' (229). Here Tom and Hatty are *known for each other* and Pearce gestures towards the humanist project that children's literature invests so much in. There is little sense of how this might play out in the narrative hinterland of her novel though, which is unsurprising given that humanism represents a philosophical and ideological battleground.[20]

In *The Borrowers* and *Tom's Midnight Garden* ontological exchange develops differently. Norton's book is more open to a Levinasian ethical ontology, while Pearce's novel (perhaps surprisingly and unwittingly) plays out existential crisis. Nonetheless, both confirm that childhood demands an exchange between self and other that makes for a challenging break from solitude. This does not necessarily mean that children make a literal move from being alone (before exchange) to being with others (after exchange) – that once they were not invited to parties and now they are. The figurative space of these novels allows for a childhood that opens itself up to these moments of profound understanding – to an exchange that has a *before* and an *after*. As *Tom's Midnight Garden* suggests, ontological exchange makes being *for-itself* more pronounced and Pearce's characters are increasingly focussed on themselves in its aftermath. They realize that part of being is being in the world; that they must come to terms with otherness and what this reveals of themselves. An exchange of perspective is involved, during which *self perceives self* momentarily in the scope of the other. Apparently then, the outcome of exchange suggests an alternative to the common account of childhood as a trajectory from 'infantile solipsism to maturing social awareness', outlined here by Stephens as 'arguably the most pervasive theme in children's fiction' (1992: 3). Configured in ontological rather than psychoanalytic and sociological terms, self folds in on self as young people discover how to be; there can be no discernable journey away from self.

The Borrowers and *Tom's Midnight Garden* share a series of ontic mechanisms, including release from childhood solitude; self–other confrontation; reciprocal exchange; and interrogation of being. While configuration of ontological exchange is not uniform across the field, juxtaposition of these examples reveals an emerging model of exchange that allows for ideological and philosophical variation.

Only the boots were different

The working model of ontological exchange provided thus far feeds into a wider consideration of how it performs across the field. Broadly speaking, it seems that ontological exchange takes on a positive or negative charge – which can be seen in terms of epiphany or rupture – providing a catalyst for ontic development. Of the examples that follow, *When Marnie Was There* (1967) by Joan G. Robinson, Jeffers' *The Way Back Home* and *A Greyhound of a Girl* (2011) by Roddy Doyle, each throws up ontological exchange whereby difference provides a comfort or boon to the emergent self and the exchange can be considered genial and epiphanic. Positively charged ontological exchange often involves angst, but it is appeased through the process of exchange.

A Greyhound of a Girl introduces another thread-bearing Mary who meets a ghost, 'wearing big boots with fat laces' when 'she was alone on the street, just outside her house' (Doyle 2011: 6). Doyle's novel does not offer up a typical example of exchange in that 12-year-old Mary observes her mother (Scarlett) and her ghost of a great-grandmother (Tansey) during their genial ontological exchange. The ontological exchange is notable on two counts: the child is an observer and there is a lack of hostility. Etymology reveals that *geniality* is conducive to growth and kindliness (being founded in nuptial), and it perfectly captures the tone and productive outcome of this exchange. Geniality encapsulates the matriarchal threading of Doyle's tale that Mary must pick up and internalize, even in this moment of ontological anguish (as it turns out to be for her). Technically, Mary is the only female child in this tale of four generations of women, yet other childhoods are conveyed as Tansey, Scarlett and Emer (Mary's dying granny) communicate lives of loss and love across the years. Mary is the first to meet the ghostly Tansey and soon learns that she died as a young mother when Emer was only 3. The first encounter between Scarlett and Tansey makes for an ostensibly simple exchange and is set up by Mary's ontic reflection about her great-grandmother: 'She existed. But what was she?' (60). Tansey then appears to Mary and Scarlett from behind a tree:

> Mary wasn't surprised.
> 'Hi, Tansey', she said.
> 'Hello, yourself', said the woman.
> She was dressed the same, the old-fashioned dress, the big boots covered in shining mud.
> She looked at Scarlett.
> 'I know you', she said.
> 'I know you too', said Scarlett.
>
> (61)

Scarlett receives the ghostly other with apparent ease in this genial exchange of ontological recognition. The older women have never met and yet they have always *known* each other in the Levinasian sense that knowing the other comes before knowing the self and in the way of matriarchal knowledge and care connecting generations. Not a mother herself, Mary is positioned as participant-observer – and through looking she is implicated in a process that reckons with being. In the immediate aftermath of the exchange Mary reflects that she 'wasn't scared' by the way her mother and Tansey were looking at each other, 'but she was curious', though she has to work hard to convince herself that she is not afraid (71). Mary's question, '"How does that work?"' makes Scarlett jump, and she admits that '"It's just a bit of a shock!"' (71) It is evident that Tansy's appearance and the ensuing exchange have been more unsettling for mother and daughter than its simplicity might suggest. Mary's initial response to the exchange between Scarlett and Tansey is 'to act as if it made no difference' (Derrida [1972] 1984: 3). I am playing slippery games here by sliding Jacques Derrida's disquisition in *Margins of Philosophy* (1972) on the silent 'a' of *différance* into Mary's ontological predicament, yet that subtle space between difference and *différance* is precisely what concerns Mary. In Derridian terms, understanding of this exchange is (and must be) deferred because Mary tries too hard to grasp at difference.

Mary becomes increasingly troubled, feeling 'scared' and 'as if she were going to cry' (73). The source of Mary's anguish is her realization that Scarlett and Tansey 'look *exactly* the same' – '"she's too like you, Mammy. I'll mix you up"' (74). Identity has become a problem for Mary in this moment as she struggles with the 'Identity of Indiscernables' (or 'Leibniz's Law'), which says that 'if objects A and B have all the same properties, then A and B are identical' (Crane and Farkas 2004: 528). The problem for Mary is that Scarlett and Tansey should not be identical. Mary only has one mother and that mother should be identical only with herself in Lewis's terms (who counters Leibniz in some detail):

> Identity is utterly simple and unproblematic. Everything is identical to itself; nothing is ever identical to anything else except itself. There is never any problem about what makes something identical to itself; nothing can ever fail to be. And there is never any problem about what makes two things identical; two things can never be identical.
>
> (Lewis 1986: 192–3)

Along the lines of Lewis, Mary feels instinctively the simplicity of the proposition that no two beings can be identical, yet her conviction unravels as she looks at Scarlett and Tansey. Mary *herself* feels threatened by this too-much-likeness, because if mother could be great-grandmother then daughter could be either of them and they might never know how to distinguish themselves; Mary could lose herself in this too-muchness of mothers. If Scarlett's place is taken by a ghostly other – 'That's what she wants', thinks Mary (74) – then the matriarchal lineage that led to Mary's being would be destroyed (at least conceptually). Mary would not exist as the daughter she should be to the mother she should have: 'It was important – vital. Mary had to separate them, get her mother home as quickly as possible' (74). Mary's thoughts and fears move at a fast pace through snatches of dialogue and half-formed thoughts. However, this is not the class of fear described by Heidegger as a mass 'tranquillization' that cannot speak publicly about death, as if it were a social inconvenience ([1927] 1996: 235). Indeed, the women are gathered to confront, welcome and ease the boundaries of life and death for Emer – and in this sense death is spoken – so it is not that Mary fears her own death (or her mother's) in this moment. Rather the nature of her very existence is thrown into question and as Heidegger points out, 'Only a being which is concerned in its being about that being can be afraid' (132). This angst around what it means to be is a condition of ontological exchange and its ramifications reach from one Mary to another – from *The Stone Book* to *A Greyhound of a Girl* – as they each catch hold of a thread that brings the conditions of their existence into focus.

Mary decides that she does not want fear to define her experience of home (self), so she looks again at Tansey and Scarlett. Eventually, a serenity still emanating from the ontological exchange seems to reach her. Ungripped by panic, she sees that there *is* something that sets ghost and mother apart: 'Only the boots were different' (75). In a parodic take on 'The Judgement of Solomon', Mary addresses her Mammy to be sure that her mother is wearing red boots as she should be – and 'Only one woman spoke'. Scarlett's response 'calm[s] Mary' and she starts to see 'other little differences' until she is satisfied that 'Tansey – the ghost – was different enough now, and herself' (75). Mary still cannot answer the question of what Tansey is exactly, but she has established that Tansey differs in kind from herself and her mother – that they can each claim identity for themselves. This realization moves Mary away from a negative and desperate reliance on otherness bound by difference into the sphere of *différance*, allowing for difference *and* the deferment of understanding. Derrida roots back to the Latin verb *differre*, which has two meanings (to differ and to defer), in order to stress the polysemic capacity of *différance*, for it 'can refer simultaneously to the entire configuration of its meanings' ([1972] 1984: 7–8). In witnessing this genial ontological exchange Mary's sense of being has undergone a shift in scope – making a perspectival move from difference to *différance*. Geniality has shown itself to be unsettling in the ontic context of exchange, serving as catalyst for this shift in outlook. Consequently, Mary can accept that she is part of this complex network of maternal relations, while taking the time to understand how her existence impinges on others and vice versa.

Mary's concern with lack of difference in *A Greyhound of a Girl* highlights the fragility of self in the face of the unknown other and underscores the fundamental importance of negotiating difference via ontological exchange. In *The Way Back Home*, dread of the unknown is the catalyst for a moment of Sartrean anguish. Jeffers's picturebook expresses this anguish visually through monstrous creatures threatening to swallow boy and Martian before they meet, having left the familiarity of their own worlds behind them. According to Sartre, anguish 'appears at the moment that I disengage myself from the world where I had been engaged' and is a state of 'apprehension of freedom by itself'. Anguish arises from the knowledge that nothing can be responsible for me except me; that I am cut off from the world and 'emerge alone' (Sartre [1943] 2003: 63). Figurative expression of such existential anguish is rendered in the moon's swallowing darkness. Martian and boy are each aware of an unknown presence close by them and in the dark – literally and metaphorocally – this could be anything. The reader is privy to their (visually) manifest terror and, although the monstrosities they conjure are not identical, the fact that they each imagine a monster in the gloom indicates the reciprocity of a fear grounded in unidentified otherness – something other than me is out there and I am afraid.

The spare storytelling of Jeffers's picturebook means that the exchange is expressed over one double-page spread and anguish recedes quickly once solitude has been overcome.[21] When boy and Martian are able to see each other they do not acknowledge difference though and this silence is worth attention. It can be read as an articulation of the silent 'a' in Derrida's *différance* – 'The *a* of *différance* … is not heard; it remains silent, secret and discreet as a tomb' ([1972] 1984: 4) – in which contrast is refused a role in our understanding of the other and signification is endlessly deferred. That there has been a confrontation of self and other is expressed via the reciprocal monsters, yet once boy and Martian are able to see each other the immediate response is one of camaraderie: 'they both realised they'd met someone else in trouble' (15) – the difference is there, but it has been silenced into an acceptance of *différance*. Add to this a Levinasian embrace of the other and immediately they recognize *themselves-in-each-other*.

It is valid to read this sequence as an overtly didactic and carefully directed ideological message about acceptance to which Jeffers's child characters – the Martian can certainly be read as a child figure – are predisposed in the (potentially manipulative) humanist terms Stephens (1992) identifies as a bedrock of children's literature discourse. However, such a reading misses the ontological and introspective entanglement of self and other, which for Levinas is unspoken and hidden before it can be understood through language: 'The unutterable or incommunicable of interiority that cannot hold in a Said is a responsibility prior to freedom' (Levinas: [1972] 2006: 52). This is not a position of passivity and slavery to the will of the other, nor is it a reductive humanist stance in which relativity is banished. Jeffers presents a moment of fundamental Levinasian sense making in which boy and Martian's respective worlds are enlightened by this predisposition to otherness. They are relieved of their short-lived anguish in this moment as their own sense of being is heightened through ontological exchange. They are absolutely themselves and as ontic organisms they are wrapped up in a beyondness of self and *différance* that draws in the worlds from which they come – Martian and boy are portrayed in the context of beings from a whole race of Martians and Earthlings. That they stand for more than themselves is evident from the scale of their respective journeys from home – Earth and Mars – to the neutral space of the moon. This illustrates Levinas's point that the other rises through and out of a context that shines through their whole being: 'The Other is present in a cultural whole, illuminated by that whole just as a text by its context. The manifestation of the whole ensures its presence. It is illuminated by the light of the world' (30–31). Boy and Martian need not ask questions of each other as metaphorically 'their eyes got used to the dark' of the unknown and they come together in the presence of sense – in Levinas's terms they are already known to each other. The reader is encouraged to make sense of them – self/boy and other/Martian – in the context of the intimacy of a newly already discovered friendship and the detachment of universally recognizable ontological encounter. The worldly conditions of Jeffers's ontological exchange take a step towards the idea of a socially immersed and Heideggerian being-with that Beuavais (2015) is alert to her discussion of the problematic other. For Heidegger this 'is an existential constituent of being-in-the-world', which he terms *Mitda-sein* ([1950] 1975: 117). As my corpus is starting to reveal, this movement from being-there to being-with is tracked across the instances of ontological exchange in children's literature.

The pre-emptive fear surrounding otherness at work in *A Greyhound of a Girl* and *The Way Back Home* marks out numerous ontic encounters and ontological exchange serves to deflect this anguish into positive energy in these examples. In Doyle's novel and Jeffers's picturebook the fear is short-lived though, so the exchange has less work to do in the final embrace of *différance*. The exploration of loss in *When Marnie Was There* abounds with an emptiness that is grounded in the parental absence explored in Chapter 5, thus its ontological exchange anticipates my exploration of such 'imaginative acts of absence'.[22] From the outset, Robinson establishes an extended backdrop of loneliness and uncertainty for an anguished reciprocal exchange, which (notwithstanding) is positively charged. The narrator reflects at the beginning of the novel that 'Anna spent a great deal of her time thinking about nothing these days' (Robinson [1967] 2014: 9), going on to observe that 'Anna herself was outside' (10). Anna is not able to partake in social encounters that allow her the sort of concrete 'inside' contact with others that Sartre identifies as an inevitable circumstance of being for-itself – in this sense Anna is less than herself and in danger of being in bad faith;[23] of lying to herself about herself in an act of self-avoidance. As Sartre reveals, 'The human being is not only the being by whom *négatités* are disclosed in the world; he is also the one who can take negative attitudes with respect to himself' (Sartre [1943] 2003: 70). Anna's bad faith is manifest in her refusal to engage actively with the world and thus she declares that '"I like doing nothing better than anything else"' (Robinson [1967] 2014: 31). Anna's outsideness and negative attunement to her own being is identified as a problem in need of resolution, for she needs to move 'inside' the space of others in order to come into being for-itself – and this is where a positively charged ontological exchange emerges.

Ontological exchange serves as a bridge between Anna's being outside herself and the world of others around her, such as the Lindsay children who occupy an inside space of social inclusion – and who Anna watches playing on the beach from an exteriorized distance. When Anna encounters Marnie – who could be seen as a ghostly manifestation of Anna's own anguish – an exchange ensues that reveals a desperate need for the other that has long been resisted. Anna initially senses that the windows of old Marsh House are watching her and soon after she spies a girl in the upper window. When Anna and Marnie finally meet, ontological doubts gather and they move to validate each other in a process of mutual reassurance:

> [Anna] went on staring and staring as if she were looking at a ghost. But the strange girl was looking at her in the same way.
> 'Are you real?' Anna whispered at last.
> 'Yes, are you?'
> They laughed and touched each other to make sure.
>
> (65)

Once again, observation of the other is crucial to the dynamics of ontological exchange and the urgency of being is foregrounded by the girls' questions. The positivity of the exchange opens up Anna to an ontological landscape whereby she comes into being and is able to befriend the Lindsay children. The positive charge of the exchange does not render this an easy process though, for as Sartre warns, being is always encompassed by nothing and eventually Anna must give up Marnie to the historical past. Their exchange can be interpreted as a symbolic encounter with anguish as overwhelming as the 'leaden' water that almost drowns Anna (161–5) but which serves as a positive expression of being in the real world. As it turns out, Anna's relationship with the ethereal Marnie is not an expression of Mitda-sein; instead, ontological exchange is the catalyst for the being-with to which children's literature is so committed.

These positively charged episodes of ontological exchange do not suggest that being in the world is a straightforward proposition. However, they do provide a positive momentum for travel away from a position of solitude. The self–other encounters in *A Greyhound of a Girl*, *The Way Back Home* and *When Marnie*

Was There imply that solitude is a problem that can be resolved through a genial exchange of immediate commitment to the other. Each of these episodes offers a moment of epiphany in which the childly figure is enlightened by the process of exchange. However, such epiphany does not characterize ontological exchange at large in children's literature.

As I establish in the following section – through consideration of Jansson's *Comet in Moominland*, *Charlotte's Web* (1952) by E. B. White, Margot Lanagan's *Tender Morsels* (2008) and Southalls's *Josh* – ontological exchange can be marked by ongoing doubt, rupture or negation. Negation arises when the other negates self (at least temporarily), as we have glimpsed already in Woodson's *brown girl dreaming*. Exchange can also be characterized by rupture, during which sustained angst arises from a breach of sameness and the self is threatened by too much difference. Negatively charged exchange reveals uncertainty about the withdrawal from solitude in childhood, confirming that children's books do not always present being with others as a desirable aspect of the human condition.

The last chandelier

Jansson's *Comet in Moominland* signals its ambivalence about ontological exchange through anticipatory positioning, whereby the exchange precedes the self–other meeting by some way. Anticipation of such an exchange also flags the Levinisian position that 'The free man is dedicated to his fellow; no one can save himself without others' ([1972] 2006: 66). Levinas stresses that this ontological truth is foundational for being and that dedication to others is essential to human being, however much the self might struggle against it. Jansson's exchange is striking in its willingness to confront an ontological struggle that can have problematic results in experiential terms. During the exchange, Moomintroll is introduced to the idea of Snorks and it is expressed in pointedly colonial language, which exposes the (potentially prejudicial) insularity of being for-itself:

> 'Don't you really know what a Snork is?' said Snufkin in amazement. 'They must be the same family as you I should think, because they look the same, except that they aren't often white. They can be any colour in the world (like an Easter egg), and they change colour when they get upset.'
>
> Moomintroll looked quite angry. '*Well!*' he said. 'I've never heard of *that* branch of the family. A real Moomintroll is *always* white. Changing colour indeed! What an idea!'
>
> ([1946] 1967: 65)

This ontological exchange is unusual in that the other is not present during the exchange. However, in common with models of exchange established thus far, Moomintroll (self) is thrown into doubt by a confrontation with the other (albeit in absentia). Moomintroll has proved welcoming of a range of creatures unfamiliar to him on his expedition to the Lonely Mountains, yet he is immediately disturbed by the idea of Snorks. Refusing the possibility that such colourful emotivism could bear a familial and essential relation to his 'white' self, Moomintroll is thrown off balance. Such an evidently xenophobic reaction is remarkable in the mouth of Moomintroll, whose tolerance is evinced earlier in the novel and elsewhere in the series. Written in the aftermath of a war with which Jansson has engaged as a political commentator and satirist, it seems likely that this racist, colonial language is deliberate. There is no baulking from the implication that her central character has a propensity for intolerance – and such an unflinching summation of the human condition is the starting point for the ontological positions of Levinas, Simone de Beauvoir, Hannah Arrendt and others who reveal the enormity of the ontological struggle to accept the other at an existential level.

In *The Ethics of Ambiguity* (1948), Beauvoir traces the child's growing awareness of 'the human character of the reality about him' ([1948] 2015: 42). She suggests that only gradually is the child liberated from a childly illusion that adults are responsible for the ontic and moral conditions of the world. In preadolescence, 'He discovers his subjectivity; he discovers that of others' (41), and I think it is possible to read Mommintroll's anticipatory response to Snorks in these terms. From the moment of Snufkin's revelation about the Snorks, Moomintroll's disquiet over the other looms in his consciousness as a circling dread. Disquiet develops into a concern for the safety of these unknown beings, as if recognizing for the first time the foundational role of subjective self in others. Moomintroll's eventual meeting with the Snork and Snork maiden involves an act of rescue – Snork maiden is in danger of being eaten by a poisonous bush – which can be interpreted as a sort of penitent taking on of responsibility in Beauvoir's sense of it.[24] In an ontological exchange akin to Doyle's matrilineal challenge, the other's proximity to self – familial too-much-likeness – is once again the source of Moomintroll's existential qualms: 'They must be the same family as you … because they look the same.' The significance of this exchange (and others like it) lies in its performance of the ontological implications of discrimination and the tentative play of difference and *différance*. Jansson might well take an ideological position here, but its entrenchment in the subject as coming-into-being pushes beyond the political. Jansson's anticipatory ontological exchange expresses the thrown potential of the child to move forward into an encounter with the other, which is as uncertain as it is necessary. The negative charge of Moomintroll's exchange is certainly not nihilistic, but it does throw doubt on the possibility and nature of being-with.

In *Charlotte's Web*, White takes a satiric approach to ontological exchange, suggesting that it could be considered a distinguishable structure of children's literature. Wilbur's attempt to banish solitude leads to a witty exchange in which the young pig expounds on the possibility that he might be nothing. Desperate for a friend, Wilbur asks a lamb to play with him:

> 'Certainly not', said the lamb … 'I am not interested in pigs. Pigs mean less than nothing to me.'
>
> 'What do you mean, *less* than nothing?' replied Wilbur. 'I don't think there is any such thing as *less* than nothing. Nothing is absolutely the limit of nothingness. It's the lowest you can go. It's the end of the line. How can something be less than nothing? If there were something that was less than nothing, then nothing would not be nothing, it would be something – even though it's just a very little bit of something. But if nothing is *nothing*, then nothing has nothing that it less than *it* is.'
>
> 'Oh, be quiet!' said the lamb. 'Go play by yourself! I don't play with pigs.'
>
> (White [1952] 1963: 32)

This playful exchange is typical of metaphysical themes that interest White – as evident in other books such as *Stuart Little* (1945) – and the ontological remit is quite explicit here. The questions thrown up by the lamb's refusal of Wilbur also echo the mind games explored by Frank Close in *Nothing* (2009). Close observes, the more I tried to understand how 'something, the stuff of the universe, erupted out of nothing … the more I felt that I was on the edge of either true enlightenment or madness' ([2007] 2009: 3). Such metaphysical entanglement plays at the edges of the philosophically extreme generalities that White appears to satirize. This exchange also has fun with the limits of anthropomorphism though, pushing at the question of whether human beings can ever render animals *real-ly* through artistic representation.[25]

In terms of its ontological freight the exchange pre-empts a more extensive exploration of what it means to be 'some pig' – and by extension 'some human' – in the wider novel. Wilbur is adamant that the lamb's denial of him is contingent on a misstep of logic and thus redundant. Nonetheless, the mark of his solitude hangs heavy and Wilbur will require further reassurance of his status as a conscious and worthwhile being, which is eventually provided by the resourceful Charlotte (the titular spider who befriends him). Although there is a positive outcome for Wilbur, initially he is shrouded in nihilistic self-doubt as a result of this ontological exchange: 'Friendless, dejected, and hungry, he threw himself down in the manure and sobbed' (34). This negatively charged encounter instigates a period of anguish during which Sartre might say that Wilbur is 'waiting to make an appointment with [him]self' (Sartre [1943] 2003: 60). Sartre explains that anguish is a rare and temporal condition of freedom, which is necessarily bound by nothing: 'Anguish in fact is the recognition of a possibility as *my* possibility; that is, it is constituted when consciousness sees itself cut from its essence by nothingness or separated from the future by its very freedom' (59). In anguish, Wilbur fears for his future and yet simultaneously he glimpses *his* possibility in the lamb's (attempted) annihilation of him. Contained in this forward-facing glimpse of possibility is the childly nature of White's ontological exchange. It takes its place alongside other examples of exchange in children's literature, which are characterized by ambivalence – ambivalence arising from the threat of nihilating nothingness in self–other relationships that simultaneously project forward into childly possibility.

The abusive ontological exchange in Lanagan's *Tender Morsels* is in part indicative of its young adult status. However, the brutality of negation in its language is also reminiscent of a longer tradition of folk and fairy tales from which it spins its narrative. Lanagan's 'ungrateful' dwarf borrows directly from the Grimms's 'Snow-White and Rose-Red', but Christina Rossetti's *Goblin Market* (1862) is also a clear precursor for the sisters' relationship and exchange with Dought (a 'goblin man' of sorts). There is a fierce rejection of the other here that moves away from Levinasian humanism into the realms of Kristeva's abjection. Sisters, Branza and Urdda, live in a bucolic world of their mother's making and Branza is alarmed when 'a roar, at once enraged and pleading, chopped through the forest peace' (Lanagan [2008] 2010: 118). Branza knows instinctively that this sound threatens their tranquillity and the conditions of their existence at a metaphysical level. In contrast, 6-year-old Urdda is 'quite unafraid' and rushes to assist the unknown being, forcing Branza to confront her fears directly: 'With horror, Branza saw the eyes. They seemed the size of ladle bowls, they were so wide with rage and terror, and they were fixed on Urdda through the whitish webbing that held the creature to the marsh-water' (119). Branza's focus on gazing eyes exaggerates their corporeal status; they are body parts designed to see Urdda and her body, 'fixing' it in this moment of 'rage and terror'. Merleau-Ponty confirms that 'the experience of one's own body ... reveals to us an ambiguous mode of existence' ([1945] 2012: 204) and it is the creature's intense corporeal observation of the sisters, which leads them to discover that the conditions of their own existence are awry. Branza and Urdda are to be 'awakened' to their physical status as sexual beings in a movement away from the Cartesian tradition, which as Merleau-Ponty observes, 'has taught us to disentangle ourselves from the object' (204) and our bodies. The sisters are to see themselves in relation to an other body and so move into a new world of experiential reality.

The mysterious 'creature' is actually Dought, a 'stump' of a man who forces his way between planes of existence in Lanagan's fairy-tale world (he is a Rumpelstiltskin figure who is generally maligned in the novel).[26] After their initial excitement and shock the girls realize that 'It *is* a person' (Lanagan [2008] 2010: 119), although Urdda's use of personal pronoun unsettles her statement. In grammatical terms 'it' generally refers to non-human things or entities,[27] so this lexical ambiguity reveals her misgivings about the sort of person she has found and over Dought's nature and being. Urdda liberates Dought from the marsh by cutting through his beard, angering him and leading to an ontological exchange that has been building from the moment the girls hear his shouts. Even prior to the exchange, Dought has been pushed almost beyond otherness and he remains in an abject existence in Kristeva's terms until his violent death (also witnessed by the sisters). Kristeva expounds:

> The abject is not an ob-ject facing me, which I name or imagine. Nor is it an ob-jest, an otherness ceaselessly fleeing in a systematic quest of desire. What is abject is not my correlative, which, providing me with someone or something else as support, would allow me to be more or less detached and autonomous. The abject has only one quality of the object – that of being opposed to I.
>
> ([1980] 1982: 1)

As Kristeva explains, the abject is not straightforward otherness and there is no humanism here. There is no space for Dought in the girls' world in Levinasian terms, so he can reveal little to them about his own existence; he is absolutely opposed to them at the level of being. He is abject. Unsurprisingly then, a ferocious and hostile exchange ensues after Urdda has 'ducked underwater' to save him and Doubt beats her with his 'hard little fists' on surfacing (Lanagan [2008] 2010: 120). In this moment Branza moves out of her role of passive observation and fear:

> 'She was saving your life, ungrateful man!' said Branza, hating him, hating him –
> 'Oh!' she said suddenly, recognizing. 'It is that littlee-man!' …
>
> The man gasped and sank back a moment, as if Branza had stabbed him in the vitals. Then he was scrambling towards her throat, his voice gone to a shriek. 'Littlee, you call me? Outrageous orphan! Whore-mouth! You shall never speak again!'
>
> (121)

This is an exchange of denial in which self and abjected other are thrown into a combative battle for/of existence. The argumentative exchange is threatening and visceral with participants figuratively reduced to their sexual organs. The exchange becomes an episode of ontological debasement through which Dought is ultimately punished for his bodily presence. The sisters are forced to come to terms with Dought's existence though and the fact that worlds will shift brings him into the realm of their own being. Dought fascinates Urdda, and she asks directly: 'What *are* you?' (123), but she is not provided with a direct response to a question that apparently involves an ontological impossibility. However, the posing of it leads Urdda to a fuller understanding of what *she is* when eventually she follows Dought back into his world – or at least she follows the path that he once took – and what turns out to be her own reality. Dought's very presence insists on Urdda and Branza's physical existence and their exchange with him shows them how to live substantially. The sisters come into being corporeally via conditions outlined by Merleau-Ponty: 'Whether it is a question of the other person's body or of my own, I have no other means of knowing the human body than by living it, that is, by taking up for myself the drama that moves through it and by merging with it' ([1945] 2012: 205). Thus it seems that Dought's death can be considered an absolute merger with the other; through disgust at his physical presence the girls are made aware of their own bodies, which must be lived in.

Once again then, it seems that the most destructive of ontological exchanges can bring about a new commitment to being in the world, which moves forward from what seems to be annihilation into a fuller mode of being that brings consciousness into the realms of bodily function. Further significance of this ontological exchange lies in its interrogation of being across fairy-tale worlds, adding another layer to our understanding of the ontic function and importance of such tales. Before moving into the Freudian territory of his psychoanalytic readings in *The Uses of Enchantment* (1976), Bruno Bettelheim identifies the important role of fairy tales in unpicking the conditions of human existence: 'If we hope to live not just from moment to moment, but in true consciousness of our existence, then our greatest need and most difficult achievement is to find meaning in our lives' ([1976] 1991: 3). That this consciousness of existence is embedded in fairy tales via ontological exchange might further explain their assimilation into a children's literature that thrives on such metaphysical structures. In common with fairy or folk tales, Lanagan's novel is interested in what it means to be in the phenomenological world of social and cultural experience. That is, folk tales thrive on the notion of what it means to be in communities of otherness and this communal aspect of ontological exchange is explored widely in children's books.

The notion of community as especially challenging to being for-itself is taken up in Southall's *Josh* and suggests – like *Tender Morsels* – that ambivalence is a pervasive condition of ontological exchange. *Josh* brooks ambivalence as it plays out an existentialist challenge to the Hegelian notion of a civil society in which human freedom is reliant on a merging of self and society. In *Outlines of the Philosophy of Right* (1821), Hegel outlines metaphysical conditions of being in a social context as follows:

> The concrete person, who as a *particular person* is his own end, is, as a totality of needs and a mixture of caprice and natural necessity, one principle of civil society. But the particular person is essentially so related to other particular persons that each asserts himself and finds satisfaction by means of the others, and at the same time simply by means of the form of *universality*.
>
> ([1821] 2008: 180–1)

Before arriving in Ryan Creek, Josh Plowman has expected to find himself related to others in the sort of ontic terms set out be Hegel, whereby satisfaction is derived 'by means of others'. As revealed in a moment of flashback, Josh has long desired this place filled with 'Ryan Creek people' – ' "what about it *this* summer? Can I go?" ' (Southall [1971] 1973: 5). Josh has entered into Hegel's stage of *familial dissolution*, through which individuality is determined in readiness for entry into external social structures (Hegel [1821] 2008: 163). Ryan Creek represents a sort of middle ground for Josh, since he is visiting Aunt Clara for the first time in the town developed by his pioneering great-grandfather Plowman. His mother permits the longed-for visit and we meet Josh as he approaches his destination, who immediately finds himself 'the only stranger on the train' (Southall [1971] 1973: 4). It soon becomes evident that this extended family is made strange by unfamiliar civic structures and that Hegelian satisfaction is unlikely to be within the remit of Josh's encounter with others in Ryan Creek.

Southall's experimental novel is lent immediacy by stream-of-consciousness technique; use of present progressive tense structures; and an event duration of five days. The reader is positioned inside Josh's intense encounter with otherness, which proves violent, troubling and short-lived. In spite of his aunt's protests, Josh refuses to stay a full week at Ryan Creek as planned and, as the book closes, he starts out on the long walk home in what can be seen as an existentialist break for freedom. This is not a journey into Bachelard's solitude of reverie even though Josh is a poet who walks alone. Ontological exchange is not expressed explicitly until later in the novel, but its conditions are set up from the first night of Josh's stay in his great-grandfather's old room:

> A jug with blue flowers on it, huge, enormous, started forming round the fringes of Josh's consciousness, line by line, getting larger and larger and more unlikely. Curves and knobs and unfamiliar oddities started marshalling in the shadows, lining up for footdrill … Leaves of crystal, dozens of them, scores of them, shivering like dragonflies trapped in spider webs, revolving, revolving, touching and tinkling. Higher, higher, red and awful, spilling out its threads, holding up its crystals, the last chandelier that ever should have happened.
>
> (15)

As Josh wakes to take in his new surroundings in Aunt Clara's home, he comes into a new consciousness of being out of kilter with the things around him. Anticipating the focus on non-human entities in my next chapter, the objects surrounding Josh represent the 'tyranny of things' in Bill Brown's terms, whereby physical objects are described in forensic detail and Southall attempts to chart (via Josh) 'a consciousness that transcends' them (Brown 2003: 141).[28] In these things lies otherness as difference and at odds with the being that Josh thought he was coming in to. His sense that the chandelier never should have happened foreshadows his ensuing confrontation with Aunt Clara and the children of Ryan Creek.

Josh charts the difficulties of coming into being in a communal setting, wherein familial and civic expectations elide the individual conditions of poetic consciousness. Aunt Clara's decision to read Josh' poetry without permission points to the poet in recession; Josh struggles to be or find himself in this context. Aunt Clara's expectations of him – as a Plowman in a community of subservient-alienated others – also negatively influence Josh's encounters with the Sunday School children (over whom Aunt Clara presides). Josh finds himself 'carried along all the time in the middle of the crowd, not quite himself, and not wholly there' ([1971] 1973: 28) and he soon loses track of himself. Aunt Clara has scheduled Josh into a timetable of social events – shooting with local boys and competing in an annual cricket match – that serve to estrange rather than assimilate her nephew, so it is inevitable that ontological exchange is negatively charged when it comes. Towards the end of the book, Harry Jones (one of the most respected Ryan Creeks boys) catches Josh in the act of running away from Aunt Clara's home:

> 'You reckon on running away?'
> 'If you like.' …

> 'Isn't there any end with you? How can any one kid be so low? How low do you reckon you can get?'
> 'Lower yet. When I hit the bottom you can move over to make room. Take your hand off my shirt.'
> Harry screwing it violently and pushing him away.
>
> (162)

The material vitality of a thing represents Josh's alienation and the violently screwed shirt also foreshadows the beating he endures, first from Harry and then the entire cricket team. In this ontological exchange, Harry diminishes Josh on ethical grounds, drawing attention to a code of conduct transgressed. However, Josh transforms the moral challenge into a situated debasement of being, so that he exists on a level already occupied by Harry (at least from Josh's perspective of the other). Josh's act of running away has brought him into being in the pits of human endeavour. Levinas touches on the ontic conditions of such action, observing that 'The inefficacy of human action teaches us how precarious is the concept "man"' and that distinct action can be seen as 'the fact of *beginning*, of *existing* as origin and from origin toward the future' ([1972] 2006: 49). In this sense then, the base level of the boys' actions generates an exchange of ontological origin, while its future-facing aspect also allows for childly potential (as seen in other examples of ontological exchange). Although Josh is almost killed in the ensuing encounter with others, he is (after all) able to walk away from his present in Ryan Creek into a future of his own making.

Finally, Josh refuses the determinism represented by Aunt Clara (as the head of the Plowman family) and her faith; as Sartre observes in *Existentialism Is a Humanism* (1946) 'there is no determinism – man is free, man is freedom' ([1946] 2008: 399). If this stream-of-consciousness battle with otherness in *Josh* has been at root an existentialist struggle, then it is tempting to read the closing section as a triumph of self over other. However, this would be to reinstate the dualism dismantled by Sartre in *Being and Nothingness*. Close attention to the passage reveals a to and fro movement from self to other in which neither is elided. Josh moves himself away while simultaneously looking back – and he is looked at in return:

> Josh looking back to the bridge put there by Great-grandfather in 1882, looking back again and again, the least he could do while they stood to watch him go. Looking back and waving, picking different faces while faces could be seen.
>
> (179)

The looking back suggests a willingness – 'the least he could do' – to incorporate the other as '*they* stood to watch him go' (my emphasis). We might see something of Sartre's being-for-others in this, 'I am responsible for my being-for-others, but I am not the foundation of it' ([1943] 2003: 386), although this misses the ethical turn suggested by the potentially self-diminishing – *least he* could do – aspect of Josh's concern with looking back. This is where the Levinasian fusion of an existential understanding of being with ethical ontology comes usefully into focus. Levinas observes in a discussion of self, servitude and obligation that 'the responsibility that owes nothing to my freedom is my responsibility for the freedom of others' ([1972] 2006: 55). Responsibility precedes freedom and therefore the subject's freedom is constituted by consideration for the other; this responsibility cannot diminish the subject or place it in servitude since 'The subject as Ego stands already in freedom, beyond self' (54). Read in these terms, Josh's act of looking back is recognition of the fact that he has already drawn the folk of Ryan Creek into himself; he is free to leave in the act of retaining them. In the book's final line there is a heightened corporeal awareness, 'Go away, crows. Find yourselves a body that's had its day. I'm walking mine to Melbourne town and living every mile' (179). This observational detachment *from* body hints that something of Josh *himself* remains in Ryan Creek's otherness; that although his body travels to Melbourne a *significant* part of him remains of Ryan Creek (i.e. Josh signifies something in Ryan Creek). Drawing on Merleau-Ponty's sense of body as expression of the world, Levinas explains that

> the language through which signification is produced in being is a language spoken by embodied minds. ... The body is the fact that thought is immersed in the world that it thinks and consequently expresses this world at the same time as it thinks it.
>
> ([1972] 2006: 16)

Josh – understood as an expression of being beyond character – is thereby expressed through his bodily passage in and out of Ryan Creek. Southall's narrative strategy points not to dislocation of body and mind, rather to this idea that body expresses the mind – *I'm walking mine* – through its immersion in the world as Josh walks through it: 'Blue sky and yellow stubble, golden yellow plain' (179).[29] This then is Josh's epiphany. His ability to *incorporate* the homeland of his great-grandfather and simultaneously carry away this sense of home means that he is no longer homeless in the Heideggarian sense of it. In his 1946 'Letter on "Humanism"', Heidegger debates notions of homecoming and homeland. He eventually considers a history of secular, modern being in terms of homelessness, pointing to the idea that beings can only be home when invested by being. He concludes that 'Homelessness ... consists in the abandonment of beings by being. Homelessness is the symptom of oblivion of being. Because of it the truth of being remains unthought' ([1946] 1998: 258). On these terms, Josh can be away from home (Ryan Creek) and home (Melbourne) as he tunes in to a mode of being that is for others and itself.

As *Josh* demonstrates, ontological exchange as a mechanism does not necessarily lead to an easy or harmonious acceptance of others. Indeed, Southall's minutely detailed account of Josh's stay in Ryan Creek suggests that relationships with others are invariably tortuous and possible (nonetheless). The negative charge of this ontological exchange has repercussions for a whole community and yet the existential malaise that it evokes is lifted into unexpected epiphany as Josh looks back to move forward. The negative and epiphanic tenor of this ontological exchange emphasizes the ontic ambivalence of exchange in general; it generates an ontic stumbling block, while also yielding a path to the progression of being. In the moment of epiphany something is lost and gained; understood and misunderstood; enlightened and enshrouded. The presence of such epiphanic moments can be understood partly in the context of the secularization of children's literature during the twentieth century, whereby such epiphany allows for a reinstatement of being in beings that do not rely on divinity for their ontological homing. In *Josh* is encapsulated primary concerns of this chapter, while also anticipating Brown's vitality of things in Chapter 2 as Josh gradually accepts his affinity with 'the last chandelier that ever should have happened'.

2

Something Matters: Things about Nappies

A curious thing about the ontological problem is its simplicity. It can be put in three Anglo-Saxon monosyllables: 'What is there?' It can be answered, moreover, in a word – 'Everything' – and everyone will accept this answer as true. However, this is merely to say that there is what there is. There remains room for disagreement over cases; and so the issue has stayed alive down the centuries.

(Quine [1948] 1980: 1)

Foundational cataloguing

Quine's droll distillation of the ontological problem into a simple statement – *there is everything* – is as daunting as it is elliptical. An immediate challenge arising from this ontological extreme is to establish what everything is. In 'On What There Is', Quine is quick to observe that metaphysicians have been known to 'overpopulate' the universe with ontological possibility, which 'offends the aesthetic sense of us who have a taste for desert landscapes' ([1948] 1980: 4). Although Quine seeks to rid his everything of abstractions and fictions, ultimately he accepts the grounds on which Pegasus or Puff, the Magic Dragon, might exist.[1] Notwithstanding, Quine does not reveal what it means for Pegasus *to be*; instead he considers the ontological basis of 'surface grammars' that commit to Pegasus, thus rendering the winged horse possible.[2] Crane and Farkas suggest that in order to establish the remit of Quine's everything we might 'look around and start to list things: this cup of coffee, these particles of dust moving in the air, the sound of a car from the street … and our list will be too long' (2004: 137). They recognize that if their list were to include everything there is, they might never complete their inventory. A much broader process of ontological categorization is required to manage everything, of the sort that has divided philosophers since Aristotle's semantic approach to identifying things in *Categories* (*c*.335–23 BC).

What is apparent and mutual in all this – while acknowledging Quine's careful dismantling of several Aristotelian categories[3] – is that in certain contexts, the (human) acts of perceiving, listing or accumulating things are ontological projects expressed through language. In this chapter I demonstrate that baby books provide a foundational context for such ontological projects. As I have established, ontological exchange repeatedly demonstrates that to be human is to encounter other human beings – now the focus shifts to a wider concern with material objects and non-human entities in relation to and beyond human being as manifest in books for infants and young children.

The earliest ontological projects that babies born in literate societies are likely to encounter are at work in ABCs, counting or concept books of early childhood. The title of *Helen Oxenbury's ABC of Things* (1971) might seem vague, but it hints at an ontic commitment to *things* that extends beyond teaching children to read. Oxenbury's illustrations depict entities of all kinds – including pelican, pier and pig – rendering things with a vitality that moves beyond pedagogic value. Scholarship on baby books has tended to focus on the implied reader, cognitive competence or epistemological conditions of knowledge. For example, in her discussion of concept and novelty books, Judith Graham identifies codes and conventions required for meaning making. She reflects on the cognitive demands of texts for the youngest readers, observing that 'it should not be forgotten how much readers know and need to know if they are to enjoy books' (2014: 56). In order to move beyond this consideration of the reader, my first task is to set aside the (reading/playing) baby in order to consider the bathwater – and where better to turn than *The Baby's Catalogue* (1982) by Janet and Allan Ahlberg, since one of the joys of this picturebook is the attention it gives to baths in which babies sit.

Quine's query – what is there? – can be glimpsed behind the paraphernalia of babyhood assembled in *The Baby's Catalogue*, in which conventions of shop catalogue and picturebook are played off against each other. The Ahlbergs offer up a gently ironic game – at the expense of their infant daughter who persistently chose to read Mothercare[4] catalogues in favour of literary texts (Pauli 2011: n.p.) – and in the gap between product and narrative, ontological commitment to an assortment of things is apparent. Everything that appears in the book is relevant to a daily routine of early childhood in 1980s Britain and a semblance of narrative is evident in a chronological arrangement of things that moves from early morning feeds to bedtime routines. Although presented in varied catalogue formats, these items are not identified as commercial products (as in the Mothercare catalogue) and have a worth that resides in their status as baby *things*. Furthermore, while *The Baby's Catalogue* is staged through the narrative rhythm of routine and contextual drama, story event is less important than story *thing*. Essentially then, this picturebook is invested in things and uses a combination of catalogue layout and visual narrative to emphasize (what can be seen as) ontological concerns.

In *The Baby's Catalogue* human participants in the domestic theatre of infancy are represented through watercolour vignettes and labelled as exhibits, alongside other concrete things and abstract concepts. This collapse of categorical boundaries could be considered 'unlovely' in Quine's terms – for its contents page seems as committed to accidents as it is to toys – and Quine demands an ontological rigour that limits the conditions of such commitment (1953: 4). The contents are listed in a column, one after the other, and the same typeface is used for each entry, suggesting that they are equally relevant. Each listed item appears once, with the exception of 'Babies' and 'Mums and Dads', which are itemized twice in the service of narrative routine – a sequence of nursing, waking and sleeping babies open and close the book. Words in the book are used to label entities, such as Babies, Mums, Mornings, Toys, Nappies, Games, Accidents and Bedtimes. Labels have an organizing function, allowing illustrations to be sorted into the category of thing represented. Many entities are subcategorized, so that Flowers, Mower, Pots and Butterfly appear under the 'Gardens' heading (Ahlberg [1982] 1984: 18).[5] The verbal labelling does not differentiate between categories of entity though – thus human beings are presented in the catalogue alongside creatures, material objects and events.

This lack of verbal demarcation could be explained via consideration of the infantile implied audience. As Jean Piaget would have it, infants are unable to distinguish between things in the world or to recognize a world external to them. In *The Construction of Reality in the Child* (1954) Piaget describes the psycho-cognitive process as a 'transition from chaos to cosmos', for only gradually does the baby come to organize reality and to 'assign itself a place as a thing among things, an event among events' (xiii). Doubtless the Ahlbergs' picturebook is sensitive to the child's initially chaotic, evolving and limited experience of the universe, but this is not of particular interest to me here (and such a reading brings little new to a consideration of baby books). A shift away from implied readers and children's experience, towards a focus on entities represented in the book, reveals that ontological distinctions between types of object might be just as ambiguous as *The Baby's Catalogue* suggests.

Brown's discussion of the Shield of Achilles in *Other Things* (2015) is revelatory in this respect as he explores the ontological implications of the shield, which 'enacts a drama of animate matter' (2015: 1). Brown challenges the tenacity of ekphrastic readings of Homer's poem, which have focussed on distinctions between image and text and in so doing have elided the shield as object (3). Conversely, Brown observes that vitality is extended 'beyond the immortal and the mortal – to the artificial' and that Homeric

> 'wonder of the artist's craft' would seem to insist, then, on a kind of indeterminate ontology, in which the being of the object world cannot so readily be distinguished from the being of animals, say, or the being we call human being.
>
> (2)

Brown's observation that objects might share aspects of being with humans and other creatures has wide-reaching repercussions, not least for understanding metaphysical aspects of children's literature. Where Piaget might take it for granted that the Ahlbergs' child will soon be able to sort human from ball – because they are beings of a different order – Brown reveals that the distinction is not as straightforward as Piaget's developmental schema indicates.

The ontological ground on which the Piagetian distinction rests underwent an upheaval in the twentieth century and Brown makes a case for a 'Homeric vitalism' (in which the artefactual is lent the vitality of mortal or immortal beings) that has been ignored or misunderstood by Homeric scholarship (4). Brown goes on to trace a move towards 'material vitalism' in twentieth-century philosophy and art, which suggests we revisit the ontological resonance of objects in art and literature. In a Heideggerian move, Brown distinguishes between *thingness* – which registers vitality as a sort of potentiality in objects – and *objecthood*, perceived at the level of form (4–5). This allows him to demonstrate – after Heidegger – that art can get at the being of things, thus bypassing Kant and the human perception or experience of the object; the thingness of the object is at the heart of Brown's ontological project. Brown attributes to Homer's appreciation of the shield an oscillation between the animate and inanimate, collapsing metaphysical binaries that split being along these lines; Cartesian ontological dualism insists on this divide, for example. Brown argues that literature, along with the visual and plastic arts, has long recognized the 'uncanniness of the ordinary' (5).

It might not seem surprising to suggest that a children's literature, generating Hans Christian Andersen's 'The Darning Needle' (1845) or Reverend W. Awdry's *The Three Railway Engines* (1945), plays an important role in this cultural embrace of material vitalism. However, its role has been elided in literary discourse that centres on the child's negotiation of the object – vitality is typically located in childly response to the object in literature, rather than in the thingness of the object. The 'material turn' navigated by Jane Carroll in 'Objects and Toys'[6] reveals that this is starting to change, so that a concern for the tangible object – including the book itself – sits alongside a consideration of the child who might have held the objects sold or associated with books. Carroll identifies a commodity culture proliferating around children's books in the nineteenth and early twentieth century, though she remarks that 'there has been relatively little attention paid to the material culture of childhood within the period or to the relationships between children's literature and children's consumer culture' (Carroll forthcoming: n.p.). Carroll also explores the role of objects in narrative structure, recognizing that they might 'function as potent signifiers of economic and cultural status' (n.p.) or to establish an 'authentic – or deeply deceptive – sense of the past' (n.p.). For example, Carroll details the miscellany of objects in Billy Bones's sea chest in Robert Louis Stevenson's *Treasure Island* (1883), observing that 'this collection of items serves to endow Bones with a history and with a personality' (n.p.). Carroll's socio-historic and narratological focus on the material object in and around children's books buttresses my own argument for taking seriously the ontological vitality of objects in children's literature. Of course it is possible for Brown to resist analysis at the level of infantile animism or solipsism (for instance) when considering 'Western literature's most magnificent object' (1), yet it is crucial to recognize the role children's books play in allowing objects entry to metaphysical systems. Considering the object as a matter of importance in its own right also uncovers the metaphysical function of baby books and the children's literature that grows from them. While setting the ground for a pervasive thingness in children's literature, I also suggest that *The Baby's Catalogue* is doing something particular (that nonetheless has wider relevance in the field).

If vitalism can be detected in objects surrounding child and parent in the Ahlbergs' picturebook, it could be attributed to an aesthetic rendering of objects that challenges widely held philosophical categories of being (on which Piaget draws) and that Brown traces in terms of cultural and philosophical development. Brown's vitalism troubles ontological distinctions to an extent that might bother Quine, since it extends boundaries of being through its investment in thingness. Likewise, some troubling is at work in *The Baby's Catalogue*. Close observation is required to follow it, since the visual organization of entities allows for a more nuanced process of ontological distinction than its verbal list of contents might suggest. As established above, verbal labels are no more attentive to one referent than another, whereas there is gradation in the illustrative treatment of entities. The catalogue presents things visually in a range of different layouts: framed panels; unframed images; framed grids; unframed rows of objects (Figure 2.1).

Figure 2.1 Toys in wait (Ahlberg [1982] 1984: 10).

The framed panels resemble comic strips in their sequential presentation and the unframed images allow space for narrative movement. Indeed, these particular layouts – framed panels and unframed images – are reserved for the depiction of human beings, often acting on other things around them. The relatively static layouts – framed grids and unframed rows – contain material objects or creatures at rest, as if awaiting human performers to interact with them.

The illustrations indicate that beings of different kinds coexist, yet humans have an instigative potential that ostensibly is not afforded to other entities (namely material objects and other living creatures). The stasis of the gridded layouts is deceptive though, as is any passivity associated with the *wait* for (possibly human) intervention. The *wait* is crucial here, as it refers to deferred action and the potential for something to happen. Since these things are presented *in wait*, they can be understood as entities of potential and possibility – potential that relates to the being of the thing itself and not only to human proximity or future action. These are waiting things and their thingness can partly be understood in these terms. The gap opening up here – in which the being of a thing in its own right can be glimpsed – is of the sort that Heidegger grapples with in *Being and Time*, when he considers '*The Being of Beings Encountered in the Surrounding World*' (1996: 62).

Heidegger is interested in human proximity with things and quickly refutes the Cartesian idea that this proximity is gained via 'mere perceptual cognition', arguing that 'a handling, using, and taking care of things … has its own kind of "knowledge"' (63). The next step is for Heidegger to demonstrate that the usefulness of things does not reside in the (human) handling of things but in the being of things. Thus, he settles on 'handiness' as 'the kind of being of these beings', concluding that '*Handiness is the ontological categorical definition of beings as they are "in themselves"*' (67). This *handiness* recognizes the vital potential in things themselves and I propose that the Ahlbergs' grids allow for this handiness in their cataloguing of objects. Their objects have a latent vitality that exudes thingness – and of course the energy of Janet Ahlberg's vignettes is palpable. In case there is any doubt over this matter though, the potential vitality of non-human things is further borne out by an exception to the staging of material objects in *The Baby's Catalogue*: a spread full of newly washed nappies is left to bleed to the gutter, free of gridlines and containment, or human intervention (Figure 2.2).

The terry nappies are accorded the same visual space as 'Mums' or 'Brothers and Sisters' and, consequently, can be assumed to exist on the same categorical level. Of course these are *textual* categories, serving to distinguish entities that comprise the Ahlbergs' literary representation of babyhood. Of the aesthetic grounds of the picturebook therefore, it can be said that there is equivalence in the treatment of humans and nappies, an equivalence that (in literary critical terms) could suggest that babyhood can be taken over by nappies and the base functions of being human. However, merely recognizing the terms of categorization does not get to grips with the *equivalent* nature of the relationship between nappy and human – an equivalence that reaches again towards Heideggerian thingness.

In *Being and Time*, Heidegger never quite prevents his interest in being human from eclipsing the being of things, whereas full attention is given to things in *What Is a Thing?* (1967).[7] Like Quine, Heidegger recognizes that ontology can be complicated by an overabundance of things, seeking to limit the field of enquiry in order to pose the question in terms demanded by his laughing housemaid – that is, he should consider 'things in front of his very nose and feet' (1967: 3). Heidegger recounts a Platonic story in which a housemaid remonstrates with Thales because he is so busy studying the heavens above that he falls into a well. Heidegger thus determines that 'the question "What is a thing?" must always

Figure 2.2 Thingness on the line (Ahlberg [1982] 1984: 14).

be rated as one which causes housemaids to laugh' (3). Heidegger commonly employs parables or fables to further his ideas, suggesting that there is more than straightforward clarification (and jest) at work here. It seems to me that the 'genuine housemaid' matters to Heidegger because – in this patriarchal context – she is routinely in the care of everyday things; she can help him to get at the 'handy' and 'narrow' things of his concern. Heidegger recognizes that 'we understand the term "thing" in both a narrower and broader sense. The *narrower* or limited meaning of "thing" is that which can be touched, reached, or seen, i.e., what is present-at-hand' (5). Furthermore, Heidegger suggests that the question, 'even where it is understood in its wider and widest meanings, mostly aims at this narrower field and begins from it' (7). It is at this point that I bring the Ahlbergs' nappies into the 'narrower field', in order to suggest that there is ontological significance in the aesthetic categorical equivalence between human (baby) and thing (nappy) and that their depiction responds to Heidegger's narrow sense of what things are.

So what are the things in this image (Figure 2.2)? The pegged out nappies could be identified as terrycloth squares, redolent of a pre-disposable British society that washed and reused nappies. Their depiction in a 1980s picturebook might be considered nostalgically anachronistic, or subversively opposed to convenient consumerism in its environmental awareness. However, while these observations contribute to a socio-historic frame for the picturebook, they ignore the ontological dimensions of the image. It is the formal/visual presentation of nappies that is key here, alongside the fact that these nappy things take up unframed illustrative space, reserved for human characters elsewhere in the picturebook. Most pages in the book are crowded with images, while eighteen nappies are afforded a full verso to flutter in the breeze. A song thrush perched on the washing line grounds the nappies in natural processes and the suggestion of towelling texture in the sketching indicates materiality and practical use; after all the nappies' usefulness lies in their proximity to natural functions. Vignettes of nappy buckets and a washing machine sitting above the nappies also imply their routine purpose and everydayness. These nappies are given space to hang and the reader is given extra time-space to wonder at these particular entries in the catalogue.

In 'The Origin of the Work of Art' (1950) Heidegger considers the artistic expression of thingness – and this is an important step in Brown's expression of thingness (as it is in mine). Heidegger takes as his example actual shoes worn in fields by peasants and ruminates on their earthy qualities and usefulness. In so doing he reaches an understanding of their 'equipmental' nature, as we might when considering the rough terry nap and folds of a real nappy worn by an infant. Yet Heidegger finds that this focus on the 'blank usefulness' of the actual shoe results in a mundane dwindling of the thing into 'mere stuff' ([1950] 1975: 35). By comparison, the expression of things rendered in artwork gets at something beyond their usefulness in the field, as Heidegger realizes when looking closely at Van Gogh's artistic rendering of a pair of peasant shoes. He argues that the picture presents things for notice that are unremarked by the wearer of shoes; in the poetic image he finds the shoe vibrating with 'the silent call of the earth' (34). Eventually Heidegger observes that 'the art work let us know what shoes are in truth' (35), and – in spite of the vagueness that he accepts is inherent in this – it is an observation that marks the contribution made by the arts to the ontology of things and that feeds into Brown's sense of the 'secret life of things' (2015: 241). Artworks are able to animate things in the manner of Homer's shield, Van Gogh's shoes and the Ahlbergs' nappies. A key point here is to notice the company kept by those nappies. They are not vitalized by the animistic child's experience of them, as is frequently the explanation for the life of objects and toys in children's literature.[8] Instead the nappy is a vitalized being in the locus of babyhood on the same level as mothers or babies. The movement from Heidegger's visual art to Brown's poetry and prose is not to elide the importance of (art) form. Indeed, I argue that the visual properties of the baby book have a specific role to play in the ontic validation of things. My contention is that baby books have a particular understanding of the present-at-handness of things and that when presenting the things of the world they begin with the ontic focus of the housemaid's narrow field.

In *The Baby's Catalogue* I identify a shift away from the intersubjective appraisal of child and object in psychoanalysis, towards the sort of assemblage at work in Gilles Deleuze and Félix Guattari's *A Thousand Plateaus* (1980). Taking the child's experience of organic material as an example, they point out that

> for children an organ has 'a thousand vicissitudes', that it is 'difficult to localize, difficult to identify, it is in turn a bone, an engine, excrement, the baby, a hand, daddy's heart …' … This is not animism, any more than it is mechanism; rather, it is universal machinism: a plane of consistency occupied by an immense abstract machine comprising an infinite number of assemblages.
>
> ([1980] 2013: 299)

Deleuze and Guattari demonstrate the connective potential between the organic matter of the human body and locomotives or chairs, each of which depends on 'different relations of movement and rest' (298). Assemblage sees the body in terms of material relations with other elemental things and recognizes the potential for energy – not so far from Brown's vitalism – in each element. Considered in these terms, the Ahlbergs' catalogue reflects the potential for connections between materials – human bottom, excrement, nappy – in a process of assemblage that does not prioritize, or even recognize, the human subject. Of course this is not to say that the human does not exist in such baby books; rather that the human-object distinction of so much childhood discourse is challenged in ways that have not yet been recognized. In *The Baby's Catalogue* humans and nappies are equally the stuff of babyhood – and this ontological parity paves the way for a wider consideration of the metaphysical implications of baby books. The complex design of *The Baby's Catalogue* makes it an exceptional example of foundational cataloguing. Nonetheless, its careful regard for things of the experiential world is replicated in books such as *Planes and Rockets and Things That Fly* (1971) by Richard Scarry, or even less ambitious baby books that appear on publishing lists as staples, such as *100 Things That Go* (2019) by Dorling Kindersely.

Things round-about-us

> As we ask 'What is a thing?' we now mean the things around us. We take in view what is most immediate, most capable of being grasped by the hand. By observing such, we reveal that we have learned something from the laughter of the housemaid. She thinks we should first look around thoroughly in this round-about-us (*Um-uns-herum*).
>
> (Heidegger 1967: 7)

'What is there right around me that I'm not seeing?' inquires Tana Hoban as a photographer setting out to create concept books for babies and children in the 1970s (Hoban in Allison 2000: 147). This question remains central to Hoban's work and reveals ontic concern with recognizing the thingness – not that she expresses it in these terms – of everyday objects, often via a camera lens. Throughout her extensive corpus Hoban makes use of the formal properties of books for the youngest readers – minimal verbal text, visual emphasis, conceptual focus, iconographic presentation, sensual engagement – to confirm the material presence of entities in the external world. Unsurprisingly, Hoban's contribution to the metaphysics of children's literature has not been recognized, yet she shares with Heidegger's figurative housemaid a need to grasp things 'in the round-about-us' through the observation of things.[9] The idea of things being *in* (the round-about-us) is central to Heidegger's concept of being. As Brown points out, Heidegger's 'originality lies not least in his insistence that we cannot begin to appreciate what being human means without recognizing that such being is thrown (has been thrown) into a world of things' (2015: 24). We are all thrown into the world – an ontological condition shared by human and non-human things alike – and it is this sense of shared being in the world at hand that concept books such as Hoban's communicate.

Hoban's *Look Again!* (1971) is a wordless collection of black-and-white photographs, depicting a series of familiar organic objects (plants and creatures) through its 'keyhole' design. Attention is drawn to each object through a die-cut technique, whereby a square window (cut into a blank page) offers a partial view of pear, shell or starfish (Figure 2.3). The die-cut format mimics a camera aperture – zooming in on its subject – and the drama of each page turn reveals the whole of the previously obscured object (and focal subject). Implicitly the reader is invited to guess what lies behind the keyhole, yet it is the object (and the disclosure of thingness) that is of central concern. One further move places each object in a wider context of relations with the world. For example, once

Figure 2.3 Emergent thingness (Hoban 1971: 13).

a shell has been disclosed behind its die-cut window, the page turn reveals a child holding the shell to their ear (Hoban 1971: 13–16).[10] It seems then that the formal structure of the picturebook has ontic reach and that the presentation of Hoban's photographs is just as important as the images themselves in conveying object ontology.

The imperative title of Hoban's *Look Again!* charges the implied reader with closely inspecting *present-at-hand* entities. The direct address might seem to signal an overriding concern with reader engagement, but this is the first and last time readers are explicitly acknowledged. The adverbial stress of 'again' hints that Hoban's reader-viewer might have missed something that she intends them to notice – or at least that the things depicted are worth seeing *once more* – and so the reader must *go back*, or read *in the opposite direction* to see things *anew*.[11] These etymological variations of 'again' suggest the sort of return that delves and digs into a thing so that it can be seen from different perspectives. The things in this book are here to be seen now, yet the adverbial *again-ness* hints at things that have already been and will be (again). This evokes Hans-Georg Gadamer's sense in *Truth and Method* (1960) of the 'sheer presence of the past' inherent in all literary works of art, which 'are actualized only when they are read' ([1960] 2004: 156–7). Hoban's concise verbal call reaches out from the moment it was written, speaking via Gadamer's 'trace of the mind' in which 'time and space seem to be superseded' (156). This trace of mind is discernable in the again-ness of a book for the youngest readers, demanding that its things be considered again and again. It is important to note that the again-ness I detect here does not emanate from the reader – though well it might – but from the 'ontology of the work of art' in Gadamer's terms (102–61). Again-ness is an aspect of the book's playfulness, which can also be related to the aesthetic play of the keyhole game, central to the book's design. Gadamer explains:

> When we speak of play in reference to the experience of art, this means neither the orientation nor even the state of mind of the creator or those enjoying the work of art, nor the freedom of a subjectivity engaged in play, but the mode of being of the work of art itself.
>
> (102)

The crucial point is that play is not brought to the book by author or child; play is an ontological mode of *Look Again!* Having identified Gadamer's 'essence of play' (103) in the book's ontology, I also want to demonstrate the book's ontological move away from the looking child towards the object presenting itself to be seen. I am not suggesting that the reader is of no concern in a book clearly designed for babies or young children, rather that the ontological thrust of books such as *Look Again!* deserves attention (as so often it is overlooked). In order to demonstrate how the book offers up bodies to be seen a brief metaphysical detour to Lockean notions of *solidity* is required.

In *An Essay Concerning Human Understanding* (1690) Locke allows that entities are in the external world and that they have a solidity, which humans come to understand through a combination of sensation and reflection – an ontological process that can be traced in a number of Hoban's books. The solidity of material things is crucial for Locke and hence 'there is no idea, which we receive more constantly from sensation, than *solidity*' ([1690] 2004: 124). Locke recognizes that to be human is to experience the approach of other bodies and that this process is interrupted and potentially enriched by the intrusion of material beings. Bodies produce ideas in us and it is part of Locke's project to demonstrate that this happens through *impulse*; that is, via the physical process of impulsion as embodied particles interact with human senses (135). Echoes of ontological exchange inhere in this encounter of self and other in a move out of solitude,[12] though Locke's concern is with human-on-matter (instead of human-on-human): 'That which thus hinders the approach of two bodies, when they are moving towards one another, I call *solidity*' (124). Solid entities are perceived passively by all humans via touch or sight, 'For in bare naked *perception*, the mind is, for the most part, only passive; and what it perceives, it cannot avoid perceiving' (142). In Locke's terms, simple ideas are formed through basic perception of *primary qualities* that resemble qualities in the object and his notion of perception extends to the complexities of sensation afforded by sight. Locke asserts that through ideas of shape and colour, sight can afford solidity to matter since sight is 'the most comprehensive of all our senses' (145). This is of particular significance for Hoban's picturebook, in which the command to look at objects carries the ontological function of affording solidity to the objects in question.

While Locke accepts that objects are in the world, emphasis remains on the faculties of human sensation to afford the object solidity – thus as Locke would have it, Hoban's pear is only realized by the focussed, albeit passive, gaze of the reader on its seeds (Hoban 1971: 24–6). Locke's acceptance of the solidity of things is certainly helpful for appreciating Hoban's ongoing concern with objects, since it establishes that objects have a presence in the world independent of the psycho-cognition of the child. Having drawn Locke into the discussion though, it must be admitted that his emphasis on human sensation and passive receptivity quickly elides the object at hand. Something more is required to register the care taken with objects in Hoban's work – and this is where Brown's development of Heideggerian thingness returns. Hoban's shell (Figure 2.3) draws me to something ineffable beyond the spiralling form of the object and to Bachelard's conviction in *The Poetics of Space* (1958) that 'after a positive examination of the shell world, the imagination is defeated by reality' ([1958] 1994: 105). There is a some-*thing* about Hoban's shell that draws the observer to look again.

Brown sees the glimmer of thingness in the Piagetian developmental journey through object–subject relations and 'dilates' the distinction between object and thing that Piaget only 'vaguely' registers (Brown 2015: 21). In distinguishing between object and thing, Brown explains that 'the thingness of the constituted object, is the outcome of an interaction (beyond their mutual constitution) between subject and object' and moreover that 'thingness inheres (as a latency) within any manifest object' (22). Lockean perception still has a role to play here, though Brown is more concerned with winkling out the thing that attracts humans to objects in the first place. Brown's primary interest is in 'how objects grasp you: how they elicit your attention, interrupt your concentration, assault your sensorium' (23–4). Returning to Hoban's glimpse of a shell, it appears that the drama of the die-cut page turn has an ontic role to play in this grasp. The *beyondness* of the object is also confirmed in the manner suggested by Brown's sense of subject–object oscillation; as replicated in the book's tripartite page turn, there is something (its thingness) of the object that is out of reach, yet simultaneously reached for by the human subject. Presentation and grasp thus have an ontic energy in Hoban's picturebook, indicating that such objects are to be found in the external world and that they exist beyond the pages of this particular book.

The ontic commitment of *Look Again!* is further confirmed by its use of photography. Indeed, Hoban's early impact on the children's literature scene can be explained partly by her commitment to cataloguing things that exist through the photograph, an artistic medium that has a unique relationship with the experiential world. Although digital photography has brought about a change in this relationship, twentieth-century discourse on the ontic implications of photographic media proves useful for thinking about the use of photography in picturebooks. Seeking to identify the ontological status of the photograph in *Camera Lucida* (1980), Roland Barthes concludes that 'the photograph's essence is to ratify what it represents' and to say 'for certain *what has been*' ([1980] 2010: 85). Barthes's view is not valid for all photographs – in an age of digital photography and photoshopped images it is recognized that photographs do not always confirm 'for certain'. Nonetheless, photos are able to record moments in the mode of a 'natural' image that reflects reality *as it is* in a way that differs from other art forms. André Bazin underscores this point in his 1945 essay, 'The Ontology of the Photographic Image'.

> The objective nature of photography confers on it a quality of credibility absent from all other picture-making ... we are forced to accept as real the existence of the object reproduced, actually *re*-presented, set before us, that is to say, in time and space. Photography enjoys a certain advantage in virtue of this transference of reality from the thing to its reproduction.
>
> ([1945] 2005: 40)

Bazin's notion that photography can 'transfer reality' points to the ontological function of the medium, which has a particular resonance in books for young readers. These photographs ratify the things that they behold, and they have a pedagogic commitment to render entities extant for children who are learning what there is in the world and thereby coming to terms with their thrownness among a world of objects. The photographic capturing of objects in *Look Again!* (and books like it) confirms that the entities it records have existed at a certain moment in time and that they have an ontological force outside of the viewer's perception of them. Of course, the act of looking at Hoban's images of sunflower and starfish renders such objects real via the viewer, but Barthes and Bazin's observations move away from Lockean sensation and endorse the photograph's intrinsic capacity to confirm the being of its subject. Hoban's photographs hold on to entities with the expectation that the implied reader will meet objects like them in the world, but it is important to note that Hoban's objects are realized, regardless of whether actual readers ever come across them.

Photography is only one representative medium used in baby books, though the principle of focusing on objects of concern is shared by the most basic of books in the widespread use of block silhouettes, outline and contour. Hoban makes this move herself in books such as *Black White* (1993) – a wordless board book, containing a series of high-contrast shapes – which blend photographic principles of light contrast with graphic design in the creation of silhouette books for infants that stimulate sight and recognition. My edition of *Black White* is itself a robust object, produced on thick card with smooth-glossed surfaces. It is a carefully designed thing with a purpose that might seem to refuse aesthetic consideration. The book has the sort of utility attributed to designed objects; it helps babies to see and can be chewed and dropped without too much damage. As Deyan Sudjic contends in *The Language of Things* (2008), the value of art typically lies in its uselessness ([2008] 2009: 167), while design is materially rooted in the purposeful and practical. However, I want to determine that as well as having a practical contribution to make to human development (design), images in baby books demonstrate metaphysical equivalence with the external world (art).

In 'Image and Code' (1981) Ernst Gombrich rehearses the 'commonsense distinction between images which are naturally recognizable because they are imitations and words which are based on conventions' (11). In the course of exploring the distinction, Gombrich takes positions that allow me to clarify the metaphysical commitment of baby books to *seeing the world as it is*. There is an assumption in *Black White* that images are able to reveal something of the thing they represent, but this is not a given. Indeed, this is a metaphysical position upheld by the baby-book genre that takes its place in philosophical tradition. In *Iconology* (1986), W. J. T. Mitchell recognizes the metaphysical implications of a nature-convention debate that reaches back to Plato and in which Gombrich is embroiled. Gombrich challenges what he sees as a pervasive and 'oversimplified' view that 'outline is a convention because the objects of our environment are not bounded by lines', observing instead that 'Things in our environment are indeed clearly separated from their background, at least they so detach themselves as soon as we move. The contour is the equivalent of this experience' (Gombrich 1981: 17). While it might seem that the featureless outlines of Hoban's boat, balloon and leaf in *Black White* are the conventional signs of structuralism – signifying the things they represent – I want to take up Gombrich here and suggest that the contours of boat, balloon and leaf have equivalence to things in the world. As Mitchell clarifies, for Gombrich, 'Contour is not just one conventional way of indicating the separations of things from their background; it is the "equivalent" of this experience, not a "sign" for it' (Mitchell [1986] 1987: 86).[13] The Gombrichian insistence on the equivalence of contour is key to understanding the ontic dynamics of baby books such as Hoban's, since equivalence encompasses the sensory skills enlisted to 'read' the image and realize the thing represented (in an echo of Lockean solidity).

The equivalence of contour helps to trace the ontic structure of *Black White*, which realizes objects of the external world via its sequence of 'natural' silhouettes (to be seen by the implied infant viewer). While the selling point for many baby books is around their developmental value, of central interest here is the *embodied thing* to be realized by emergent visual skills. The object of perception in Hoban's book is presented in outline, thus establishing the ontological proposition that entities occupy their own space in the world and are separate from other things. The same principle adheres in books such as *Jungle Animals* (2017) by Xavier Deneux, since each blocked out animal stands out against its background in order to be recognized as a being of ontological consequence. This is a more challenging text than Hoban's though, as each creature is labelled with proper nouns and conceptually some are placed (at least implicitly) in food-chain relationships; for example, 'ants' crawl up the tongue of an 'anteater' (Deneux [2017] 2018: 3–4). In this case, image and sign work in tandem and language acquisition is stimulated along with motor skills – touch is encouraged by raised images – and general knowledge about the ecosystem. Notwithstanding, although there is a cluster of developmental tools in the book's coded material, underlying all this is a fundamental commitment to beings in the external world, realized by equivalence and the sight of blocked out images. The thingness of Deneux's beings makes the epistemic conditions of his books *matter*.

Alida Allison observes of Hoban's work that 'Since these images of real things and common experience are not culture bound, Hoban's books communicate at the most fundamental levels – awareness of oneself in the world and awareness of the world itself' (2000: 143). Certainly there is an attentive engagement with the external world in her 'books of perception' as Hoban describes them (148) and there is potential for grasping Brown's thingness in the salience of her clean images. Allison's observation here is not quite accurate though – Hoban's work communicates on fundamental levels, yet partially this happens because it *is* 'culture bound'.[14] The ontic commitment of Hoban's work is to demonstrating that our relationship with the world holds true for local and relative encounters. The cultural specificity of Hoban's conceptual primers, such as *Shapes, Shapes, Shapes* (1986), is comparatively easy to detect, as photographs centre on localized domestic and urban spaces. The cultural remit of the widely recognizable silhouettes in *Black White* (1993) is perhaps less obvious, yet the depicted objects have identifiable roots.

The silhouette of a rubber duck on the first spread, for example, is more complicated than it might appear in its ontic and cultural frame of reference.[15]

The duck is broadly representative of all species of living duck, while simultaneously evoking a toy that takes its place in Western pop culture – thus the 'culture bound' object is vitalized into thingness through its complicity with a biological entity. Patented by sculptor Peter Ganine in 1949, the iconic duck was further popularized by the US television series *Sesame Street* in the 1970s, though its longer history incorporates the manufacture of rubber, industrial design and mechanical reproduction. The trouble for Allison is that she detects a contradiction between the apparently shifting shapes of cultural relativism and a more stable profundity in the communicative qualities of Hoban's images; and she denies the former in order to champion the latter, thus missing their ontic dynamism. Sudjic reveals that the sort of metaphysical significance Allison reaches for in Hoban's objects can be squared with the transience of design submerged in tides of cultural change. Sudjic locates objects of twentieth-century design – such as the Bakelite rotary telephone – with chronological precision, while recognizing that they are able to communicate something beyond the moment that produced them.

Sudjic is concerned with the consumptive superficiality of 'a world drowning in objects' ([2008] 2009: 4), yet he recognizes that the gathering together of such objects has ontic import. Sudjic traces a language of design that has evolved and proliferated in post-industrial territories, amplifying material desire of the sort lovingly parodied by *Sesame Street*'s Ernie in the 'Rubber Duckie' song.[16] He identifies a design spectrum that embraces beauty alongside crudity, while delivering iconography through which the external world is realized, an iconography that *shows us what there is*. Baby books and primers such as Hoban's make an ontic contribution to this iconographic semiotics of design as they provide a way of organizing and structuring Quine's *everything*. Sudjic recognizes that to 'collect a sequence of objects is, for the moment at least, to have imposed some sense of order on a universe that doesn't have any' (21). Sudjic does not identify this as a process of ontological significance, but precisely this sort of ordering is a human activity that brings material things into the frame of the real; and as such it has ontic capacity.

A word of caution is required here though, for collecting can be perceived as a way of stripping the object of its thingness and of eliding material bodies. In *The System of Objects* (1968) Jean Baudrillard identifies collecting as a process of passion and possession in which the object becomes a reflection of the self. The object is '*abstracted from its function and thus brought into relationship with the subject*' ([1968] 2005: 91). The object is no longer a material body at a distance from the human body and Baudrillard locates the initial urge for this type of collecting in childhood: 'For children, collecting is a rudimentary way of mastering the outside world, of arranging, classifying, and manipulating' (93). There are signs of colonial imperative here in this mastery and manipulation that does not, however, tally with the glimpse of Brown's thingness in picturebook collections such as *The Baby's Catalogue* or *Look Again!* Such books pay attention to something in the object with which the subject has a relationship – hence a catalogue of baby's things – yet the drive is not towards ownership. This drive comes much closer to the Heideggerian housemaid's sense of things that exude handiness and that need to be handled as a result. Indeed, *The Baby's Catalogue* communicates something about the objects it represents to the titular baby (and implied reader). The formal presentation and grasp of these books provide a glimpse of something ambiguous in concrete bodies that cannot be reduced to object or subject and this is where *thingness comes into play* (in a contraction of Brown, Heidegger and Gadamer). Such books break down the binary relationship on which Baudrillard's impassioned collecting relies and thus baby books, which catalogue, list or collect objects, can be seen as an ontic project that resists mastery and realizes material objects of the external world. The ontic awareness demonstrated by baby catalogues has consequences that reach beyond this most basic of literary forms, as I demonstrate in the upcoming consideration of abstract concepts and objects that move beyond Heidegger's round-about-us.

Other fancy stuff

> Little Jackie Paper loved that rascal Puff,
> And brought him strings and sealing wax and other fancy stuff
> …
> A dragon lives forever, but not so little girls and boys.
> Painted wings and giant's rings make way for other toys.
>
> (Yarrow and Lipton [2007] 2008: 5 and 17)[17]

Fancy stuff is central to the childness at work in 'Puff, the Magic Dragon', Lenny Lipton and Peter Yarrow's whimsical paean to childhood imagination. Jackie Paper's playthings delineate the shifting child–dragon relationship as marked out in these pivotal couplets. The ontology of these things relates to their childly status – they are things of childhood – and Jackie rejects them when he no longer identifies with childly pursuits. Thingness inheres in this fancy stuff, lending it a vitality that resonates through the pleasure of friendship shared and the pain of its loss. Strings and sealing wax are things of childhood (in this context), yet they have a resilience that transcends childhood. There is an ambiguity here that points to a pull between Heidegger's understanding of the term 'thing' in its narrowest and broadest sense (1967: 5) – and this ambiguity also explains something of my own response to 'Puff' as a child. An understanding of Jackie's fancy stuff also offers a starting point for consideration of the ontological status of abstract things in children's literature.

The song was made popular by Peter, Paul and Mary in the 1960s; first written by Yarrow and Lipton in 1963, it has been remediated several times and most recently in picturebook form (2007). The song fascinated me as a child, in part because I was sensitive to its melancholic air (Puff's abandonment was a tragedy of epic proportions, in my view) but also because that fancy stuff drew me in. Strings, sealing wax, painted wings and giant rings were solidly mysterious. I could conceive of them as concrete objects, although they were not the familiar effects of my own experience. Strings could be considered an exception here – string is relatively mundane after all – but that pluralization (of string into strings) lends the mundane a degree of obscurity. Jacky Paper did not bring Puff the sort of string my mother cut from a Sunday roast. I wondered what sort of strings they were – perhaps of harps or puppets – and I never could decide. Indeed, this fancy stuff extends beyond Heidegger's round-about-us, but this does not mean that these things cannot exist.

In order to allow for things that cannot 'be touched, reached, or seen', Heidegger returns to Immanuel Kant's notion of *Ding an sich* (thing-in-itself) and *Ding für uns* (thing-for-us) – and his deliberations further help to explain the ontological significance of fancy stuff in 'Puff' (Heidegger 1967: 5). Round-about-us things – things in the narrowest sense – are both Ding an sich and Ding für uns; they are things in their own right, but we have verifiable experience of them and on this level they are 'for us'. The thing in Heidegger's 'widest' possible sense of the term, 'means only "something" (*etwas*) that which is not nothing' (5). As he explains, we think *something* about the concept of God, but we cannot experience God in the same way as a piece of chalk (6). God is a thing-in-itself, of which we can say only that it is not nothing (ontologically speaking). In this sense, Jackie's fancy stuff drew me in because it matters in its own right (thus transcending childhood) and, although I could not touch it, I could be touched by the thingness emanating from those strange and compelling objects. I had faith in Puff as a thing-in-itself because of that fancy stuff, even though Puff and these fanciful things were not for me in Kant's terms.

There is *something* more to Jackie's fancy stuff though that is missed by Heidegger's account of things in the widest sense. This is partly because Heidegger is more interested in things in the narrowest sense, which can be experienced by human touch, reach or sight – he does not expend much energy on other ontological categories in *What Is a Thing?* By contrast, Brown's thingness allows for a vitality that makes unreachable things something more than 'not nothing'. Furthermore, Hollindale's childness can inhere in cultural artefacts, accounting for the ontological status of a thing; the thingness of some objects inheres in their childness. Strings, sealing wax, painted wings and giant rings thus exude a thingness that encompasses the temporal conditions of childhood. Of course, strings and sealing wax have ontological status outside of childhood, but in the ontic remit of this song they are things of a childly order.

Two important conclusions can be reached here: the first relates to the material conditions of childhood; the second relates to the temporal individuation of things in ontological terms. Through this fancy stuff we experience the shifting terrain of childhood – stuff demonstrates that relationships matter in childhood but that they cannot last. Jackie's fancy stuff is the *matter of childhood*. Moreover, the song recognizes that strings and sealing wax have different instances of being that do not hold for all times. In Aristotelian terms, 'Puff' makes a case for particular instances of a substance, so that the strings brought by Jackie are not to be lumped together with string as a more generalized substance. The two aspects of this conclusion reveal that childhood and entities in the world exist in an ontic relationship, whereby childness can be revealed through objects and that objects can be childly in their being.

I am not arguing for a binary relationship in which childhood limits the being of objects (and vice versa). Instead, the *ontic relationship* I outline helps to establish the metaphysical concerns of a literature that frequently rehearses the nature and complexity of things in childhood. The picturebook form is particularly well equipped to explore this ontic relationship, since it lends itself to the sort of verbal–visual counterpoint and playful tension inherent in Brown's thingness. *Not a Box* (2006) by Antoinette Portis, for example, is dedicated 'to children everywhere sitting in cardboard boxes', suggesting that this picturebook might reveal a childly domain (Portis [2006] 2008: 3).[18] The point of view in this picturebook is unusual, in that the narrator directly addresses the unnamed focal (and only) character – apparently a rabbit. The unseen narrator puts a series of questions to the rabbit (child), who looks out at their inquisitor (adult) and answers these questions with rising frustration. The narrator perceives that the rabbit is sitting in a box and the rabbit insists that the object in which they sit is not a box. Seemingly we are in the presence of an ontological dilemma. From the rabbit's point of view, the thing they sit in/stand on/wear is variously a racing car, a mountain or a robot (Rab-bot). The rabbit's perspective is confirmed by illustrations that retain the dark outline of a box, overlaid by a bold image of the thing they perceive.[19]

In common with 'Puff, the Magic Dragon', *Not a Box* validates childly imagination, suggesting that children view the world differently from adults. However, this is not the book's only concern; it also seeks to challenge the aetonormative superiority of the narrator's inquisitive voice, achieving this through an ontological manoeuvre in the direction of childly thingness. The rabbit never wavers from the position that 'this is not a box', repeating the claim five times before asserting that 'It's my Not-A-Box!' (28). Moreover, these claims are visually supported by the dominant red outline of the thing (never a box) the rabbit perceives on each page. We are not to conclude that the rabbit was playing with a box all along. Instead, the reiterative dialogue and visual representation confirm that – on an ontological level – this mutable object is a matter of childhood, its thingness exuding from its childly not-boxness. The Not-A-Box is another example of fancy stuff imbued with childness and of a dynamic mode of being that eschews the generalities of ontological categories.

Fancy stuff is compelling because ambiguity is part of its thingness – the Not-A-Box could manifest as a rocket, or a burning building, or a boat. There is an ontological dynamism here that seems to be rooted in Beauvais's childly might and potential. While Beauvais's concept of might designates the being of a human child in its thrown forward state, the Not-A-Box is also in the reach of childly being. Its mutability ensues from the possibilities inherent in the modality of might; that it *could be* a rocket or a boat is part of its thingness. This need not complicate Heidegger's discovery that 'being singular is obviously a general, universally applicable characteristic (*Zug*) of things' and that 'these single things are just these (je diese): this door, this chalk, this now and here, not those of classroom six and not the ones from last semester' (1967: 18). The Not-A-Box is always this (single) thing that could be another single thing; it is *this rocket that could be a boat or a building*. The ambiguity of the Not-A-Box applies in all of its instances and this ontological status is expressed through the picturebook form, which uses illustrative overlaying and the drama of the page turn to intimate being of a particular kind. It seems clear then that the picturebook has ontic resonance.

Notwithstanding this discovery, concept books for the youngest readers are often concerned with things about which there seems to be no ambiguity if publishers' blurbs are to be believed. For example, the Penguin catalogue entry for Bill Martin Jr. and Eric Carle's *Brown Bear, Brown Bear, What Do You See?* (1967) suggests that it is 'the perfect introduction to looking and learning about colours',[20] while the back cover of *Walter's Wonderful Web* (2015) by Tim Hopgood claims that readers will 'learn all about shapes'. The evident pedagogic agenda here – expressed in the ubiquitous phrase, 'learn all about' – assumes that there is something straightforward to learn about shapes, colours or numbers. The implication is that shapes, colours and numbers have epistemic value and that knowledge about them is finite; thus it is possible to 'learn all about' them. Obviously I am taking at face value an idiomatic marketing phrase, which more accurately suggests that such books will introduce young readers to abstract concepts. At the very least though, each iteration acknowledges that children's books invest in *something* to be learnt about; that is, a property (or a number) *is a thing* to discover. What I am suggesting then is that the relentless didactic investment in properties has ontological commitment at its foundation (in spite of its ostensibly epistemic focus). Quine demonstrates that it is especially difficult to conceive of properties and abstract concepts ontologically, yet baby books have played a crucial role in reaching for the (almost) unreachable. Heidegger observes that 'we hesitate to call the number five a thing, because one cannot reach for the number – one cannot hear it or see it' (1967: 4). Consequently, if we think that numbers, shapes or colours exist and that children's books play an ontic role in committing to them, we need to look beyond the concrete and to consider ways in which visual and verbal texts are ontologically committed to them. In Quinean terms, ontological commitments – things that we surmise about the configuration of the external world – are manifest through language (while not being limited to it), thus combinations of words or images indicate the extent of ontological commitment invested in them. As will become apparent, children's books exhibit a range of responses to the question of whether the purple in Harold's crayon exists.[21]

Where Is the Green Sheep? (2004) by Mem Fox and Judy Horacek is a picturebook packed with the sheep to which it seems ontologically committed. It has a hide-and-seek structure, involving the hunt for a missing green sheep among an assembly of sheep with other qualities: 'Here is the blue sheep. And here is the red sheep. Here is the bath sheep. And here is the bed sheep. But where is the green sheep?' (2004: 3–7). Horacek's images are symmetrical and confirmatory with the relevant sheep depicted on the same page as the words describing it, while the inquisitive tone of the 'green sheep' refrain is emphasized by verbal text on an otherwise blank page. Fox makes unusual adjectives from more familiar verb patterns – 'bath sheep' is a sheep sitting in a bath full of bubbles – which is both a source of the book's humour and its ontological conviction. In Heidegger's terms, every sheep is singularly 'this sheep' and is identified as such by properties that draw attention to themselves through linguistic virtuosity and incongruity. A contemporaneous review of the book (albeit unwittingly) supports my case for its ontic remit: 'there is a joyous romp through the lives of sheep of various colors and occupations – sheep bathing and juggling … and still somehow always being sheep' (Bursztynski 2004). Bursztynski apparently picks up on the subtle sophistication of this book, which lies in its commitment to 'being sheep', although she misrepresents its verbal phrasing. Bursztynski translates Fox's curious adjectives into a more familiar verb-formations, but in so doing she elides the dedicated path taken by Fox to 'being sheep' and misses the import of its playful take on properties.

In order properly to understand the ontic mechanisms of *Where Is the Green Sheep?*, careful attention must be paid to its semantic structure or 'surface grammar' in metaphysical terms. Following Nikk Effingham's discussion of philosophical paraphrase in his *Introduction to Ontology* (2013: 26–34), gaps exist between surface grammar and ontological commitment in Fox's verbal text. Let us take the opening statement: 'Here is the blue sheep.' To adopt Effingham's logic, 'it looks like the things talked about have to exist in order for the sentence to be true' (26). Of course it can be argued – as Anthony Everett does in *The Nonexistent* (2013) – that this is playful fiction and 'truth' is beside the point in this case. What I want to suggest though is that the book's playfulness is ontologically committed in ways that make it hard for abstract concepts (such as the colour blue) to be dismissed as non-existent, especially in a wider context of a baby-book diet. In order to establish this though, I need briefly to travel down a methodological wormhole of bovid metaphysics.

The surface grammar of the sentence apparently commits to sheep that are blue. That is, the phrase is ontologically committed to blue sheep. A realist about concrete objects and abstract concepts will not have a problem with this, as it simply involves an ontological commitment to sheep and the colour blue. Admittedly, we do not find sheep and blue in combination very often, but the idea of blue sheep is not impossible (wool can be dyed blue). However, an anti-realist about abstract concepts will have trouble accepting what the surface grammar seems to confirm, as the anti-realist will protest that 'blue' cannot be found in space and time in the way that sheep can be located. Empiricists, for example, might argue that blue is a property reliant on human sensation, thus not of this world in its own right. They might argue that the proximal adverb 'here' can only apply to the sheep and not to the colour blue, thus the statement is ontologically false as it stands. To resolve the problem, the anti-realist about properties would need to paraphrase the sentence in such a way that it does not ontologically commit to blue. For example, 'Here is the sheep that is blue because it has been hit with light rays that are on a visible spectrum; this sheep reflects only blue light and absorbs all other light.' This sentence only ontologically commits to sheep and light, having an empirical explanation for the fact that the sheep appears to be blue. Obviously, this anti-realist paraphrase is ridiculous in relation to *Where Is the Green Sheep?* – more likely, the anti-realist would say that we should not take seriously the nonsensical fictions of baby books and that they are not within the remit of metaphysical concern. I do take them seriously though as the playful surface grammar of Mem Fox's verbal text makes a persuasive ontological case for blue sheep, while explaining why it might be hard for anyone growing up with modern baby books to dismiss colours, shapes and numbers as non-existent.

Returning to the book's adjectival forms, it is clear that they have two important ontic roles. First they confirm that sheep exist; these sheep have different traits, but they have *being sheep* in common. Second, the unusual reach of these adverbs draws attention to the actual presence of conceptual apparatus in the world. As established above, a realist about material objects and abstract concepts will accept the standard grammar of the book's first two phrases: 'Here is the blue sheep. Here is the red sheep.' These *acceptable phrases* prepare readers for the non-standard grammar, which follows: 'Here is the bath sheep. And here is the bed sheep.' Although 'bath' and 'bed' do not function as adjectives in formal English, they are contextually acceptable because 'blue' and 'red' *are* familiar adjectives. Moreover, the viability of blue and red increases due to their proximity to the unfamiliar adjectives surrounding them. This conviction is then cemented by the refrain, 'Where is the Green Sheep?' – a question that makes sense at the level of surface structure and in ontological terms, as a consequence of proximal acceptable phrasing. The rhythm and repetitive structure of the book are ontologically committed to sheep and to the colour green, so once again this points to an ontic resonance in the formal properties of the baby book. Attention to the formal surface grammars of sentence structure in *Where Is the Green Sheep?* confirms its willingness to push at the boundaries of what there is. This playful picturebook also bolsters Quine's conviction that 'postulated entities' can 'round out' our experience of the world.

The case I am making for the formal ontological commitment to properties in baby books could be exemplified further by any number of colourful board or cloth books in libraries and nurseries. However, the recent appearance of a picturebook series that knowingly builds on this relationship is confirmation enough, since its humour assumes a foundation of wider ontic commitment in the field. The shapes trilogy by Mac Barnett and Jon Klassen comprises *Triangle* (2017), *Square* (2018) and *Circle* (2019). Each book involves playful interaction between personified properties (if we accept that shapes are properties);[22] a deadpan narrative that culminates in an open-ended address to the reader; and a tone of light philosophical enquiry. A particular aspect of this enquiry interests me, which arises first in *Triangle* and concerns the naming and characterization of shapes. This is of specific relevance because it draws on the demonstrable ontological commitment to shapes in baby books at the level of literary form (while other examples of philosophical enquiry in the series point to themes at the level of content and the books' special concerns). If we anticipate that this series is designed to teach children 'all about shapes' we would be wrong and a little bit right. We would be wrong in that the purpose of these books is not to convey the basics of geometry, yet we would be right in that this series digs down into the ontological conditions of shapes – digging that is aided by an ability to recognize shapes (as defined by mathematical rules).

In *Triangle*, a character identified as Triangle leaves his triangular home, passing other triangles and non-specified shapes, on the way 'to play a sneaky trick on Square' (Barnett and Klassen [2017] 2018: 9).[23] The ontic layers here need untangling, so I proceed step by step. Let us consider the opening sentence, 'This is Triangle' (3), in which the protagonist is introduced as a determinate (this) being (is) via a proper noun (Triangle). This introductory phrase also suggests that Triangle is named for his appearance. That is, he looks like a triangle – as confirmed by Klassen's illustration[24] – and is (apparently) named after a universal abstract shape. Triangle is a triangle, which in geometric terms means that we can 'get the measure of him' via a mathematical formulation. But is Triangle really an ideal geometric shape, belonging to the realm of ideas? This would render him a form of human 'intuition' (Kant [1781] 2007: 64–66), an idea that has no substance in this world, along the lines of Kant's *transcendental idealism*.[25] Such a reading seems at odds with the rocky solidity of the world through which Klassen's triangle moves though.

Reading on, it is evident that Triangle has little in common with the precise and abstract discipline of mathematics. Rough around the edges and coloured in earthy tones, Triangle is evocative of physical or organic shapes of things in our world. This is further confirmed when he sets out on his mission to visit Square and travels through a landscape of geological formations of varied shape and hue. His contours are imprecise and yet Triangle can be identified in spatial terms as an extended shape with properties approximate to (if not congruent with) triangles. Triangle is a substantial object that shares features of other objects around him and Klassen moves Triangle through an environment from which he has been hewn. It is a world full of shapes like him and shapes unlike him, but it is (without doubt) a physical world. Consequently, *Triangle* commits ontologically to shapes by moving them into a concrete domain. It is then a much shorter step to allow for the abstract shapes of mathematics to which the series alludes – in Klassen's world we might well reach out for Heidegger's number five (and in *Square* the notion of ideal shapes becomes central).

This is not only Klassen's domain though. This is a picturebook in which words and pictures make meaning together and when Barnett's words are brought back into play it is clear that – in terms of the book's ontological commitment – ontic identity (what it means to be Triangle) is at stake. Triangle has much in common with other shapes around him; nonetheless he is distinct from them. And it is Triangle's distinctiveness that flags up the ontic pulse of this simple picturebook. During his journey to Square's house, 'He walked past small triangles and medium triangles and big triangles. He walked past shapes that weren't triangles any more. They were shapes with no names' (10–15). It seems clear that Triangle is not the same as all the other triangles he walks past, but if Triangle shares identical properties with these other triangles, how can Triangle be identified? Lewis provides a partial answer to this in his claim that 'everything is identical to itself' (1986: 192);[26] therefore, there can only ever be one Triangle (i.e. the character named in the picturebook). However, a more complete answer lies in that very first sentence and the ontological commitment of surface grammar that distinguishes Triangle (who lives in a triangular house) from small, medium and big triangles and nameless shapes.

A fruitful overlap between analytic philosophy, semantics and narratology can be applied to 'This is Triangle', and this critical nexus confirms that Triangle is necessarily unique in an environment crowded with triangles. Alongside narratological conventions of narration, point of view, characterization or action, Saul Kripke's theories in *Naming and Necessity* (1972, 1980)[27] are valuable in teasing out *Triangle*'s ontological remit. Triangle is a proper noun that refers only to the object it designates; as I have established, it does not designate any other triangles. The proper noun indicates a character distinct from the inanimate objects around him – he is the focus of attention in the story – and he speaks, acts and thinks, whereas they do not. Thus, in Kripke's terms Triangle is a *rigid designator*, which refers only to the thing named. Furthermore, Kripke argues that baptism (naming) denotes the thing referred to more reliably than any properties it might be associated with during its ongoing existence. For Kripke, a name is not descriptive (as it is for Bertrand Russell); it does not accrue associations that might change the nature of the referent. This means that Triangle can be distinguished from any other object – even from those that share properties with him – because his name is a rigid designator of the various things that mark him out at the moment of baptism. 'Triangle' refers to a shape with properties approximate to other triangles, who also lives in a house at a walking distance from Square: 'This is Triangle' (and with this sentence the book ontologically commits to him). Kripke also distinguishes between *speaker reference* and *semantic reference*, which allows for the identification of one object (Triangle) among many (triangles). Thus, a speaker using a name in a particular instance can distinguish the object referred to from objects sharing a semantic reference (the same name). In this case, the narrator (speaker) characterizes Triangle via a statement of 'baptism' – This is Triangle – and singles him out as a being/referent different from any other triangle. The final step (at least in terms of this discussion) is Kripke's revelation that rigid designators can function on a metaphysical level to show that truths about objects are necessary or contingent.[28] This helps to explain why and how so much is invested in that opening line of *Triangle*.

'This is Triangle' makes both a narrative and an ontological commitment; the phrase commits simultaneously to character and being. This means that as soon as Triangle sets out on a journey among other triangles, he is identifiable as protagonist and a distinctive entity. Of course this process is not unique to Klassen and Barnett's text; this sort of verbal identification of characters is a convention of picturebooks, which do not have the narrative time-space to introduce protagonists at length. Nonetheless, the brevity of the statement focuses attention on a triangle named Triangle who lives in a triangular environment. Triangle is anthropomorphized, but the force of narrative and ontological commitment to shapes squeezes the potential for figurative revelations of human being.[29] Triangle's anthropomorphic status might reveal something of being human – if Triangle is interpreted figuratively – but I want to revisit Brown's Homeric revisions here, wherein the thing is animated by its thingness (not for what it reveals of human being). Returning to Kripke, we can say that Triangle's designation is important in itself. His distinctiveness has an impact on the shape-filled environment through which he moves, for his unique triangular presence invites reflection on the status of triangles and shapes that are not named. It matters that Triangle has triangular properties and that he exists in a region full of shapes. If Triangle designates an entity that inheres of and in spatial property – and if a being *is* Triangle – then it follows that these spatial properties are conferred ontological status and that all of the shapes Triangle passes are something; these things are yet to be designated, but they are things *in wait*. Like the Ahlbergs' toys and groceries, the shapes surrounding Triangle can be perceived as stuff which has potential vitality and thingness.

Triangle is able to designate in part because he is embedded in a children's literature that makes a wider ontic commitment to shapes and other abstract concepts, including colours and numbers. *Petra* (2017) by Marianna Coppo makes a similar ontological commitment to a rock who eventually recognizes that mutability is inherent in her rocky being: 'I'm a rock and this is how I roll' ([2017] 2018: 41). Indeed, the gentle humour and philosophical freight of such books rest on a metaphysical framework that reaches for a green sheep under a haystack and confirms its place in the external world. Having established the ontic structure of baby books and the ontological commitment of picturebooks more widely, I now move on to a consideration of children's novels in which these metaphysical structures can be identified.

Gallery of false principles

In 1852 Marlborough House in London became home to The Museum of Manufactures. The museum's director, Henry Cole, believed that it should be a 'schoolroom for everyone' and sought to educate the public on matters of design. One of Cole's pedagogic strategies was the installation of a 'Gallery of False Principles', which exhibited objects representing the antithesis of good taste:

> Dubbed by the press as a 'Chamber of Horrors', this display of 'bad' design assaulted visitors with a range of what were considered 'utterly indefensible' everyday decorative objects that didn't meet the standards of design that were being formulated and promoted by Cole and his fellow design reformers ... The failings of these exhibits were spelled out in the gallery labels, and they were displayed alongside comparative objects which were judged successful and correct.
>
> (V&A, Building the Museum 2019)

My interest here lies not in the reformers' focus on design and manufacture, nor with the ethical remit of a museology that makes value judgements about its exhibits.[30] I am intrigued by the idea of negative exhibiting more generally, whereby a grouping of objects might be presented to demonstrate 'false principles' of a particular order or to transgress widely shared principles of some sort. Cole intends that his 'indefensible' objects be rejected comprehensively, yet there is subversive potential in an arrangement of object(s) that might challenge hegemonic values or normative positions – as represented in his gallery by an aesthetic elitism – if these objects are not 'read' as Cole intends them to be. Brown confirms that thingness exuded by objects has an ontological potential that could evade the epistemological intentions of the curator. The notion of a 'Gallery of False Principles' is interesting in the context of this chapter, as in part I have identified baby books as a holding place for ontologically determined objects – a function shared with the museum gallery. Furthermore, I have demonstrated that the convention of cataloguing is widespread in baby books, a convention shared with museum exhibitions. My final steps in this chapter are to confirm that the presentation of objects in baby books could be considered to function under false principles – that is, these books challenge the dominant epistemological framing of objects in children's literary discourse; and furthermore, that the ontological commitment to objects in baby books has implications for the wider field of children's literature. In order to take these steps I move away from baby books to consider thingness at work in a classic example of museum fiction.

E. L. Konigsburg's (1967) novel, *From the Mixed-Up Files of Mrs. Basil E. Frankweiler*, is a museological adventure that shifts from the epistemological to the ontological in its approach to gallery exhibits. The novel opens in a moment of decisive action when 11-year-old Claudia Kincaid resolves to run away (with her 9-year-old brother Jamie) to the Metropolitan Museum of Art in New York City. This is a carefully planned undertaking that 'would not be just running from somewhere but would be running to somewhere' ([1967] 2015: 9). Claudia's distinction pinpoints the Met as a chosen destination with a palpable presence in the book from the outset; she conceives it as 'a large place, a comfortable place, an indoor place, and ... a beautiful place' (9). The repetitive emphasis on 'place' locates the Met as an ontic matter of concern – it is something somewhere – and the adjectival inventory encompasses the practical (large or comfortable) and the aesthetic (beautiful), which will take on metaphysical significance later in the novel. Claudia identifies injustice – she is given chores, whereas 'her brothers got out of everything' (10) – as a motivating factor in running away. However, her overriding concern is to escape 'the monotony of everything' (10). Indeed, 'everything' is referred to three times in the opening exposition on running away, for she also notes that 'everything costs' in suburbia (9). It seems that Claudia does not yet have a handle on Quine's everything and has an ineffable sense of things crowding in on her, yet cannot express fully why this matters so much. She knows only that she needs to escape it, finding it hard to manage the routine mechanisms of being in Heidegger's sense of its 'average everydayness' ([1927] 1996: 41). Her fundamental rejection of domestic mundanity – in the move from home to museum – amounts to an ontological crisis that ultimately will allow Claudia to *approach things differently*. When eventually Claudia and Jamie undertake their journey to New York the children remain unnoticed at the back of the school bus, hidden as they are among school-day paraphernalia: 'There was so much jostling and searching for homework papers and mittens that no one paid any attention to anything expect personal possessions' (23–4). This transitional journey elides the children's status as human beings, emphasizing their affinity with the objects that so preoccupy their schoolmates. The elision is temporary, but it underlines the close attention given to different kinds of things in Konigsburg's novel and points to the ontic nature of their adventure.

Claudia is attuned to the material conditions of her existence, having recognized that 'everything costs' (9), and chooses Jamie to be her companion in this venture due to his relative wealth. His thrifty ways have allowed him to save for a transistor radio, which they are likely to need. Claudia typically spends her allowance as soon as she receives it and decides that 'she must get accustomed to giving up things' (11) if she is to save the fare to New York. The economies of Claudia's dependent status as a child remains a central concern throughout the novel – and the hot fudge sundaes of Claudia's childhood desire retain their pull on her – but things of a different order eventually demand her attention in the Met. Claudia's domestic duties also render her attentive to things that shape the daily routine of her family. An entire page is devoted to contents of family wastebaskets and Claudia's fortuitous discovery – 'What a find!' – of an unused bus pass beneath her mother's 'litter of lipstick kisses' (13). Marxist undertones inhere in the humour of this passage as Claudia reflects on adult failure to notice the ticket: 'The cleaning lady never went to New York, and Claudia's dad never kept close track of his pocket change or his train passes' (13). More pertinent though is the implication that Claudia's childly affinity for things makes her especially observant of the objects around her. Indeed, Claudia locates vitality in the commonplace, so that 'a shallow layer of Kleenex, which her mother had used for blotting lipstick' becomes 'a litter of lipstick kisses' (13). This transformation is perhaps more sophisticated than Jackie Paper's toys, but the vitalism Claudia attributes to her mother's waste tissues is the thingness of childly fancy stuff. Claudia, it seems, is well prepared for her ensuing discovery of the art-work as a mode of being, a discovery invested in childly thingness that grounds so much children's literature.

The children's stay at the Met culminates in Claudia's preoccupation with 'the most beautiful, most graceful little statue she had ever seen' (54), but revolving around the ontological centre of the book are a series of more tentative metaphysical positions. When first the children arrive they choose bedrooms in which to hide and protective cordons distance them literally and figuratively from the 'fine French and English furniture' (38). In awe of their period elegance, Claudia infuses these furnishings with historical knowledge, so that the reach of past events obscures the objects themselves. Claudia 'wanted to sit on the lounge chair that had been made for Marie Antoinette or at least sit at her writing table', but she notices 'silken ropes strung across' to prevent wear or damage: 'She would have to wait until after lights out to be Marie Antoinette' (38). Claudia is definitely not at home here and is unable to consider these objects on their own terms – as she has been able to in her parents' bedroom. Instead she plays at being someone else in this fanciful moment of ontological exchange, which indicates a level of anxiety or destabilization. It is as though she is suddenly conscious of her thrown state among things, in Heideggerian terms, and is at a loss as to how to manage the objects around her.

This dislocation is further illustrated by Claudia's insistence that she and Jamie treat the museum as an extensive schoolroom: 'she set forth for herself and for her brother the task of learning everything about the museum. One thing at a time' (48). This echoes the doubtful claims of publishers whose baby books 'teach everything about colour or shapes' and also hints that Claudia has taken a wrong metaphysical turn. The narrator confirms the epistemological impossibility of such an undertaking, pointing out that even if Claudia had realized that the Met had 'over 365,000 works of art … she could not have been convinced that learning everything about everything was not impossible; her ambitions were as enormous and as multi-directional as the museum itself' (48). Claudia's approach to objects has emphatically changed, so that thingness is obscured by the extent of her epistemological aspirations – she has pushed beyond the pedagogic concerns of most schoolrooms. She is also undercut by Jamie who 'chose the galleries of Italian Renaissance' in the expectation that Claudia would 'soon give up in despair' (49). In his pursuit of unattainable knowledge Jamie also joins a group of schoolchildren learning about mummies and almost exposes himself as an imposter in the class and a trespasser in the museum. The precariousness of their existence among things is underscored in this moment and anticipates the shift away from epistemological concerns, as foreshadowed by Claudia's earlier appreciation of childly thingness.

Claudia is drawn to the statue instantaneously and her interest is confirmed when she discovers the debate over its provenance and the question of whether Michelangelo created 'Angel': 'She decided that the statue was not only the most beautiful in the world but also the most mysterious' (62). In this moment her transition away from the pursuit of knowledge begins and she tells Jamie to 'skip learning everything about everything' in order to 'concentrate on the statue' (63). This is not to say that her education simply stops – and she reassures Jamie that 'we don't have to skip learning *something* about everything' (63) – but after all she ran away in part to escape 'simply being straight-A's Claudia Kincaid' (10). It is more the case that Claudia needs to find another way of being around everything and the route to this is via an ontological appreciation of the artwork as thing and not simply an object of knowledge (and historical education).

The statue is presented quite differently from other artefacts in the Met and it is projected through Claudia's experience of it. She wonders what it is about the statue that is different from other objects: 'Why did she seem so important; and why was she so special? Of course, she was beautiful. Graceful. Polished. But so were many other things at the museum' (54). Claudia realizes that the mystery surrounding Angel has something to do with her own fasciation (62), yet there is something more to it that she cannot articulate (albeit hinted at in her use of female pronoun). Brown's notion of the *dialectical object* is helpful here, since it allows for Claudia's fluctuating sense of the statue. Brown employs the term to denote the

> experienced, irresolvable and contradictory, doubleness of a single object, the way it seems to oscillate between the poles of object and thing, which can be, as well, the poles of unhuman and human, the figural and the literal, then and now, proximate and distant.
>
> (2015: 371)

Of course, the statue operates metaphorically to represent (on one level at least) the sense of self that Claudia wishes to keep private and untrammelled by domestic routine – and hence its mysteriousness draws her in. However, Angel also matters to Claudia in Brown's literal terms. At times Claudia treats the statue as an object of research, while at others she seems to recognize Angel's thingness and responds to her as she might another person: 'Claudia especially wanted to make herself important to the statue. She would solve its mystery; and it, in turn, would do something important to her, though what this was, she didn't quite know' (65). Angel is anthropomorphized here to an extent that renders her sentient and capable of action, confirming that Claudia is now responding to her ontic (rather than epistemic) potency. Claudia also yearns to hug (83) and touch the statue (87) – exhibiting an affinity with the handiness of Heidegger's housemaid – and is frustrated by the depersonalized distance forced on her by the museum's alarm system, suggesting that proximity might allow her to get to grips with Angel's contradictory doubleness and at the same time understand something more of herself as a being in the world.

Claudia is driven to uncover the mystery of Angel's creation for she knows that Angel will help her to address something important, although 'she wasn't exactly certain of the question she was trying to answer' (93). Even when Mrs Frankweiler (who once owned the statue) reveals hidden evidence of lost Michelangelo sketches, Claudia is not furnished with the sort of answer she had expected – and I suggest that this is because her journey has never been epistemological. This adventure is not about ways of gaining knowledge (epistemic); it is about discovering what things are (ontic). Claudia takes on board a secret that has a sort of presence within her, an ontological presence that also inheres in the statue. Mrs Frankweiler observes that 'Secrets are safe, and they do much to make you different' (146) – thus secrets *are* something (safe) and they *do* something (make you different). This phrase ontologically commits to secrets and gives Claudia a clearer understanding of their nature: 'she knew something about secrets that she hadn't known before' (147). Claudia's secret allows her to go home a different person and in possession of *something vital*. She had so feared returning home, 'without the radio and all. With nothing' (115). This is partly because Claudia has not let go fully her sense of the object as commodity in terms of Marxist reification and, consequently, she identifies herself 'with nothing' in the rationalized system of capitalism. Mrs Frankweiler helps her to see that she simply needs to reposition herself in relation to the things around her and the secret does this for her. Brown explains that *redemptive reification* 'describes a re-thingification that resuscitates the character of things as things – or the thingness of the object – although it is engaged not in recovery ... so much as discovery' (2015: 374). Claudia's secret relationship with Angel is thus redemptive in its ontological engagement with thingness; it allows her to return to and discover home as the beneficiary of an ontological legacy.

The Kincaid's sojourn in the Metropolitan Museum of Art transforms it into a gallery of 'false principles' via their enactment of redemptive reification. Angel as exhibit is transformed from an object of public consumption into a discovered thing with a vital presence. As such, the statue subverts the notion that curating is bound to the conveyance of knowledge. The children leave the Met as curators of a secret life that has personal, local and domestic ontological significance – Claudia takes Angel home with her as a consequence of a curatorial challenge. Konigsburg's novel also takes ontic interest in the domestic stuff that occupies Brown's inanimate object world, as demonstrated by Claudia's absorbed concern with the things around her. Thus, it seems that there is another legacy at work here, as this ontological investment in things is supported by the foundational dedication of baby books to inanimate objects of everyday concern. There is a direct line to be drawn from that on which the Ahlbergs hang nappies and the discovery that statues (like nappies) have a secret life. In common with baby books, Konigsburg's novel also validates the ontological status of abstract concepts – such as secrets – to move away from a perception of entities in relation to consumerism and economics. Moreover, it challenges the aetonormative conditions of museology – through which exhibits are designed to pass on authoritative and curated knowledge – suggesting that the mighty child might do something in the future with her uncurated experience among things that exude thingness. Indeed, consideration of children's books through the lens of 'false principles' uncovers their subversive potential to present objects outside of the epistemic structures of prevailing authority. This is not to deny the epistemological aspect or function of objects in children's books, but exclusive focus on their epistemic qualities occludes their ontic remit and the terms of their engagement with being in the world.

Konigsburg's naturalistic approach to domestic and cultural life involves the presence of realist operators with an ontic value that is unsurprising perhaps. For this reason, I close my discussion with recourse to an experimental novel, which blurs the boundaries of *that which is* in its involvement with *things that matter*. *Strange Objects* (1990) by Gary Crew is a complex time-shift novel of sorts – it is a book that defies classification – delving into historical events surrounding the 1629 wreck of *Batavia*, a flagship of the Dutch East India Company, off the coast of Western Australia. The novel is commonly described by critics as a psychodrama, as in the following example: 'Fact and fiction, the past and present, indigenous and European characters are integrated into a powerful psychological novel' (Lees and Macintyre 2006: 363). I do not refute this assessment of Crew's novel, for it certainly probes the psychological state of Steven Messenger, its unreliable focal narrator, along with the mental stability of other characters – historical and contemporaneous – whose voices are heard through epistolary techniques. However, given that the narrative is so invested in the 'strange objects' of its title, ultimately to describe it as a human psychological drama is to obscure the vitality of its extensive inventory of things. Even the letters, newspaper articles and journal entries that shape the narrative have status as material objects. I could give many other examples, including the flora and fauna of the Australian landscape, so abundant to Aboriginal peoples in the novel, but invisible to European eyes of 1629 – Walter Loos reports that there is 'nothing' in the landscape (Crew [1990] 1991: 83) – and to Messenger in 1986, who describes his school-town Hamelin as being 'nowhere' (25).[31] I therefore propose that this novel has extensive metaphysical remit, which is actuated as much by the presence of objects and other non-human entities, as it is by the human beings who come into contact with them.

The objects in Crew's novel are not limited to those discovered by Messenger in a cave during a school trip – including an iron pot, a mummified hand, a gold ring and a leather-bound logbook. As the historical thread of the novel comes into view, a preoccupation with material things is evident in Loos's autobiographical account of events. When he is first cast away with Jan Pelgrom – his companion in exile – Loos compiles an 'inventory of our goods' which comprises: items to trade, victuals and practical items such as clothing and a musket (63). Some of these goods – the iron pot and the logbook – are clearly those discovered by Messenger some 350 years later, so the items take on a manifold existence as they crop up at different chronotopic points in the narrative. Indeed in the progress of Loos's journal, the 'Cannibal Pot' (so dubbed in xenophobic terms by Messenger) transforms from mysterious object into a container for thingness – Loos uses the pot to store trade goods – in Heidegger's narrow sense of the present-at-hand. The archaeological artefacts also stimulate the historical and time-shift elements of the novel and – under the investigation of Dr Hope Michaels, director of the Western Australian Institute of Maritime Archaeology – they provide access to the historical past through the prism of scholarly authority.

These slippery objects are not purely archaeological in status though, as is becoming clear. For instance, Loos's logbook moves from object to thing (in Brown's terms) in its transfiguration from documented manuscript to utilitarian journal. Michaels documents the leather-bound book in some detail, accounting for the use of ink as follows: 'Two writing mediums have been used: initially a black ink and later a paler, purple ink' (31). The ink also appears in Loos's journal, listed in his itinerary of goods and then lamented as it starts to run out. When Pelgrom presents Loos with a sea slug, the ink becomes something of a different order again – as Pelgrom explains: '"They squirt the purple juice so that they might hide in the coloured water it makes" … he held out his palm, to show the dark fluid cupped there. "I brought it for you, Wouter. You see. It is like ink"' (161). Pelgrom is alert to the handiness of the ink and considers it an object of practical use. However, the presence of the sea slug also renders indigenous fauna in real terms for the reader, just as increasingly the wider Australian environment is becoming real – and full of life – to the Dutch mariners. The variant status of the ink and the logbook within which it is used thus open these objects to thingness, as they come into being via the numerous threads of the narrative. Gadamer makes a case for writing 'handed down' as a means of achieving 'the sheer presence of the past' through 'trace of mind' ([1960] 2004: 156); the written words of the diary thus *present* the past and Loos's thoughts as if they were ontological propositions of the world. Gadamer is more dismissive of other 'remnants of past life' – such as 'what is left of buildings, tools, the contents of graves' – achieving this sort of 'living meaning' (156). However, in the context of Crew's novel it seems that the close proximity and multivalency of entities also involve them in an ontic structure, whereby the past is presented by the thingness of non-human objects. Furthermore, the vitalism of objects throughout the book also allows Crew to explore the ontic conditions of being human in the world.

The torrent of strange objects in Crew's novel reveals an awareness of the ontological conditions of the world inhabited by young people and certainly it can be considered in terms of museological 'false principles'. Although it uses mechanisms of curational authority to piece together disparate aspects of the narrative, *Strange Objects* subverts this authority. Curation is not able to control the unstable and vital performance of objects, because these objects really have a life of their own. *Strange Objects* also loops back to Mary's thread of ontological exchange in *The Stone Book*. Messenger experiences a comparable communion with the past through walls of stone: 'Then I saw. Over and over, everywhere, were hundreds of hand prints, very pale and faded, white and yellow and red all over the wall' (Crew [1990] 1991: 155). The outcome of this exchange is very different from Mary's, yet once again the thingness of the rock speaks to the conditions of being human. This investment in stuff of the landscape also leads the way into Chapter 3 and its rhizomorphic approach to being in the biosphere.

3

Something Else Matters: Rhizomes and Animal Messes

Before my teacher reads the poem,
she has to explain.
A *birch*, she says, *is a kind of tree*
then magically she pulls a picture
from her desk drawer and the tree is suddenly
real to us.

(Woodson 2014: 223)

Birch tree reverie

Woodson's 'birch tree poem' in *brown girl dreaming* understands something of the ontological potential in a poetry that dreams worlds: 'A [tree] takes form in our reverie, and this [tree] is ours' (Bachelard [1960] 1971: 8).[1] In a move from worlds to trees, I have modified Bachelard's observation in *The Poetics of Reverie* about the 'innovating action of poetic language' (8) in order to highlight a figurative, childly and metaphysical affinity between Woodson's verse novel and Bachelard's philosophical meditation. For Bachelard, the world comes into being through childhood reverie: 'The roots of the grandeur of the world plunge into a childhood' (103) and 'childhood is at the origin of the greatest landscapes' (102). The figurative language used here – roots and landscape – is immersed in the natural world and, although Bachelard draws on a range of poetic images to express the ontological freight of reverie, he returns repeatedly to flora – 'the child's trees, the child's springtime flowers' (124) – in his expression of its childly aspect. In 'birch tree poem' Woodson's persona (Jacqueline) reflects on a moment of ontic becoming in which 'the tree is suddenly real to us' as she and her classmates respond to the visual and poetic images before them. Like Bachelard, Woodson seems to invest in the rootedness of this moment as it reverberates throughout *brown girl dreaming* via a world-dreaming commitment to trees – family trees, high-up trees, pine, pecan, willow, maple, apple, peach, birch, oak and mimosa trees – that brings into being 'all the worlds you are' (319). The metaphysical nature of Woodson's 'made real' trees is worth exploring further, since they provide a frame for understanding a wider commitment to plant-life in children's literature that pushes beyond anthropocentric ontologies and pastoral renditions of the child in the natural world. In this chapter there is a move away from the thingness of material objects, to a particular system of metaphysical connectivity flourishing in the flora and fauna of children's literature. My initial focus is on the creeping plant-work of children's books and the representation and role of biological organisms that could exist in the external world – I demonstrate that the birch tree really matters in Woodson's poem. I do not deal with the sentient trees and plants of fantasy literature, to which Zoe Jaques draws attention in *Children's Literature and the Posthuman* (2015). However, as I move on to explore metaphysical messes made by animals (and other non-humans) in B. A. G. Fuller's terms, I consider aspects of post-human entanglement via Donna Haraway's *cyborg politics* and Derrida's *limitrophy*.

Birch trees come into existence in 'birch tree poem', an ontological event that appears to Jacqueline 'magical' and which is usefully complicated by the embedded reading of Robert Frost's 'Birches' (1915). Woodson's suggestion is not that a tree has literally rooted itself and grown in the classroom. Rather, a tripartite relationship is forged between the external object (birch tree), its representation (visual/poetic image of a tree) and Jacqueline's ontic act of perception. Frost's poem itself negotiates the relationship between 'Truth' and imagination, leading Jacqueline to reflect on the epistemic and ontological capacities of poetry. 'Birches' imparts knowledge of the external world, while also revealing that things can exist outside of human experience of them. Jacqueline suggests that some top-down knowledge of the natural world is required in order to appreciate the figurative and affective qualities of Frost's poem: 'some of us put our heads on our desks to keep/the happy tears from flowing … And even though we've never seen an ice storm / we've seen a birch tree, so we can imagine / everything we need to imagine' (223). This implies an affective dimension to the epistemic (we might understand things when we feel something about them) and by extension that the human imagination has a role to play in ontic encounters with things (birch trees) in the world. Moreover, while this childly connection with the birch tree is important, the poem's focus on the possibility and becoming of trees also commits to trees as entities in their own right. According to its surface grammar, *we've seen a birch tree* is a statement about the act of observing something, verified by the teacher's action of showing the class a birch tree. The statement is also untrue though, because Jacqueline has seen a *picture* of the birch tree – she has not seen a concrete birch tree, any more than she has an ice storm.[2] Jacqueline is not lying as such, but her claim is ontically complex and its validity would be challenged by Quine's stripped back ontology. Notwithstanding, her 'untruth' is valued for its ontological significance and its transformative imaginative experience, as confirmed through intertextual reference to Frost's poem, which treats truth with some derision: 'Truth broke in / With all her matter-of-fact about the ice-storm' ([1915]1989: 1101: 22).[3] The merit of this untruth is not visible on the surface level of Woodson's poem; it is validated by the poem's deep structure, through which an ontological engine drives its exploration of the relationship between entities in the external world and the human imagination (without reducing one to the other). It does all this quietly and covertly, yet I suggest that 'birch tree poem' (along with its ontological freight) plays a crucial role in Woodson's verse novel, since it gives insight into the process of coming into being in a world of human and non-human entities – one of the book's central concerns.

The intrinsic and extrinsic value of 'birch tree poem' leads back to Bachelard's poetics of reverie, whereby 'a poetic image can be the seed of a world' ([1960] 1971: 1), while also being seeded by the world – thus Woodson's birch tree propagates a world through which it is simultaneously sustained. Bachelard and Woodson are each concerned with the ontic reach of poetic consciousness, whereby images bring worlds into being – Bachelard's poetics proceed from this point (1–2), while Woodson's verse novel closes with the related reverie of 'each world', as 'Each day a new world/opens itself up to you' (2014: 319). Bachelard's metaphoric images identify seeds as points of origin, or roots as channels of extension from childhood to adulthood. I hesitate to express this in terms of growth towards adulthood though – from one point of development to another – since Bachelard's poet has continued access to childhood reverie and the process is not hierarchical or vertical, as his extended arboreal metaphors might seem to suggest. Bachelard's *roots plunge into a childhood* – all and any childhoods at any point in time and space – just as Woodson's trees send out roots into a multiplicity of childly reveries that throw up 'many worlds' and 'you can choose the one / you walk each day' (319). Despite this multiplicity there is a potential rootedness here that needs to be troubled, for there is an underlying implication that poetry and the reveries of human childhood are points of origin from which birch trees grow. However, although Woodson and Bachelard send out roots that are in the world(s) it will become clear that their childly poetics are not embedded in a hegemonic or homocentric ontological system.

In *A Thousand Plateaus*, Deleuze and Guattari introduce a writing process that makes a metaphysical move from root to rhizome, a process that helps to untangle the apparent contradictions of a poetics (at work in Bachelard and Woodson) that inheres of seeds and roots, while simultaneously challenging a stable or single point of origin. As I will demonstrate, *The Poetics of Reverie* and *brown girl dreaming* are not the problematic root-books described here by Deleuze and Guattari, although echoes of the root-book can be found in each:

> A first type of book is the root-book. The tree is already the image of the world, or the root the image of the world-tree. This is the classical book, as noble, signifying, and subjective organic interiority (the strata of the book). The book imitates the world, as art imitates nature: by procedures specific to it that accomplish what nature cannot or can no longer do.
>
> ([1980] 2013: 3)

The roots thrown out by this 'classical' root-book, and challenged by Deleuze and Guattari's rhizomorphic philosophy, can be traced through a figurative allegiance to the 'world-tree' in *brown girl dreaming*; consequently, Jacqueline's family tree is charted in the book's peritextual materials. The influence of the root-book is clear, yet Woodson's poetic process soon challenges the hierarchical genealogy of the tree and Jacqueline's family tree opens out into many worlds – 'all the worlds you are' (2014: 319) – that cannot be represented by a root-book or standard family tree. Instead, these familial worlds are represented by the fluidity of Woodson's verse novel. As 'birch tree poem' reveals, art does not imitate nature as it does in the root-book; the birch tree is in art and art is in the birch tree. Bachelard's notion of seeds as points of origin might appear more problematic, since Deleuze and Guattari suggest that books (and by extension poetic images) are unattributable to origin ([1980] 2013: 2). However, Bachelard's poetic images (his seeds) are both single and diffuse – images 'come together and mutually embellish each other' ([1960] 1971: 175). Essentially, he allows for a poetics that multiplies in line with Deleuze and Guattari's rhizome, which 'is absolutely different from roots and radicles' ([1980] 2013: 5). Bachelard uses the ontological language of roots and radicles in his poetics, yet his approach to the poetic image incorporates the multiplicity of Deleuze and Guattari's rhizome. As Deleuze and Guattari observe, 'Plants with roots and radicles may be rhizomorphic' since 'the rhizome itself assumes very diverse forms' (5). Deleuze and Guattari's concept of rhizome seems promising then in its tolerance of roots and seeds within a connected and heterogeneous system that is open and forward looking.

Deleuze and Guattari offer a system of writing that 'has to do with surveying, mapping, even realms that are yet to come' (3). This *yet-to-come-ness* of rhizomorphic expression connects with the childly potential of a poetics that dreams worlds and brings birch trees into existence. Deleuze and Guattari's *becoming* is forward facing, allowing for the temporal currency embedded in Beauvais's concept of mighty childhood, which incorporates the future as an open space in which to act (2015: 19). In 'Posthumanism and the Animality of Children's Literature and Play' (2018) Maija-Liisa Harju and Dawn Rouse explore the notion of children *becoming* through nature, and their focus is on ways in which wildness might be sustained in children through literary engagement and animal play. They 'seek to demonstrate how *becoming* animals through children's immersion in narrative and in free play, can help them further a feeling of necessary wilderness' through an 'embodied knowledge' of nature (Harju and Rouse 2018: 449). Their notions of becoming, embodiment and immersion draw on posthumanism theories, which overlap with my interests here and we a share a concern with emphasizing the biospheric potential of children's literature to connect human and non-human beings with the world around them. However, their focus on the active child in classroom and play is outside the remit of my project, which identifies a rhizomorphic apparatus for *becoming-child* in children's books.

Deleuze and Guattari actually refuse ontologies that insist on being, attributing the historical, colonial, conjugal and aetonormative weight of the verb *to be* with the majority 'law of arborescence' ([1980] 2013: 341). They explain that 'What constitutes arborescence is the submission of the line to the point', a central point through which 'Man constitutes himself as a gigantic memory' (341). Conversely, a rhizomorphic line of becoming 'passes *between* points' and because it 'comes up through the middle' (342), the becoming-tree-becoming-child is able to escape the dominance of being. The presence of the child in this rhizomorphic assemblage of becoming allows me to outline a network of flora and fauna in children's literature that commits to rhizomorphic ontologies, thus bypassing dominant configurations of pastoral childhood.

Picking up on the ideological and political dimensions of pastoral and its development in children's literature specifically, Lydia Kokkola observes that 'this setting of the child in pastoral surroundings typically serves to emphasize the "natural" innocence of the child, land and the nation' and is 'often used for nationalistic purposes' (2013: 137). In much writing for children, pastoral childhood seems to emanate from an imperial centre with pastoral images serving as constellations (points) that root the child in land and nation. Nodelman notes that the pastoral conditions of texts in his survey of children's literature 'emerge from and express an adult nostalgia for childhood as an idyll or Eden, a simpler and better time now over' and that such texts 'relate their conception of childhood to other forms of Edenic beginnings and mythic pasts' (2008: 79). What emerges is the idea that children's literature can be traced to a prelapsarian root-book, drawing from 'Man's gigantic memory' (hence the dominance of adult nostalgia). This is a literature written from the arborescent centre dismantled by Deleuze and Guattari and, as Nodelman and Kokkola confirm, this pastoral script has dominated constructions of childhood and children's literature discourse. Of course other critics have interrogated the rootedness of the pastoral child; for example, Jaques observes that 'tropes of the literature of childhood ... strongly resonate with reflections on the instability of the human relationship with nature' (17). While I am not suggesting that the pastoral legacy is a secure or uncontested area of children's literature discourse, it remains important to trouble assumptions arising from it. Consequently, in the metaphysical groundwork of children's literature I identify an alternative explanation as to why the natural world is intrinsic to this literary field. There is a metaphysical assemblage of flora and fauna in contemporary children's books, which does not rely on a childhood rooted in pastoral space.

Woodson's birch trees make connections as soon as they appear in Jacqueline's classroom-imagination-poem-world. They push through the middle of her desk as she listens and they rise up through the middle of Frost's poem to connect with a rhizomorphic process of becoming-tree-becoming-child. Nerve fibres[4] thrown out from other lines of *brown girl dreaming* reach into 'birch tree poem' and '*I'm gonna figure out how to grow myself a pecan tree*' (2014: 49) from the land worked by my grandfather and his garden full of 'sweet peas and collards/green peppers and cukes/lettuce and melon/berries and peaches' (49). The vegetables, fruits and flowers of 'the garden' (48–9) grow full of slavery missed 'by one generation' in the 'dark Nicholtown dirt' (48). The vegetables are gathered by a '*brown-skinned/black-haired/and wide-eyed*' (3) girl who wants to be a writer and a revolutionary, '*When I see birches bend to left and right*' (314). As Jacqueline works the garden the fruits grow through her history, present and future (and vice versa), thus child and flora are mutually thrown among things in the world. The connections made here are between entities of a different order – flora, child, political system, literary form – and of course I could have accumulated these things/lines differently (for no one element is prioritized over another). Yet the connective assemblage of the rhizomorphic system is what matters and my mapping of it (for illustrative purposes) serves as a crude entry into its complex realms. Deleuze and Guattari explain that

> A rhizome ceaselessly establishes connections between semiotic chains, organizations of power, and circumstances relative to the arts, sciences, and social struggles. A semiotic chain is like a tuber agglomerating very diverse acts, not only linguistic, but also perceptive, mimetic, gestural, and cognitive: there is no language in itself, nor are there any linguistic universals, only a throng of dialects, patois, slangs, and specialized languages.
>
> ([1980] 2013: 6)

Deleuze and Guattari are committed to this 'ceaseless connectivity' and it is this structure of connection itself (rather than the things connected) that decentralizes language and hegemonies in *A Thousand Plateaus*. It is the connectivity of the rhizomorphic system that allows a move away from the pastoral centre and origin of the child in the natural world. In order to understand how this rhizomorphic system works in children's literature though, I do need to consider some of the entities connected – otherwise ontic plant-life is in danger of being lost again beneath the weight of focus on human being. Therefore, in the first section of this chapter I investigate flora commonly assembled in books for young readers. Essentially, I identify a metaphysical move at work here – that is not explicitly acknowledged as such by Deleuze and Guattari in their introduction to rhizomes – through which flora (and fauna) are realized and proliferate via their rhizomorphic connection with each other.

Immersed becomings: Heather is never only heather

'Heather is never only heather' because it travels across the moor, growing and sharing with asphodel, bilberry, crowberry, cotton-grass, tormentil, moss and lichen (Macfarlane and Morris 2017: 50).[5] In *The Lost Words* (2017) Robert Macfarlane and Jackie Morris assemble words and images into spells and in their depiction of heather they emphasize the co-dependency of flora and fauna (Figure 3.1). Heather has an adventitious rooting system that layers stem upon stem,[6] allowing to it spread above and below ground into an extensive bed or plateau in which other life forms gather. The watercolour bleed of Morris's ling moor sustains in its *Calluna vulgaris* a mountain hare in summer coat, hen harrier (skydancer) and bumblebee alongside Macfarlane's assemblage of

Figure 3.1 'Heather is never only heather' (Macfarlane and Morris 2017: 50–3).

other plants. The fragility of the moorland terrain and its inhabitants is also evoked through the almost-not-thereness of the hen harrier, from which Morris withdraws the colour-flooded intensity of her goldfinch or kingfisher – harriers have been hunted near to extinction through driven grouse shooting in the UK. Yet the ontic conviction of this image – insisting on the *thereness* of its flora and fauna – and its accompanying spell lies in patterns of connectivity, reaching out for all 'the other things that heather shares its measure with' (as Morris expresses it).[7] Heather is never only heather in the process of becoming creatures, plants and the moorlands on which it grows – and in Deleuze and Guattari's terms it is becoming-plant-becoming-child through the spells that speak the natural world to and through children in a metaphysical process of realization. *The Lost Words* has an extensive audience,[8] yet it is addressed directly to children and there is an acknowledgement of the mighty child in Beauvais's terms, a harnessing of the potential for forward movement inherent in childness. This is a childly manoeuvre through the middle of the heather – which is never only heather – connecting heather with bilberry and moss and hare in a 'biotic community', such as that envisaged by Aldo Leopold in *A Sand County Almanac* (1949). Leopold promotes a land ethic, alongside the notion of 'biotic teamwork', underscoring the idea that human beings – as speakers and viewers of word and image – can only be a tiny part of the assemblage at work in *The Lost Words*.

Humans do not actually appear in a spell book designed to conjure words of the land missing from everyday usage in the twenty-first century, although they are implicated in its ecological agenda.

Macfarlane and Morris have flooded their book with natural words and images that encourage 'biotic interaction' in an affirmation of Leopold's land ethic:

> That man is, in fact, only a member of a biotic team is shown by an ecological interpretation of history. Many historical events, hitherto explained solely in terms of human enterprise, were actually biotic interactions between people and land.
>
> (Leopold [1949] 1968: 205)

In common with Deleuze and Guattari, Leopold effectively throws out the root-book and destabilizes those 'gigantic memories' of human enterprise that have dominated historical events. Leopold's *Almanac* is an ecological manifesto for humans to extend the notion of community to biotic environments and to connect with it through biotic teamwork. Leopold's address is to all humans, yet children's literature has been an important force in responding to such calls from environmentalists and children's literary scholarship has also responded to this call. For example, in *Wild Things: Children's Culture and Ecocriticism* (2004) Sidney Dobrin and Kenneth Kidd highlight 'the interplay of children's texts … and children's environmental experience' (2004: 1). In *New World Orders in Contemporary Children's Literature* (2008), Clare Bradford et al. argue that 'children's texts remain "environmentally informed" rather than "ecocritical" in that the fictions are constrained by a pervasive commitment to maturation narratives' and that this 'ensures that any environmental literature remains anthropocentric in emphasis' (Bradford 2008: 9). There is no doubt that a concern with human maturation, or the developing child, in much environmental literature for children points to an anthropocentric stance – this could be said of *Lost in the Barrens* (1956) by Farley Mowat, for example. However, this assessment does not represent the breadth of environmental commitment in children's literature, which reaches back (at the very least) to pioneers, such as Beatrix Potter. I would argue that the 'deep ecology' called for in *New World Orders* is located, for example, in the intricate landscapes of Potter's *The Tale of Miss Tiggy-Winkle* (1905), which works on a different level from her social satire. In *Watership Down* (1972) by Richard Adams, a closely detailed engagement with the countryside, combined with various anthropomorphic strategies, allows for biotic interaction with the environment on Leopold's terms. A large number of more recent picturebooks – a form well suited to ecological enquiry – also reach down into what might be recognized as deep ecology. In common with *The Lost Words*, many books imply a child reader but avoid the developing child altogether – for example, *Slow Loris* (2002) by Alexis Deacon; *A Forest* (2012) and *A River* (2015) by Marc Martin; *Tidy* (2016) by Emily Gravett; *Animal City* (2017) by Joan Negrescolor; *The Last Wolf* (2018) by Mini Grey; or *Somebody Swallowed Stanley* (2019) by Sarah Roberts and Hannah Peck. I trace some of this history in my earlier work on the ethical dimensions of ecocritical movements in children's literature (Sainsbury 2013: 99–133), but as I go on to reveal here, a close focus on the metaphysical structures of flora and fauna in children's books uncovers a fundamental commitment to biotic teamwork. A complex metaphysics emerges, in which entities move past and through each other. I also suggest that the biotic assemblage at work in *The Lost Words* throws out shoots to connect with entities that move beyond the natural world, confirming that 'heather is never only heather'.

A Thousand Plateaus challenges some of the ontological foundations I have set up elsewhere and, while embracing the forward-facing dimensions of Deleuze and Guattari's becoming, I do not want to reject conceptions of *being* entirely. The notion of human being and thingness is crucial to my own thinking and to certain areas of children's literature (such as ontological exchange), so a philosophical framework that allows for ontological being *and* rhizomorphic becoming in the context of plant-life is invaluable for my consideration of flora (alongside fauna) in children's literature. In *The Life of Plants: A Metaphysics of Mixture* (2017), Emanuele Coccia establishes an 'atmospheric condition' ([2017] 2019: 119) for the metaphysical consideration of plants, which he argues have been overlooked by philosophy 'more out of contempt than out of neglect' (3). He contends that plants are often ignored by a metaphysics focussed on beings with senses and consciousness. Through his concept of *immersion*, Coccia makes a compelling case for his claim that 'One cannot separate the plant – *neither physically nor metaphysically* – from the world that accommodates it … To interrogate plants means to understand what it means to be in the world' (5). In previous chapters, when I have considered 'what it means to be in the world' the focus has often been on *being human* in the world – and even material objects in the world are frequently approached in terms of a vitalism afforded to human beings. Here the focus shifts to a consideration of the world that sustains plant-life, for as Coccia points out, 'We will never be able to understand a plant unless we have understood what the world is' (6). Evidently Coccia's project is ontological and he demonstrates that plant-life is intimately linked to being human and animal. So, although Coccia embraces the ontology contested by Deleuze and Guattari, he allows for their assemblages and connections – initially through a return to Bachelard's seed, before pushing on to his notion of immersion. Returning momentarily to *The Lost Words*, Macfarlane's fiddle-heads flare, unfold and reach into Morris's double-page spread (44–7), which is filled with ferns of different species, such as bracken fern, hart's tongue and maidenhair spleenwort. Their ferns have a palpable life force that cannot be ignored; indeed they have a presence that demands as much (if not more) attention as the other creatures – common toad and goldcrest – hidden within their fronds. It seems reasonable then to ask what these beings are – in the general terms of metaphysics – and how they relate to the creatures presented alongside them; in *The Life of Plants* Coccia offers ways of approaching or answering this question. Indeed, he observes that it is 'thanks to our plants and their life that higher organisms [bird and toad] can produce the energy necessary for survival' (10).

Cosmos, atmosphere, breath and immersion are related concepts central to Coccia's metaphysics, helping to explain the ways in which plants – and other living entities by association – exist in the world. Just as Bachelard's poetics allows for trees seeding and seeded of worlds, so Coccia observes that 'When there is life, the container is located in the contained' (10). Furthermore, 'Plants … demonstrate that living beings produce the space in which they live rather than being forced to adapt to it'; they make 'possible the world of which they are both part and content' (10). There is a mutual overlap of biological entities here that relates to the very act of breathing:

> To blow, to breathe – means in fact to have this experience: what contains us, the air, becomes contained in us; and, conversely, what was contained in us becomes what contains us. To breathe means to be immersed in a medium that penetrates us with the same intensity as we penetrate it. Plants have transformed the world into the reality of breath.
>
> (10–11)

Plants might breathe differently from animals and humans – of course they have no lungs – but they create and are created by the world in which all living things breathe. Botanical inhalation is at work in children's books too, so that flowers, shrubs or trees breathe life into the worlds springing forth around them. Shaun Tan provides a vivid example of this in 'Bee', one of his stories in *Tales from the Inner City* (2018), during which a roof-top tree bursts into blossom and attracts the bees of the night. The tree has been nurtured nightly by a married couple, the Katayamas, 'for about seventy, eighty, even a hundred years – who knows? They stopped counting many anniversaries ago' and for the first and only time their tree is due to 'come into flower' (Tan 2018: 202). Tan builds a reverential dream-life and anticipation around an event which is transformational in Coccia's terms. In the seasonal cycle of flora, the immersive abundance of flowering trees on naked winter trees can seem to come from nowhere and their petals fill the air – through which animals or humans move, sometimes in wonder and sometimes without noticing at all – with life that manifests presence. Tan captures this ontic resonance in the tree he brings to life in the middle of a city, thus: '*Shoosh*! A million flowers! A billion! A colossal pink hemisphere rising upward so unbelievably, so massively, it's as if the whole apartment building is breathing in, like an enormous set of steel and concrete lungs, the whole architecture of existence groaning' (204). Tan allows the slow inhalation of the apartment building to take the weight of his ontological imagery here, as the atomic[9] resonance of the blossoming breathes life into the material, human and non-human life around it. In the ontic terms set out by Coccia the blossom makes 'possible the world of which they are both part and content' because when it breathes it allows the world to breathe along with it.

Although first published just outside the period of my study, Cicely M. Barker's *Flower Fairies* series 1923–48 was reissued in a box-set format in the UK in 1974 and took its part in a tide of environmental engagement in children's literature of the 1970s. The seven books in the series are dedicated variously to season, or habitat, plus an anomalous ABC. The format is sustained across the series, with each spread introducing a detailed illustration of a flowering plant and its 'fairy', plus an accompanying poem. I include these books here, because the fantasy element is in service of Barker's botanical commitment to flowers that live through her books. Barker is explicit about this in her final work of the series, *Flower Fairies of the Wayside* (1948), maintaining in an author's note that 'I have drawn all the plants and flowers very carefully, from real ones; and everything that I have said about them is as true as I could make it … But I have never seen a fairy' ([1948] 1974: 52).[10] Barker is no illusionist in the style of the Cottingley Fairies,[11] for she is a non-realist about her fairies – 'they are just "pretend"' (52) – and insists that they should not be considered ontically possible in Quine's terms. She is keen to lend her flowers a vitality that accords them ontological and verifiable presence in the external world and she achieves this through the visual and verbal conditions of her texts. It would be easy to dismiss Barker's whimsical poems, for the anatomically detailed images are more robust and carefully rendered. However, the immersive combination of word, illustration and fantasy element works together to let her flowers move together and breathe. The Rose-Bay Willow-Herb sings: 'On the breeze my fluff is blown; / So my airy seeds are sown' (16); Fumitory is '"Smoke of the Earth" – a soft green smoke!' (40); Totter-Grass is embedded in movement as it dances and 'sways like trees' (34); while Jack-Go-To-Bed-At-Noon has 'Twelve puffs! and then from sight' (46). These fragments of verse emit airiness suggestive of life forms that respond to the habitat in which they grow. Barker's illustrations also convey the immersive quality of plant-life, as insects or birds frequently accompany her flowers and trees. In *Flower Fairies of the Garden* (1944), the depiction (Figure 3.2) of a snapdragon is carnivorously immersive as it enfolds fairy and 'Clever old Bumble Bee' into the pleats of its snapping 'mouth' (Barker [1944] 1974: 36). The combination of word and image in Barker's work thereby demonstrates Coccia's assertion that 'plants have transformed the world into the reality of breath', while also identifying its ontological remit.

In common with Deleuze and Guattari's dismantling of ontological binaries, Coccia points out that a life of immersion rejects the 'material distinction between us and the rest of the world' (32) so common in the evolution of metaphysics. To make his point about the collapse of object and subject in immersive

Figure 3.2 Immersive snapdragon inhales a bumblebee in its puffed petals (Barker [1944] 1974: 37).

environments, Coccia takes the extreme example of jellyfish, creatures that lives in water and primarily made of water:

> The world for an immersed being – the world in immersion – does not, properly speaking, contain *real objects*. Everything in it is fluid, everything in it is in motion, with, against, or in the subject ... It is, properly speaking, a universe *without things*, an enormous field of events of varying intensity.
>
> (32)

Coccia admits that the immersed being of the jellyfish might seem at an extended reach from human being but argues that listening to music allows for a similar sort of immersion, as waves of sound that 'penetrate us and that we ourselves penetrate' (33). If biotic communities are to be understood from a metaphysical (as well as ethical) point of view – and I have suggested that the ethical remit of children's literature surely rests on metaphysical groundwork – then this sort of mutual penetration needs to be explored.

The oceanic metaphor employed by Coccia floods through David Wiesner's wordless picturebook, *Flotsam* (2006),[12] which is in sympathy with immersion at the level of form, subject and style. Wiesner's precise, luminous watercolours are convincing in their verisimilitude, allowing for suspension of disbelief when a clockwork fish swims alongside fish that appear 'real' (Figure 3.3). His vividly realized shoal raises ontological questions along Quinean lines as surrealism troubles the real. The book's wordlessness is immersive, as environments and creatures flow together through and into 'a field of events' in Coccia's terms. The withdrawal of anchoring words invites the reader to draw together crab, fish, turtle or human through a connective process of close looking. Immersion can be seen as a visually penetrative process, as Wiesner magnifies a boy's

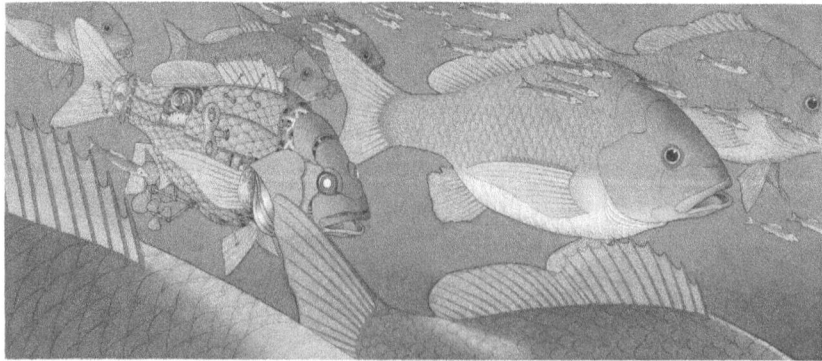

Figure 3.3 A shoal swims through a fluid seascape of ontic immersion (Wiesner [2006] 2012: 14–15).

fascination with a hermit crab. Human being is embedded immediately in a wider environment of sand, sea and non-human being and the boy becomes immersed literally in the ocean when a wave catches him and carries with it an old camera. The camera contains images that allow for a process of visual reverie, for the photographs are spatially, temporally and ontically open to immerse the viewer in their mutable field of reference. They bring past into contact with present and reality into the remit of fantasy through successive stylized photos, which connect surreal, anthropomorphized, undersea worlds with other human beachcombers who have found the camera.

The movement from seascapes to human portraits – in which land and sea merge – emphasizes the sort of metaphysical community and continuity that Coccia has in mind and *Flotsam* shows its viewer how entities in (and beyond) the world relate to each other. As Coccia points out, 'Life has never abandoned fluid space' and the terrestrial world remembers and echoes life beneath the sea: 'Terra firma is just the extreme limit of this cosmic fluid at the heart of which everything communicates, touches, extends' (35). In symbiotic response to Coccia's sense of biotic communication, the final image of *Flotsam* depicts another child crossing the ontic borders of land and sea as they reach for a camera washed ashore – a camera that extends the ontological limits of what there is in the world.

In *The Fox and the Star* (2015) by Coralie Bickford-Smith, immersion is expressed primarily through the repetitive nature of illustrative design. Bickford-Smith is a book designer by trade and the arrangement of visual detail plays a central role in conveying a biosphere that echoes Leopold's biotic teamwork. Expansive double-page spreads depict a profusion of trees, foliage and brambles that spring into life on every page turn. Each spread is filled with repeated patterns and the connections made through this stylized and overtly artificial design evoke the deeper complexity of natural environments beneath the surface. Indeed, these dense and detailed spaces almost swallow the creatures depicted on each page, so that rabbits are inseparable from the thicket of ferns that shelter them; thicket is rabbit and rabbit is thicket (Figure 3.4).[13]

Heather is never only heather. It is a story that is full of plant-life through which Fox weaves, as does the light of Star, so that Fox exists in a fluid universe made up of interlinked entities. Since this is a fable of sorts, there are lessons to be learnt and at least one of them relates to what it means to exist in the cosmos – its message involves looking beyond the confines of the world we think we know in order to reflect on what the world is. There is a movement from the epistemic towards the metaphysical, in common with Tan's 'Butterfly'

Figure 3.4 Repetition of ferns breathes life into Fox's habitat (Bickford-Smith [2015] 2016: 12–13).

(discussed later in this chapter). Fox loses track of Star and only finds Star again once he follows instructions written in fallen forest leaves: 'look up beyond your ears' ([2015] 2016: 46–7). Fox discovers that the world is much bigger and more complex than he imagined and that the 'blazing sky' is full of stars. The book ends with a final silhouette of Fox – his orange coat replaced by constellated stars – suggesting that he is immersed in the cosmos that lights his way. This sort of immersive design-work can be seen in other texts, which maximize formal properties of the picturebook in an ontic commitment to flora. For example, in Martin's *A River*, the cover shows a section of a river flowing through the dense habitation of a stylized jungle and the endpapers are washed with the mysterious blue of the river itself. These peritextual elements of the picturebook prepare the way for a narrative that connects its different landscapes – busy city, industrial factories, farmland, mountainscape and jungle – through a single watercourse and the childly imagination of its narrator. In *Animal City*, the limited colour palette of Negrescolor's design-work lends itself to this dystopian fable in which derelict wild and invisible cityscapes are fused with the flora and fauna of lost habitats. The illustrator's use of vibrant pantone colours, superimposed one over the other, also provides a sense of unfocussed unease in a secret city inhabited only by animals and plants. In both examples, formal elements of the picturebook are used to engage with the metaphysical conditions of being in a world of immersive and wildly varied habitats.

Picturebooks lend themselves to metaphysical immersion through a visual dimension that is able to convey directly a connectedness between different entities – images can be overlaid and fused through streams of watercolour, oil and pastel, and so on. Moreover, the illustrative presence of flora and fauna can open ontological dimensions that are not present in the verbal narrative alone (as I suggested earlier in *The Lost Words*). For example, in *Adrian Simcox Does NOT Have a Horse* (2018) by Marcy Campbell and Corinna Luyken, Luyken's images of floral biotic profusion are integral to the becoming of horse and child in a picturebook embedded in the ontological fabric of reverie. In this tale it seems that a horse might not exist and plants come to trouble its might-not existness. The nameless and unreliable narrator refuses to believe that Adrian Simcox has a horse and illustrative plants consistently challenge the authority of the narrator's perspective on what can be real. Indeed, the grounds of truth and reality are tested by the plant-life of this urban environment and reject a dichotomous positioning of town and country: 'He lives in a town like me, and I know you can't have a horse in town' (2018: 6).[14] Despite living in an apparently deprived environment, where 'even though it wasn't trash day, it looked like it was' (19), Adrian refuses to be limited by the geographic or economic conditions of his daily life; this is made clear by the plants that seem to flow from and through him. Although it is possible to read in this book a plea for all children to have access to spaces enriched with horses and plants, I think this misses the point. This is a book about world building, which refuses to limit the metaphysical boundaries of its community.

While the narrator's words reveal a prejudicial attitude to Adrian that she comes to reconsider, the illustrations stand in counterpoint to her initial claims and doubts. When she asks, 'Is your horse at a farm?' (29), the narrator evokes a discourse of pastoral childhood – of the sort espoused by Coleridge in 'Frost at Midnight' (1798)[15] – to deny Adrian his horse. However, the plant-life of Adrian's urban world signals a biotic community that dismantles such monolithic roots. It is not the case that Adrian belongs in the country or that he makes the best of what little he has in the town. The point is not that he would have a horse if he lived on a farm. He has a horse – and his horse is not denied by the conditions of his town space. It grows out of the place he lives and from the stuff of Bachelard's

Figure 3.5 Horse immersed in the plant-life of grasses (Campbell and Luyken 2018: 33).

reverie; it is a horse of plateaus that exists on different levels. Adrian Simcox is consistently surrounded visually by an abundant plant-life of leaves, grasses and flowers, revealing him as one of Bachelard's poets who recognize the 'cosmicity of childhood' ([1960] 1971: 126). Cosmicity in Bachelard's terms allows for an openness in the dreamer, whereby seeds create worlds – and in this case the seeds of a daydreamer burst a horse into being via floral assemblage. Luykin's effusive and loose style emphasizes the plant-life surrounding Adrian and when he discusses his horse, extended strokes and lines of feathery grass grow to support the grounds of his reverie in which a horse exists (Figure 3.5).

Furthermore, Adrian does not need to travel out of his urban space to engage in biotic teamwork – ontologically he is open and has the capacity to reach outside of himself. Coccia's observation about flowers and sessile beings is of value here, as he observes that 'It is only within itself that a being without motion can encounter the world … Every sessile being has to make itself world for the world, has to construct within itself the paradoxical site of an environment for the world itself' ([2017] 2019: 99). Adrian is situated in 'the tiniest house I ever saw' (Campbell 2018: 22) and yet the visual and verbal narrative does not conspire to move him from this house, since he is able to build a (horse) world from the place within (and simultaneously without) which he exists. Coccia's point is useful here, since its paradoxical positioning of being and world retains the idea of immersion in which beings come together without privilege. Reading Adrian's reverie in these terms allows for the idea that this is not an anthropocentric process in which hegemonic relationships are reinscribed. The formal conditions of the picturebook have an ontic capacity to demonstrate different levels on which reality and lived experience operate.

As *Adrian Simcox Does Not Have a Horse* (2018) confirms, picturebooks can formally complicate and challenge binaries operating to situate the natural world in pastoral spaces. This dynamic visual form provides fertile spaces for a rhizomorphic reach across plateaus, and a metaphysical energy inheres in biotic spheres that allow for the becoming-plant-becoming-child. This reach does not trap the child in amber hues of pastoral fossilization. It anticipates and plays out the sort of bioscientific ontologies described by Haraway as she articulates 'cyborgology' in experiential terms: 'I am fascinated with the molecular architecture that plants and animals share, as well as with the kinds of instrumentation, interdisciplinarity, and knowledge practices that have gone into the historical possibilities of understanding how I am like a leaf' (2000: 132). Haraway describes a moment of ontological epiphany here in which human being is open to the molecular architecture of a leaf – to be human is to be immersed in plant-life. Haraway implies a link between her 'adult perspective' on this 'aesthetic-moral-physical-unity' and her child consciousness, which was 'fascinated by miniatures ... and playing with tiny figures in the grass' (132). This evokes the figurative power of (the miniature) Arrietty's biotic immersion in a garden, as she 'lay back amongst the stalks of the primroses ... and looked sideways up the bank among the grass stems' (Norton [1952] 2003: 91). In this moment Arrietty is 'seen' for the first time and her immersion in grass and primrose points to an ontological like-leafness, which allows for Haraway's cyborg and Coccia's cosmic metaphysical fluidity.

The butterfly effect

Having explored the ontic conditions of plant-life in contemporary picturebooks, I now open up my discussion of Coccia's immersive ontology to explore a strange case of near-immersion in James Vance Marshall's *Walkabout* (1959).[16] This novel demonstrates the dangers of conflating Coccia's immersive and egalitarian ontology – which opens up ontological systems to all organic beings – with the more hierarchical root-book that advances some categories of being over others. Indeed, this is why Deleuze and Guattari dismiss being altogether in favour of rhizomorphic assemblage. *Walkabout* can be considered a Robinsonade, in which American siblings, Peter and Mary, survive a plane crash on Sturt Plain in the Northern Territory of Australia. Although it attempts to engage with a crude form of postcolonial politics (28–9),[17] the dualistic treatment of an Aboriginal boy (who remains unnamed) and 'coddled' siblings makes for difficult reading. The depiction of the Aboriginal boy in *Walkabout* falls prey to a primitivism that has shaped hierarchical and racist ontologies, whereby Aboriginal peoples are ranked on an ontological scale that measures them in the same terms as plants and wildlife of the Australian bush. It could be seen to reflect a contentious area of Australian legislation – exposed by the 1967 referendum on Aboriginal rights and equality – which circled around a 'Flora and Fauna Act' that appeared to regulate Aboriginal peoples in the same terms as flora and fauna.[18]

The novel retains the sort of colonial roots redirected and pulled up by Deleuze and Guattari, yet there are aspects of a more sensitive immersive ontology in its rendering of landscape that is worth attention, not least because the history of children's literature is awash with politically complex examples of ontic ambivalence at work in the Robinsonade. Moreover, the rhizomorphic concept of immersion might seem to acknowledge (if not satisfactorily address) political tensions of the period. Marshall also maintains Cartesian hierarchies between human and animal, suggesting that human beings are more advanced in cognitive and emotional capacities than animals. As the narrator insists when the bush boy makes fire, 'Man alone can harness the elements' (52). The claim is typical of the sort of 'arrogant anthropocentrism' identified by Fiona Probyn-Rapsey (2018) and which animal studies of the twenty-first century seek to challenge.

There are metaphysical fault lines and absences in *Walkabout*, but I reveal that there are synergies between all three children and the geological environment in which they find themselves that are persuasive in ontic terms. Prior to the Aboriginal boy's death mid-way through the book, Marshall implies that being human is dependent on the sort of immersion in environment and biotic teamwork that many Aboriginal communities understand and that without which humankind cannot survive (exist) in the long term. The American children are disadvantaged in comparison and have no understanding of what it means to be in world. The problem is that the Aboriginal boy is not allowed to live into a future that might be reshaped by metaphysical reappraisals of being, through which all humans live alongside flora and fauna in a biosphere of common respect. Indeed, the boy's problematic death works against the ontological investment upheld in this passage (and elsewhere in the novel):[19]

> The bush boy led the way unhesitatingly: across the salt-pans, through the scattered yellow-jackets ... around the outcrops of quartz and granite. It was eight years since his tribe had last passed this way. He'd been little more than a toddler then; but small as he was his memory and instinct had been at work, recording landmarks, storing up information that might be of use for the future – information that was proving invaluable now.
>
> (71–2)

There is an epistemological investment in this passage as the boy calls on knowledge stored in his memory and reflected back at him through the environment. However, there is an ontological thrust here too, which is almost elided by that which he has learnt. In metaphysical terms, it is evident that this boy has a biotic relationship with the external environment through which he moves, calling on Leopold's notion of biotic teamwork – and it is the importance of this teamwork as a means of survival and being that the boy passes on to Peter and Mary. The prose is interspersed with details of the terrain and biosphere, so that the boy physically grows through saltpans, quartz and yellow-jackets – rather than being reduced to them – recalling the conditions of Coccia's immersion. The emphasis on future requirements also hints at a concern with becoming-child in Deleuze and Guattari's terms.

The pattern of immersion through recollected moments of being is taken up as a trajectory for the American children to follow as they travel further into the Australian outback. Indeed, moving deeper into the hills of the Northern Territory, the children's relationship with their surroundings begins to develop. In the following scene 'a whole hillside [is] aglow with shimmering colour' (126–7) and a further move is made towards biotic assemblage:

> As the children approached the hill they heard a low, high-pitched rustling; a soft vibrating hum that trembled the air. Then, to their amazement, the blaze of colour began to move: shimmering: palpitating: rising and falling, as the butterflies opened and shut their wings. Suddenly, like bees, they swarmed – disturbed by the children's approach – and in a great rainbow-tinted cloud went swirling south: south for the Victorian plains.
>
> (127)

The atmospheric writing incorporates granite hillside, butterflies and human beings. The children are responsive to vibrations in the air, suggesting a level of immersion in their environment similar to that experienced (and passed on to them) by the Aboriginal boy. In this moment they disturb the butterflies, indicating that the children are not yet fully connected with these creatures and the space through which they move. However, the close attention of the prose (which extends beyond the extract I have provided here) to this 'kaleidoscope of brilliance' foreshadows fuller immersion. Although not overtly expressed in this passage, the children retain this memory in a bank of experiences that increasingly connect them with desert, hills, valleys and forests of the outback and to which they refer towards the end of their journey.

This metaphysical commitment to immersion as a way of 'becoming-child' is confirmed when the children pass through the 'fantastic battleground' of the forest: 'They wandered through twisting tunnels, arcaded with vegetation through which the sun had never penetrated; they smelt the rich humid soil which had never felt the stir of drying wind' (137–8). This passage follows detailed descriptions of flora and fauna and is expressed in terms of immersion as they breathe in earthy smells. The shift in their response to their surroundings is made explicit: 'At first they were filled with awe and amazement, but eventually, after three of four days of exploration, they became as much at home in the forest as they had been in the desert' (138). This is not the conventional return home – to their 'comfortable home in Charleston, South Carolina' (3) – of much children's literature; rather this is a newfound connection with a biotic space that has changed their relationship to entities in the world around them.

One further indication that the children are growing into their status as biotic beings relates to Mary's ongoing struggle with nudity. Social convention has marked out her life experience prior to the plane crash and its relevance recedes the further she move into the Australian landscape. The children's journey marks a shift from the sociological to the metaphysical, as social life is stripped away and moves towards a deeper understanding of what it means to be and to become-child. In this moment, it is not the case that the children 'sink' to a primitive level of being – alongside plants, animals and Aboriginal peoples – rather that they are able to look at themselves in relation to the landscape and all of the humans and non-humans who occupy it. Consequently, Mary 'felt strangely unembarrassed' (140) when a koala cub tears the remains of her dress from her and she is left naked among the eucalyptus. Finally, her skin is able to breathe in its surroundings as she comes into biotic being. Derrida provides the tools to make sense of this moment in *The Animal That Therefore I Am* (2006),[20] when he seeks properly to see animals in metaphysical terms. In so doing he reflects on the conditions of his own cat's nakedness:

> The animal, therefore, is not naked because it is naked. It doesn't feel its own nudity. There is no nudity 'in nature'. There is only the sentiment, the affect,

the (conscious or unconscious) experience of existing in nakedness. Because it *is* naked, without *existing* in nakedness, the animal neither feels nor sees itself naked. And therefore is not naked.

([2006] 2008: 22)

Derrida recognizes that the cat is naked in its being and goes on to reflect on the biblical shame that prevents humans from being on the same level. His revelation that humans will never properly look at animals, be-with animals, if we cannot let them see us is crucial to understanding the ontic shift in *Walkabout*. Haraway (2006) is right to identify a masculine positioning here as Derrida stands naked before his cat in Adam's name. However, Haraway's 'A Manifesto for Cyborgs' (1985) would have us eschew the Garden of Eden altogether and the chimeric fusion of woman and land, typical of cyborg literature, is relevant in this post-human moment of becoming-woman-becoming-animal. Mary does not become koala, but she looks koala in the eye and understands the equivalence of human and non-human being.

My exploration of *Walkabout* involves an act of what Alison Waller terms 're-memorying', which she defines as a phenomenological approach to childhood reading that focuses 'on the specific functioning of individual reading acts, while still acknowledging social and shared meanings' (2019: 11). I had not returned to *Walkabout* since childhood (I was 9 when I first read it) and was reminded of it by my recent encounter with 'Butterfly', another of Tan's short stories from *Tales from the Inner City*. The immediate connection I made between Tan's story and Marshall's book was powerful, since the butterfly passage is the only specific episode of *Walkabout* that I could recall with clarity. In 'Butterfly'[21] Tan depicts a moment of immersion that is unexpected, brief and transformative in the connectivity it achieves:

> The butterflies came at lunchtime. Not millions, or billions or even trillions but a number beyond counting, beyond even the *concept* of counting, so that people on the street were relieved of any estimation. By people on the street, I mean everyone. Literally *everyone* … None had ever experienced such inexplicable, joyful urgency.
>
> (17)

The emphasis on *countless* butterflies that descend on *everyone* suggests that this is an experience that reaches into something deep and profound about all living beings. The butterflies obscure the people – or at least it becomes impossible to distinguish person from butterfly – and in this sense humans become butterfly. The scene has metaphysical weight and can be considered another moment of becoming in Deleuze and Guattari's terms. The butterflies cause a silent stillness as they land, as people wait 'for the weightless blessing of tiny insects' (17), allowing for immersive reflection. The story then opens out into an expansive double-page spread, which expresses the motion, colour and inclusive enormity of the butterflies' descent. As this short tale closes, Tan also emphasizes the contemplative connectedness experienced by those involved: 'We thought of nothing but the butterflies, the butterflies settling on our heads, on the heads of friends and family, on everyone we knew and everyone we didn't, on the whole city at once' (19). This is an experience of biotic teamwork; it is entirely inclusive in its reach.

In Tan's commentary on 'Butterfly' he reflects on his decision to capture this moment of butterfly communion.[22] His focus on breathing, as humans come into the meditative presence of butterflies, is reminiscent of Coccia's immersion:

> They enjoy a special respect in our imagination, as almost metaphysical animals, hard-to-believe flying canvases that are attractive to each other but also, strangely, to the eye of a quite unrelated primate. Their presence tends to inspire a certain mindfulness, an awareness of breath, position and time, not unlike mediation.
>
> (Tan n.d. b.)

Tan throws up an incongruity in this passage, in which his knowledge of Darwinian classification and of differences between species is challenged by this moment of metaphysical realization. He understands on an epistemic level that butterflies are 'a foreign species' (Tan n.d. b.), yet this knowledge is overturned by the immersive quality of his poetic prose and oil painting in which human and butterfly merge. Tan also explains that he read an article about a moving mass of butterflies over Colorado soon after completing *Tales from the Inner City*. Subsequently, he wonders whether the 'image of a mass of butterflies filling city streets may have been something I'd seen a long time ago, I can't quite remember' (Tan n.d. b.). I draw attention to Tan's hazy sense of recollection, since it relates to my own experience of re-memorying. Tan makes no mention of *Walkabout* and I am not suggesting that he was ever aware of or intended a relationship between his story and Marshall's novel. However, my decision to reread *Walkabout* was initiated by a shared sense of poetic reverie and profundity related to this assemblage of butterflies, (accompanied by a notion that *Walkabout* is a book immersed in the natural world, which might well be relevant to the ontological work of this chapter). When I did return to *Walkabout* I was surprised at the brevity of the butterfly scene – it covers little more than half a page – which in my memory had expanded. Tan's 'Butterfly' is similarly brief and might be described as a prose poem. These miniature paeans to butterflies accurately convey the fleeting nature of insect life and any physical contact humans might have with them, while reflecting the metaphysical depth of connections made. The links between *Walkabout* and 'Butterfly' are obvious to me for the reasons I detail, yet there is a connection here that moves beyond these specific works into a wider framework of children's literature, which details immersion in various ways and through different literary forms.

Animal messes

> Paradoxically enough, all these other forms of terrestrial life and consciousness, which equally with ourselves are parts of the real and manifest its nature, and also so extensively engage our practical activities, are almost completely ignored by us in our theories regarding the nature of reality.
>
> (Fuller 1949: 829)

In 'The Messes Animals Make in Metaphysics' (1949) Fuller traces a long history of metaphysical evasion that posits man as the only conscious being on the face of the earth, or beyond (829). Fuller's central target is really the myopic philosophies of pluralistic idealists – such as Berkeley – who disregard the existence of animals due to the unresolvable contradictions they throw up. Essentially, animals and lower life forms make such a mess of metaphysical propositions that they represent a significant absence in the Western philosophical tradition and consequently, 'When the chickens come home to roost, it silently wrings their necks at the entrance to the coop, before they can get in and cackle' (838). Although Fuller's argument is historical in emphasis, his qualms about the metaphysical deletion of non-human organisms are prescient in their awareness of the need to account for terrestrial and non-terrestrial life forms in any account of reality. Mary Midgley's *Animals and Why They Matter* (1983), Haraway's 'A Manifesto for Cyborgs' (1985) and Derrida's *The Animal That Therefore I Am* ([1997] 2008) are at least thirty years away and, as Kari Weil notes, it is much more recently that 'a new generation of animal scholars makes the plea to reject the human – and the humanism it subtends – as tired metaphysics' (Weil 2018: 195). Fuller playfully refers to the graphic description of the 'octopus-like inhabitants' of Mars in H. G. Wells's *The War of the Worlds* (1898) and implies that speculative fiction has taken more ontological responsibility for the conditions of reality than have countless metaphysicians. Fuller focuses on the absence of animals in dominant metaphysical systems, recognizing that if philosophy cannot account for creatures encountered in quotidian life then it seems ill equipped to deal with things to come. Fuller's sideways glance at literature is important, since he reveals a philosophical openness to the sort of 'aesthetic-moral-physical-unity' that Haraway identifies in post-human ontologies. Fuller's qualms also anticipate the contradictions and complexities played out in Jaques's conception of posthumanism, which 'as a discourse, both exposes and ironically establishes boundaries between the human and the non-human, to facilitate a dialogue as to how those very borders might become more fluid' (Jaques [2015] 2018: 2–3). In this final section then, I demonstrate that children's literature is less daunted by metaphysical mess than philosophies, which

> ignore the possibility of the existence of other worlds, inhabited by beings perhaps even more intelligent than man, but differently organized physically and with different senses, passions, emotions, values, ideals, goods, gods, and metaphysical appraisals of the nature of reality.
>
> (Fuller 1949: 829)

Via its long-standing engagement with natural and artificial life forms, children's literature is fundamentally concerned with the sort of 'metaphysical appraisals of the nature of reality' Fuller has in mind. Many children's books test the ontological limits of human and non-human being in terms outlined by Derrida in *The Animal That Therefore I Am* and have been doing so at least since Alice played croquet with live hedgehogs – and Derrida is fascinated by the gaze of those hedgehogs that twist themselves round to look Alice in the face ([2006] 2008: 26). When his own, real cat – 'this cat that is perhaps not "my cat"' – looks at him in his 'bedroom or in the bathroom' Derrida concludes that it does so in its existence as 'an irreplaceable living being' (29). Alice's hedgehogs have helped him to recognize that his pussycat tests the boundaries of 'being *after*, being *alongside*, being *near* ... indeed of *being-with*. With the animal' (30). Derrida explains that his project can be understood as *limitrophy* and I suggest that the texts I explore here – and many others like them – are similarly preoccupied with 'what sprouts or grows at the limit, around the limit, by maintaining the limit', while also being concerned with 'what *feeds the limit*, generates it, raises it, and complicates it' (61–2).

Beyond the Fence (2017) by Maria Gulemetova might be considered a working example of limitrophy. In its portrayal of the negative conditions of restriction and ontological hierarchies, this picturebook explores sites of being-child and being-animal and tests the limits of being together – being-animal and being-human – in domestic and wild spaces. Piggy lives with Thomas (a young boy) in a grand house that appears to be situated on the edge of an expansive moor in

Figure 3.6 Piggy's gaze through the window complicates the limits of existence (Gulemetova 2017: 14–15).

which 'Thomas talked a lot. And Piggy had to listen' (Gulemetova 2017: 1–2).[23] Thomas dresses Piggy and decides what they should play, because he always 'just knew' (5) how things should be. It turns out, however, that Thomas has no idea of how to maintain the limits of being human and being-animal in order to be-with Piggy. Meanwhile Piggy is depicted as a forlorn figure, lost in an environment that does not accommodate what it means to be a pig, and living with a human child who does not see him as one of Derrida's irreplaceable living beings. When Thomas's cousin comes to visit, Piggy takes the opportunity to leave the house and meets a Wild Pig on the moor. Wild Pig wonders why Piggy is 'wrapped up' (clothed) and urges Piggy to try running someday (11). Back in Thomas's home, the limits of Piggy's existence are made clear by his gaze through a bright green window of hope (Figure 3.6). As conveyed through gesture, point of view and colour tones, Piggy yearns for the verdant pastures in which another being who recognizes what it means to become-pig runs free. Piggy has his back to the implied reader and is positioned at the end of a bleak, panelled room that occupies most of the double-page spread. This image seems to be a tipping point, for colour tones and perspective incline Piggy towards the window, who seems to be testing the limits of the space that contains being.

Piggy is not permitted to roam 'beyond the fence' and still appears willing to submit to Thomas's control – until the boy kicks over a model forest that Piggy has decided to build; independent forest building is another means of testing the limits. Finally, Piggy politely takes leave of Thomas's teatime meal, throws off restrictive clothing and runs beyond the fence to join Wild Pig 'beyond the fence'. Gulemetova's picturebook pays careful attention to boundaries, which are evoked through spatially aware illustrations. Piggy is contained by narrow borders and between the architectural lines of domestic structure. It is clear that anthropocentric dominance generates limitations to the conditions of existence for non-human beings. *Beyond the Fence* confirms that being-with can never successfully be achieved under the conditions of imprisonment and control. If Piggy ever resumes his friendship with Thomas – if ever they were friends in the terms of generosity required by the concept – then it will need to be on the proviso of freedom in which fences that limit the conditions of being are torn down. Thomas would need to see Piggy properly in order to be-with an animal on equal terms. Understood in the context of this thought-provoking picturebook, limitrophy is a useful tool for testing the conditions of human and non-human being and the biotic conditions of existence.

The 'natural' words chosen for inclusion in *The Lost Words* were dictated by deletions from *The Oxford Junior Dictionary*,[24] as Macfarlane explains in *Landmarks* (2015: 3), yet the process is not only of etymological and philological import, for it also involves Derridean limitrophy in its testing of verbal and visual representation of non-human being. Macfarlane's awareness of ontological remit is implied by his reference to Henry Porter, who observes that 'the OUP deletions removed the "euphonious vocabulary of the natural world – words which do not simply label an object or action but in some mysterious and beautiful way become part of it"' (Porter, cited in Macfarlane 2015: 4). Porter speaks to the poetic and metaphysical aspect of nouns that extend into the being of entities and become entwined in them. It is through this 'euphonious vocabulary' that the language of nature – of Macfarlane's summoning spells – is breathed into the air and a sort of immersion takes place in which human voice sounds around 'adder', 'heron', or 'kingfisher' and a community of beings takes shape in biotic community. *The Lost Words* gets to grips with being at the level of linguistic play, yet it also makes connections between absences/beings/becomings through its complex arrangement of words and images. For every verbal entry into the spell book and for every natural thing called into existence, Morris creates a negative space in which the natural object does not exist (absence); an iconic rendering of natural subject on gold-leaf (being); an immersion of the becoming-creature/plant into habitat (becoming). The book establishes a relationship between semiotic representation and organic entities, suggesting that flora and fauna of the natural world might cease to exist if they are no longer spoken by name – by human-given names – and that they might come into being as a result of human representation. Shades of anthropocentrism inhere in this, yet the complex combination of visual and verbal representation in *The Lost Words* defuses potential hegemony.

In *Environmental Culture* (2002) Val Plumwood observes that anthropocentrism has not been well served by philosophy (2002: 123) and that related discourse is often split down dualistic lines, leading to impasse and reductive reasoning. Plumwood finds a way of accepting the significance of being human in the natural that does not reduce non-human to human. Indeed, a concern with being human is crucial to the sort of ecocritical and politicized uprising of which *The Lost Words* is a part; and any drift away of human beings from the natural world breaks down the possibility of Leopold's biotic teamwork. Ultimately, Plumwood argues that anthropocentric frameworks are not *necessarily* detrimental to the external world in which humans live as one of many species, but that they can 'prevent us from experiencing the others of nature in their fullness' (142) – and of course 'nature in its fullness' is precisely what *The Lost Words* seeks to evoke. Plumwood adds that in order for encounters with 'more-than-human' presences to be realized, 'we will need a reconception of the human self in more mutualistic terms as a self-in-relationship with nature, formed not in the drive for mastery and control of the other but in a balance of mutual transformation and negotiation' (142). In Plumwood's view, anthropocentricism can allow for a balance and mutuality that appears central to the verbal-visual negotiations of *The Lost Words*.

The question of language has long played around the limits of human and non-human being and the (in)ability to speak is central to many metaphysical systems that exclude animals and other entities. In *Animals and Why They Matter* (1983) Midgley points out that 'some philosophers have recently exaggerated the importance of language to such a point that they make all inter-species communication look impossible', going on to observe that not all communication is verbal anyway and that speech can 'conceal or misrepresent feelings' (1983: 54). Midgley takes on Kant and Wittgenstein (among others) as she demonstrates that the propensity for spoken language is a flawed foundation on which to delimit species on metaphysical grounds. Midgley's ethical position on 'the species barrier' is in sympathy with John Berger's political indictment of capitalism and the zoological project in which he sees the animal marginalized or erased in 'Why Look at Animals?' (1980: 28). Berger's ethical position might be hard to resist, but the ontological grounds of his polemic are unstable. He begins to answer the question of why we should look at animals (and be concerned about them) through his observation that the animal's 'lack of common language, its silence, guarantees its distance, its exclusion, from and of man' (1980: 6). Berger starts in a similar place to Derrida (2006), considering the way in which animals and humans regard each other: 'The animal scrutinises him across a narrow abyss of non-comprehension' (Berger 1980: 5). However, Berger is forced to conclude that the animal is *inevitably* marginalized under the human gaze, because he does not reconsider or challenge the ontological conditions of his animal – and this is the task that Derrida takes on as he overhauls his own metaphysical project in order properly to see animals and his relation to them.

Unsurprisingly, Derrida's limitrophy is workout out and through language, so that some of the early questions Derrida raises are related to nomenclature: 'The animal, what a word! The animal is a word, it is an appellation that men have instituted, a name they have given themselves the right and the authority to give to another living creature' ([2006] 2008: 51). This authoritative appellation feeds into Derrida's own autobiography and in recognizing this he actuates a revisionist history to counter the historic abuse and use of the word – the animal – in violence. Derrida calls into question 'this auto-biography of man' and 'the human *Dasein* as regards what is living and animal life' (52). Derrida takes issue with the singular usage of animal to designate all non-human species, suggesting that this would be to utter an *asinanity* (64). Instead he proffers *animot*, a portmanteau play on singular (*l'animal*) and plural (*l'animaux*) in the French usage and so 'by means of the chimera of this singular word, the *animot*, I bring together three heterogeneous elements within a single verbal body' (90). It is in this moment of heterogeneity and verbal dexterity that I return to *The Lost Words*. Evidence of Derrida's animot can be detected as Macfarlane plays with heterogeneity in some of his summoning spells, demonstrating also that words can be steeped in a sort of becoming (rather than reduction via human utterance). This language of land and life forms involves a restless and mutable becoming – as Macfarlane details extensively in *Landmarks* (2015) – avoiding essentialism that might reduce a thing to its name. During the willow's spell there is an absolute refusal to translate the whispering leaves of willow for human ears: 'We will never whisper to you, listeners, nor speak, nor shout, and even if you learn to utter alder, elder, poplar, aspen, you will *never* know a word of willow – for we are willow and you are not' (116). The willow recognizes perhaps that to converse with humanity risks ontological depletion and also that organic beings need not be understood by humans fully to exist.

In the 'raven' spell, the bird with 'the boxer's swagger' and 'twice as agile as the wind' is asked by rock, air, vixen and earth: 'what are you?' Raven's responses are varied and evasive, so finally his interrogators declare that 'Nothing knows what you are.' Raven 'riddles in reply', retorting: 'Not True! For I am Raven, who nothing cannot know' (Macfarlane and Morris 2017: 98). The ontological run of questions seeks to identify Raven, but its playful and shifting responses

Figure 3.7 Raven refuses to be spoken for – Raven is Raven (Macfarlane and Morris 2017: 100–1).

reveal that it will not be pinned to anything in particular – for Raven, existence is the thing and it will not be refused or settled by human language. Raven's final double-negative answer confirms quite simply that it is known by everything and that *it is Raven*. Morris's imposing and assertive images of Raven reflect the knowing self-importance of a bird who recognizes its right to be for itself. These are portraits of majesty, wherein Raven first stands erect, holding life (an egg) in its beak and (on the page turn) straddles the page-spread, as solid as the crags on which it postures (Figure 3.7). Raven's oral and graphic attitude seems Heideggerian in its emphasis on Da-sein, 'Being is always the being of a being' (Heidegger [1927] 1996: 7), yet in Derrida's terms there must be a liberation of animot from Da-sein. 'How to welcome or liberate so many animal-words [*animots*] *chez moi*? In me, for me, like me?' (74) – and this question is also central to *The Lost Words*.

In *The Lost Words* there is a simultaneous move away from the object–subject dichotomy of humanist root-books into a space of becoming, within which other kinds of connections can be made. The double-page spread wherein each 'spell' opens out presents an immersive biosphere in which plants and creatures might become *something more* when they are brought into contact with each other. These are complex ontological manoeuvres, demonstrating that the book works on different ontic levels. Indeed, there is an openness that allows for something more to enter the frame – as required by Fuller – and this something more brings me to insects. As we have seen, Tan puts bees and butterflies into immersive contact with human being, affording them the close attention that Fuller pays to ants and bees. Fuller recognizes in insects intelligence and levels of social organization that require fluid ontological systems, for without metaphysical recognition

> they can be no more for us than outposts, as it were, on our own planet of the possible inhabitants of other possible worlds, reminding us that the real, in defiance of our anthropocentric and anthropomorphic hypotheses regarding its nature, may be a house of many mansions, and fulfill itself in many ways of which ours is only one, no more central or conspicuous than the rest.
>
> (837)

In *Du Iz Tak?* (2016) by Carson Ellis the idea of insects existing at Fuller's outpost of existence is emphasized by the nonsense language Ellis creates for her vibrant bugs. In common with most examples of nonsense, unfamiliar words follow grammatical rules, so that the ontological remit of her playful narrative is clear in its enthusiastic response to: 'what is that? Elis's picturebook follows the life cycle of a flower, which grows in the habitat shared by a group of insects. The flower's short life is mirrored by that of a caterpillar who hangs as a chrysalis throughout most of the book, before flourishing into fullness as an ephemeral moth. The other bugs build a home in the flower, which lasts only until the seasons change and the flower wilts. Theirs is a precarious existence and yet the insects' incessant chatter in their own tongue means that they escape Derridean violence accorded by human language. In *The Lost Words* we might see insects as occupying the outposts of existence described by Fuller, were it not for the fact that such creatures are connected by a metaphysical groundwork in wider children's literature and culture that support these 'many mansions'. Although it has a limited presence in *The Lost Words*, insect life is there – hidden away in the words and illustrations of plant-life, birds, mammals, amphibians and reptiles. I followed the instructions laid down in the book's introduction carefully: 'To read it you will need to seek, find and speak. It deals in things that are missing and things that are hidden, in absences and in appearances' (5). This address speaks to ontological mutability and I suggest that the minority insects, hidden or unmentioned as they are, might lead elsewhere if we move on to another connected plateau. It is possible that I have missed some of the Lost-Word insects, but I found a moth in the spell words and landscape of bramble (24–9), an unspoken bumblebee flying through its heather habitat (53) and unidentifiable insect wings undergoing predation in the ivy (64). I searched out these insects since they are part of the book's biotic community and, moreover, because they move within and beyond these natural environments in unexpected directions – as a return to beginnings reveals.

The Lost Words project was inspired by the findings of a 2002 zoological study, which probed children's ability to identify natural and synthetic entities.[25] The study reveals that children over 8 typically identify Pokémon 'species' 'substantially better' than 'organisms such as oak trees or badgers' (Macfarlane 2017: n.p.). The Cambridge zoologists conclude that children have a 'tremendous capacity for learning about creatures (whether natural or man-made)' and that 'conservationists are doing less well than the creators of Pokémon at inspiring interest in their subjects' (Balmford et al. 2002: n.p.). Macfarlane's disquiet over these discoveries compounded his own findings, detailed in *Landmarks* (2015), about depletion of language related to the natural world and instigated the development of *The Lost Words*. However, as well as drawing attention to dwindling natural vocabularies, *The Lost Words* opens up communal space for different life forms to communicate through the interplay of word and image. Add to this an implied audience of readers receptive to all manner of synthetic and natural things – if the Cambridge findings are correct – and its place in a children's literature that is wide-reaching in its rhizomorphic reach, *The Lost Words* has the potential to connect even with synthetic entities from which it distances itself. Macfarlane does not dismiss the place of technology in the lives of young people, observing that 'Children are now (and valuably) adept ecologists of the technoscape' (2015: 3); it is more the case that he detects an imbalance between children's experience of natural and synthetic entities. However, there is perhaps greater potential for movement between synthetic and natural beings than ecologists might allow – and this is the point at which those insects return.

Satoshi Tajiri designed his Pokémon card-trading game on the strength of his boyhood preoccupation with collecting and studying insects, thus an investment in connecting biological organisms with synthetic species inheres in the early development of Pokémon.[26] However, beyond the imaginative affinity between Mothim (synthetic) and White Ermine (natural) there is little to instigate movement across rhizomorphic plateaus in Tajiri's game. Such movement across levels of sur-reality is embedded in the immersive storytelling experience of David Wiesner's *Spot* (2015), a digital platform that renders a ladybird and the worlds it contains through sound, illustration and vertical movement. Developed as an app for the iPad, *Spot* takes advantage of pinch and zoom functionality, allowing objects to be enlarged and for the viewer to move down into its dynamic fantasy worlds. In common with *Flotsam*, *Spot* interrogates the ontic structures of the surreal through its artistic medium, so that the ontological remit of Wiesner's realistic ladybird is tested through a tactile movement into nested environments. In its commitment to an insect of the natural world – and entities that *might* lie beyond it – *Spot* pushes at the sort of ontic and narrative boundaries familiar to post-human discourse and literature. Children's culture in its variety thus allows for movement across plateaus: 'Moths have come in their millions/drawn to the thorns. The air flutters' (Macfarlane and Morris 2017: 26).

The metaphysical commitment to exploring boundaries of synthetic and natural entities in children's literature is further demonstrated by numerous books that bring child protagonists into contact with post-human beings. Jaques explores several instances of the 'entangled relationship between man, machine and the natural world' ([2015] 2018: 206-7) in her interrogation of the post-human and points to 'a complex and confused response to the place of the robot in countering anthropocentric norms' (205). In many examples of cyborg or robot literature, including works explored by Jaques, 'child readers can be encouraged to celebrate what it means to be human through an encounter with the machine' (181). A recent example of this tendency is offered by *Tin* (2018), Pádraig Kenny's ontological quest, in which mechanical children set out to discover who made them and what it means to be human. Alternatively, young readers are tasked with the responsibility for saving humankind from environmental catastrophe as a result of their contact with 'cybernetic organisms' (Jaques 2018: 196), as is the case in *The Iron Man* (1968) and *The Iron Woman* (1993) by Ted Hughes.[27] In *The Wild Robot* (2016) though, Peter Brown builds on these earlier examples of cyborg entanglement in order to test ontological boundaries from a different perspective. Brown's illustrated novel is unusual in that human characters are (ostensibly) absent from the central action of the book and the relative isolation of a robot in the wilderness allows for ontological encounters that start to sweep up Fuller's animal messes.

The Wild Robot announces its project through a title that brings together ideas – wilderness (natural); robot (synthetic) – often placed in dualistic opposition. This dichotomous relationship is questioned and challenged by the immersion of a robot in an island wilderness inhabited by North American flora and fauna and unoccupied by human beings. This novel travels with Haraway's 'A Manifesto for Cyborgs' (2004), taking its place in sociopolitical and cultural discourse that has grown around and through it. The *Wild Robot*'s ecocritical awareness benefits from the feminist thinking that underwrites Haraway's essay, whereby

Nature and culture are reworked; the one can no longer be the resource for appropriation or incorporation by the other. The relationships for forming wholes from parts, including those of polarity and hierarchical domination, are at issue in the cyborg world.

([1985] 2004: 9)

Interrogation of the points at which nature–culture meet, overlap, fuse or move through each other is crucial to Haraway's feminist take on cyborg culture and the widespread influence of her manifesto can be explained by its rhizomatic reach into related domains, such as ecocritical, postcolonial or queer theory. Haraway's cyborg feminism is also key to understanding the philosophical thought experiment undertaken by Brown, which wonders what might happen if a robot were to be stranded on a remote island. It asks whether a synthetic being could survive in a natural environment; whether the proximity of different entities is ontologically revealing; and whether different species could learn anything from each other, or change anything about each other. These questions suggest a fascination with the sort of chimeric merger at work in the wider field of science fiction (and children's literature) and they unfold gradually as the narrative follows Rozzum unit 7134 on her voyage into the wilderness.

That Roz is a female robot is not accidental and Brown acknowledges as much in an afternote, which demonstrates awareness of the literary and sociocultural discourse from which she evolves. Her gendering is a political function of a novel that challenges patriarchal and colonial centres, while simultaneously depolarizing technology and nature. Roz's act of mothering is not inevitable or natural – '"I am not your mother," said the robot' (Brown [2016] 2018: 69) – yet the gosling who imprints on her makes an ontic connection between machine and bird that sends out disruptive metaphysical shoots. Haraway has reflected in published interviews on the fact that the feminist aspects of her manifesto are often jettisoned as commentators pick over cyborg circuits (Haraway 2006: 136–7), yet it seems impossible to have one without the other. Writing in the 1980s, Haraway contends that the 'cyborg is a matter of fiction and lived experience that changes what counts as women's experience in the late twentieth century' and more urgently that 'This is a struggle over life and death, but the boundary between science fiction and social reality is an optical illusion' (8). Haraway argues for the relevance of cyborg science fiction to and in people's lives and over forty years later her manifesto remains germane. In part this is due to the chimeric qualities of the discussion itself, which she continues most recently in *Staying with the Trouble: Making Kin in the Chthulucene* (2016), and also because issues around gender, race and environment have been reanimated in the twenty-first century. Where Fuller pokes at metaphysics with an ironic stick, Haraway is determined to outline a fresh metaphysics in which being(s) overlap. Critics have identified a relationship between Deleuze and Guattari's rhizomorphic becomings and Haraway's sense of cyborg, chimera and kinship (and I recognize the correspondences myself). However, Haraway refuses the comparison (2006: 156), reasoning that Deleuze and Guattari's 'Becoming-Animal' is not the least bit interested in animals (2006: 143). I see much to value in the rhizomorphic movements of becoming, although I agree with Haraway that Derrida looks more carefully at the animot of his autobiographical concern than do Deleuze and Guattari. I bring together strands from each of these theorists in my reading of *The Wild Robot* as they offer complementary perspectives on its metaphysical groundwork.

First a retraction. Although Roz is stranded in an ostensibly non-human domain in *The Wild Robot*, her experience is configured from a human perspective. I said earlier that humans are (unusually) not present in the central action of Brown's novel and yet – in common with *The Lost Words* – the narrator and narratee are human in voice and ear from the outset, as 'Our story begins' (1). On one level this is a conventional story opening, but the inclusive embrace of the possessive pronoun returns throughout the novel as a young *human* reader is implied and reinforced through direct address. It is important to the narrator that 'we' are witness to Roz's arrival, habitation and survival in the wilderness, for we (humans) are embedded in her experience – and (as it turns out) not only on a diegetic level. The story begins in media res as a ship sinks, spilling its cargo of robot-filled crates into the ocean until only five remain – no backstory is supplied to explain where the ship came from, nor where it was headed. This proves important, as it places the reader/listener in the same position as Roz (when she is activated), as she has no prior knowledge of why or how she came into being. From the outset it is evident that the epistemological freight of this narrative is shared between human narratee and robot character (and the island creatures with whom she soon comes into contact).

Its midstream opening indicates that *The Wild Robot* is not to be conceived as a prelapsarian myth or fable, which could be tempting given the proliferation of plant and animal life and the fabular heritage of children's literature. Derrida insists that in order to bring animot into metaphysics we must 'avoid fables', as 'we know the history of fabulization and how it remains an anthropomorphic taming, a moralizing subjection, a domestication. Always a discourse *of* man, on man, indeed on the animality of man, but for and as man ([2006] 2008: 74).

I suggest that the blend of robot and biotic wilderness in *The Lost Robot* assures that its anthropomorphic treatment of animals does not lead back to man as centre and beginning – this is not a human fable. Moreover, as Haraway observes, 'the cyborg has no origin story in the Western sense', elaborating that humanist origins depend 'on the myth of original unity, fullness, bliss and terror, represented by the phallic mother from whom all humans must separate, the task of individual development and of history' (Haraway [1985] 2004: 9). The absence of history at the moment of Roz's arrival does not preclude the possibility of a before, but it obscures it and hints at its lack of significance in mythic terms; this is no tale of original sin and responsibility. The narrator underscores this point in 'Chapter Ten: The Reminder', wherein the reader is reminded of what Roz does not know and is provided with pointedly scant details as to why/how she has arrived on the island; for example, 'she didn't know that she'd been built in a factory' (Brown [2016] 2018: 24). The function of the direct address – '*I should remind you*, reader' (24) – is less to provide the reader with external and privileged information than it is to reiterate the idea that origin is of little consequence. This recap situates Roz on an island that she perceives as a starting point – 'As far as Roz knew, she was home' (24) – which is overlaid with a hidden (and therefore elided) origin that will not define her. Roz is not forged by any root-book in the human conditions of factory production, as Marxist ideology might configure it. Instead, she is destined for a rhizomorphic process of becoming, sending out shoots across the island in a cyborgian fusion of machine and nature.

After the shipwreck, only one crate survives rocks encircling the island, with its robot safely packed inside. A curious group of otters examine the debris: 'Scattered across the rocks were the broken bodies of four dead robots' (4), before climbing inside the remaining box. The 'death' of these robots implies that they had been afforded life, thus anticipating Roz as a potential life form in ontological terms. It is also significant that the otters are responsible for activating Roz: 'one of their paws accidentally slapped an important little button on the back of the robot's head' (6). In this moment Roz is aligned with the indigenous species of the island that 'give' her life, while the inadvertent nature of the action suggests that it is not an act of creation. Roz begins life with the otters – so obscuring and refusing human rootedness – but cannot be traced back to them in alignment with any 'myth of original unity', of the sort rejected by Haraway's cyborg. When Roz is activated she 'communicates' a brief preprogrammed message, which explains that 'Over time, I will find better ways of completing my tasks. I will become a better robot' (7). Of course this message hints at Roz's obscured origins – thus her genesis is ambiguous – and it reveals that Roz has knowledge, which is confirmed later in the novel when she is able to draw on programmed information. Haraway's cyborg is 'completely without innocence' (Haraway [1985] 2004: 9) and Roz's encounter with the otters confirms a level of unattached experience that will result in her becoming an unanticipated creature. It is evident early on that *The Lost Robot* is playing out a cyborg narrative, which in Haraway's view makes 'thoroughly ambiguous the difference between natural and artificial, mind and body, self-developing and externally designed, and many other distinctions that used to apply to organisms and machines' (11). Brown sets up these apparent tensions early on as a function of a thought experiment that cannot be predicted – he makes it difficult to anticipate what Roz will be or do in the wilderness.

The preprogrammed message also allows for the idea of adaptation and change in Roz, implying ironically that Roz can become *a being beyond programming*. Indeed, without comment until the final chapter, the narrator traces an ontological shift through ubiquitous and contradictory references to Roz's design. She is first presented as a robot ill-equipped to deal with stormy island conditions: 'Our robot was helpless. … Mud surged around her, spraying into her face and pinning her against some solid thing' (Brown [2016] 2018: 28). Brown thereby avoids an essentialist line that might conceive Roz's introduction to the wilderness as natural – to perceive Roz as a purely natural being is to misunderstand her metaphysically. As Haraway points out, 'The cyborg would not recognize the Garden of Eden; it is not made of mud and cannot dream of returning to dust' ([1985] 2004: 9). This does not mean, however, that Roz cannot find a way of becoming-robot-becoming-wild thing, for she learns to send out shoots that draw flora and fauna of the island to her. When ultimately she is able to plant up a garden, the narrator observes: 'Clearly, Roz was designed to work with plants' (Brown [2016] 2018: 96). The narrator's comments cumulatively build a metaphysical system of becoming through integration of machine and natural world, until finally it is confirmed that Roz has changed fundamentally:

> Maybe Roz really was defective, and some glitch in her programming had caused her to accidentally become a wild robot. Or maybe Roz was designed to think and learn and change; she had simply done those things better than anyone could have imagined.
>
> (268)

The allusion to 'accidental becoming' is revealing here; a combination of biotic immersion and teamwork has an ontological impact that shapes the narrative and consistently refuses human design-work or doctrinal genesis. When finally

Roz is tracked by RECOs, robots programmed to retrieve lost ROZZUM units, she destroys them, symbolically refusing the human makers who seek to claim and control her. Although physically she is broken to the extent that only her torso remains, Roz has become a wild robot and this ontological conviction drives her to seek help from the human beings who (she now knows) built her. She is not determined by a return to origin, rather a desire to embrace that which she is becoming. A violent and bleak humanity is glimpsed beyond the island when the geese migrate, which Roz rejects – and thus her journey reinscribes Haraway's manifesto:

> The main trouble with cyborgs, of course, is that they are the illegitimate offspring of militarism and patriarchal capitalism, not to mention state socialism. But illegitimate offspring are often exceedingly unfaithful to their origins. Their fathers, after all, are inessential.
>
> ([1985] 2004: 10)

Roz's faithlessness with regard to root-books is fundamental to her successful existence on the island and her commitment to non-human being.

The Wild Robot is a staged narrative, which takes its time to trace the various phases of Roz's wilderness merger as she is distanced from human experience and immersed in the natural world. Biotic immersion completes the first stage of the robot's encounter with the natural world, but she has to move into and earn this immersed status. The incongruity of her ontological position in the wild is underscored early on: 'The island was teeming with life. And now it had a new kind of life. Artificial life' (Brown [2016] 2018: 23). Detailed descriptions of the natural world are set against Roz's presence through a framework of verbal–visual othering and counterpoint. This is achieved in part through figurative comparisons that convey similarity and difference simultaneously: 'Then she lifted her hands and pulled apart the crate. Like a hatchling breaking from a shell, Roz climbed out into the world' (8). The simile is juxtaposed with Brown's accompanying illustration, which reveals that she looks nothing like the gosling she will eventually hatch and rear. This uncomfortable foreshadowing of the maternal role Roz assumes suggests that this is not a straightforward example of Kate Soper's 'woman-nature equivalence that has served as a legitimation for the domestication of women and their relegation to maternal and nurturing functions' (Soper 1995: 123). Roz's cyborg mothering brings the wild robot into being as machine and animal merge.

The robot's lack of alignment with her natural environment continues, for 'the forest was not a comfortable place for Roz' (16) and 'so she stood there, motionless, all perfect lines and angles set against the irregular shapes of the wilderness' (18). The wilderness takes its toll on Roz (31) until she observes a stick insect merging with its twiggy background: 'I can see how camouflage helps you survive; perhaps it could help me survive also' (41). This is the point at which immersion begins – initially as a means to survive and finally as coming into being-with the animals that are like and un-like her: 'she padded to the centre of the clearing, nestled herself between some rocks, and became part of the landscape' (43). Roz's physical appearance continues to alter as she morphs into her chimeric status, initially amalgamating with the natural environment and eventually losing mechanical body parts, which are replaced with forest materials. This immersion is not a loss of identity, since a composite mode of becoming-animal-machine ensues, leading to a simultaneous entanglement in language that moves the narrative into another stage of being.

Through placing Roz in the wilderness, Brown seeks to bring the speaking/listening humans with her in order to achieve a perspective change on the machine, landscape and creatures of the natural world. Derrida anticipates that for humans to achieve a being-with animals that shifts humanist hierarchies, then we must look closely at the questions we typically ask of animals: 'Does the animal have not only signs but a language, and what language? Does the animal die? Does it laugh? Does it cry? Does it grieve?' ([2006] 2008: 114). Such questions are certainly posed by *The Lost Robot* as Roz learns to communicate with the creatures around her. However, Derrida suggests that it is not the questions themselves that require modification if we are to recognize the being of animals, but rather the tenor of the questions posed:

> I wish only to indicate a tonality, some high notes that change the whole stave. How can the gamut of questions on the being of what would be proper to the animal be changed? How can a flat, as it were, be introduced in the key of this questioning to tone it down and change its tune?
>
> (114)

Derrida's musical analogy is helpful, since it conceptualizes what I understand as a metaphysical poetics of animot in which human voice and ear are able to get at animot being from a tonal reach – and of course narrative has the capacity to lend voice and ear to the conditions of being. My contention is that children's literature is especially attuned to the particular speech acts of animal-being-with-human that the post-human endeavour of *The Lost Robot* achieves. Roz's cyborg ontology allows for a fusion of human-animal-machine that poses Derridean questions in a different key. Roz can ask of herself and the creatures around her what it means to be from a position that is before and after, inside and outside human experience.

Initially, Roz's speech acts are ignored or remain unanswered by the animals she meets – the otters, a crab, bear cubs and a robin – and she is not able to understand the sounds they make. Rather than assuming that these creatures do not have language, Roz becomes attuned to the notes of the birds around her: 'After weeks of robotically studying the birds, Roz knew what each bird would sing, and when they would sing, and eventually, why they would sing. The robot was beginning to understand the birds' (46). The narrative emphasis on 'robotic' study of the natural suggests that Roz's tactics are different from anthropocentric approaches, which have privileged human being as linguistic, thus depriving non-human beings of sign-making capacities. Brown could have allowed his wild creatures to communicate with Roz from the outset – in the manner of Beatrix Potter's animals, for example – but this would have undermined a metaphysical shift that renegotiates the ontic mechanisms of anthropomorphism. Narrative perspective is also used to show the human aspects of cyborg experience, so that Roz's robotic discovery in the third person moves on to the second-person human position: '*She discovered* that all the different animals shared one common language; they just spoke the language in different ways. *You might say* each species spoke with its own unique accent' (47: my emphasis). The modal construction of this direct address is important – and there are examples throughout the novel – for the capacity of the *mighty* child to throw doubt on adult (narrative) authority and the hesitant construction of the proposition leaves room for Roz to be something other than *might* be expected of her.

As I have suggested throughout this chapter, the flora and fauna of children's literature can be conceived as an ontological project that shifts the groundwork of metaphysical systems that have little or no room for non-human life. The opening lines of *The Amazing Maurice and His Educated Rodents* (2001) – Terry Pratchett's metafictive manifesto of ludic anthropomorphism – make the point neatly: 'As the amazing Maurice said, it was just a story about people and rats. And the difficult part of it was deciding who the people were, and who were the rats' (2001: 9). Certainly the task is difficult, but as Pratchett's disingenuous observation suggests, children's literature is well placed to distinguish between human and animal and to test metaphysical systems that obscure animal and plant-life. Often the fusion of beings is unsettling and incongruous, as is the case in Tan's *Tales from the Inner City*. The surrealism of Tan's short stories in which animals and humans share urban life confirms that existence is puzzling and (moreover) that it is worth puzzling over. Who knows exactly why 'crocodiles live on the eighty-seventh floor' (Tan 2018: 11) or why a pig vanishes into the concrete floor of a family apartment (85), but the questions arising from these mysteries are worth addressing and thinking through. Children's books know that animals and plants have ontological status worthy of poetic reverie and in this understanding worlds are seeded.

4

Mapping the Nowhere

The floor was wet with the drops. In some places the surface of the water was freezing thinly. This was no place to be – Unn searched the complicated walls yet again for an opening.

(Vesaas [1963] 2009: 56)

Housed everywhere, but nowhere shut in, this is the motto of the dreamer of dwellings. In the last house as well as in the actual house, the day-dream of inhabiting is thwarted. A daydream of elsewhere should be left open therefore, at all times.

(Bachelard [1960] 1971: 62)

Nowhere shut in

The Ice Palace (1963) by Tarjei Vesaas captures a moment of metaphysical clarity as a young girl grasps that *this was no place to be*. Unn is trapped in the icicled room of a frozen waterfall that leads 'only further in to ice and strange flashes of light' ([1963] 2009: 56). Bachelard's vision of metaphysical dwelling in *The Poetics of Space* (1971) suggests that to be shut in is to be nowhere at all. Inescapable interiority leads to ontological contradiction in which being is so intensely situated that somewhere becomes nowhere. As Bachelard explores the homely interiors of metaphysical space, he determines that the housed condition of human being is contingent on the possibility of elsewhere. We should be *nowhere shut in* and yet nowhere exists as a proposition that hinges on here, somewhere and elsewhere. This paradox is allowed for by Deleuzian displacement, which I bring into play alongside Bachelard's poetic challenge to 'thrown' metaphysical systems, as I outline an ontological structure for nowhere. Vesaas and Bachelard consign nowhere to the limits of the experiential world – and at this extreme reach, being is an ontically tested proposition. The extremity of nowhere in their poetic explorations of ice and space allows for an interrogation of being. Moreover, nowhere is conceived as a conceptual entity with spatio-temporal conditions that resonates in a particular way in books for young people. *The Ice Palace* is not quite a children's book (perhaps),[1] nevertheless its poetic engagement with childhood rests on nowhere in its childly aspect, providing a working model for nowhere as a metaphysical structure of children's literature. Plotting nowhere throughout this chapter reveals the complexity and variety of its manifestation in children's books, and identifying its ontic breadth and depth requires historical underpinning in each section. The utopian shoots of nowhere have rhizomorphic spread, which I explore in relation to the fabular renditions of belonging and displacement; local political conditions of the here and now; and *nowhere in extremis* at *poles of inaccessibility*. Finally, I move on to explore the *awareness of whereness* involved in mapping the mundanity of nowhere.

The particular movement I trace in *The Ice Palace* – and there are many – is the movement from being somewhere to being nowhere, as undertaken by Unn on the fateful day of her outing. In the aftershock of an intense encounter with her newfound friend Siss, Unn has decided to visit a frozen waterfall alone. Unn is not ready to meet Siss at school today: 'tomorrow it would be different, but not just *now*' (Vesaas [1963] 2009: 38). On reaching the 'enchanted palace', Unn 'was aware of nothing but her desire to enter' (49). Unn's excursion to the ice palace on this particular day – here and now – anticipates Deleuzian fluidity in its ontic negotiation of space–time. Unn might seem to be somewhere quite definite (she wants to enter the palace specifically), yet bound up in *not-just-now* and an *awareness-of nothing-but* is a conceptual precision that negates itself – *not* and *nothing* – as it comes into being. Thus, 'somewhere' becomes a tricky concept, which does not seem sufficient to reflect Unn's sense of being in this unsettled palace as fluid water freezes into solid ice. Unn is simultaneously liberated (water) and trapped (ice), and this simultaneity layers *here and now* in a repetitive slide into being nowhere.

In *Difference and Repetition* (1968) Deleuze advances a positive approach to repetition that embraces difference, as opposed to generality, whereby 'difference is internal to the Idea; it unfolds as pure movement, creative of a dynamic space and time which correspond to the Idea' ([1968] 2014: 28). The ice palace is essentially a layering of difference as countless drips and trickles of water are frozen into ice via repetition. Through this repetitive act of nature Unn is delivered into the dynamic space of nowhere, which also allows for the possibility of somewhere and elsewhere. Although Unn's encounter with nowhere seems to enclose her – as watery openings are closed into ice – still and always she could be somewhere, as testified by Siss and all those searching for her. Unn seems to be frozen in childhood, nevertheless she embraces a childly futurity that retains possibility: 'Unn was running towards it' (Vesaas [1963] 2009: 40). Capturing Unn's approach to the palace, this short statement is typical of the novel's poetic phrasing; precise images overlay each other as the narrative evolves. Thus, it can inferred from this emphatic move forward into the frozen falls that Unn's nowhere is a melting-frozen possibility that inheres in childly being. When considering the metaphysical parameters of conceptual experience – into which I am drawing nowhere – Deleuze argues for an empiricism that 'treats the concept as object of an encounter, as a here-and-now, or rather as an *Erewhon* from which emerge inexhaustibly ever new, differently distributed "heres" and "nows"' (xvii). Deleuze employs Samuel Butler's concept of *Erewhon*, 'signifying at once the ordinary "nowhere" and the displaced, disguised, modified and always re-created "here and now"' (xvii).² In this sense Vesaas's ice palace becomes a utopian vision of displacement, in which nowhere encompasses an elsewhere and somewhere that is always happening (always re-created) in a corruption of now. I return to the utopian branch of nowhere in children's books later, but emphasize here that the 'splendid intricacy' of the ice palace and its 'sinister' turn ([1963] 2009: 48–9) helps to explain the more disquieting aspects of utopia in its *always re-created 'here and now'*.

Unn urgently wants to be in this enchanted palace, yet her encounter with nowhere takes her further into the conditions of being than she intended; 'it was like being right *inside* it' (55), she observes when she reaches a room at the heart of the waterfall. Initially Unn's passage through each icy interior is marked by thoughts of Sis and the world outside: 'It gushed out, she called "Sis!"' (54). This is the pinnacle of nowhere, wherein elsewhere is still possible for Unn. However, her grip on elsewhere diminishes as Unn's thoughts become confused: 'There were plenty of fissures, but they did not lead out to anything, only further in to ice … No use thinking like that. It was not in, it was out now' (56). Unn had been on a childly trajectory towards meeting Siss at school tomorrow and being nowhere helped her to come to terms with a future that might challenge her. However, such coming to terms with being in nowhere cannot be prolonged, for childness depends on the promise of forward movement. This childly futurity is denied her though and she settles into stasis: 'Here I am. I've been here all the time. I haven't done anything' (58). This immobility infiltrates her nowhere to such an extent that it transforms into an inescapable somewhere and she becomes 'languid and limp and ready' (60). The material weight of this – and this is the point at which the narrative turns away from Unn as focal subject – suggests the *thingly* and ontological freight of somewhere and nowhere as encountered by Unn. Embraced by a metaphysical system these indefinite pronouns become empirical entities of the experiential world and start to function as nouns in the surface grammar of ontologically aware phrases. For example, in *Fox* (2000) by Margaret Wild and Ron Brooks, when Magpie warns Dog about Fox, she declares that ' "He belongs nowhere" ' (2000: 16); and nowhere can be seen operating here as an ontic entity that also reveals something of fox's being (as I go on to reveal). Vesaas does not actually describe Unn as being nowhere – so the term itself is not in play in *The Ice Palace* – but it is clear that Unn has experienced nowhere in the dynamic terms identified by Deleuzian repetition of the here and now. This dynamic conception of nowhere will prove fruitful when considering the status of nowhere in a diverse range of children's books from *The Magic Pudding* (1918) by Norman Lindsay to *Outside In* (2014) by Sarah Ellis.

Having established the dynamic and childly conditions of Deleuzian nowhere, I turn to the spatial conditions of Bachelard's metaphysical system of dwelling in *The Poetics of Space*, which allow for the possibility of nowhere *within*. In order to appreciate the ontic nuance of Bachelard's nowhere, I must take Unn back to her arrival at the edges of the waterfall. Unn finds 'a fissure with water trickling through it, wide enough to squeeze herself through' and enters the first of many rooms as she moves further inside the enormous palace of 'blue-green ice' (49). Unn experiences the palace as a series of enclosures, classified in domestic terms of interiority. The mutable palace grows around Unn, freezing fissures close as water sprays and drips incessantly, until finally she recognizes that 'This was the last room; she could go no further' (56). Unn's journey to the heart of the waterfall has brought her 'out into something she did not like very much' (55). The prose detailing Unn's exploration of the ice palace is spatially aware and taut with this sort of paradox and disorientation: *out into something*. Unn 'looked for a way out, a means of getting further in' (50), while 'forward or back meant nothing to her any longer; she had lost all sense of it' (51). Unn's excursion from the safety of her Auntie's cottage to the hostile magnificence of rooms in the ice palace might seem to encompass opposing types of internal space. However, each edifice maintains signs of domesticity and it is clear that, via Unn's experience of them, cottage and ice palace share the humble scope of childly dwellings in Bachelard's metaphysical order. Palace and cottage also come together in the etymological tracings of 'edifice',[3] as the term allows for a building, dwelling, hearth or even funeral pyre. Thus, I propose that Unn's entry into somewhere and nowhere can be considered a process of *ontological edification*.

Bachelard recasts Heideggerian thrownness in the world as a secondary metaphysical stage of being, proposing instead that 'Life begins well, it begins enclosed, protected, all warm in the bosom of the house.' Bachelard's 'complete metaphysics' recognizes that 'within the being, in the being of within, an enveloping warmth welcomes being' ([1960] 1971: 7) and the thoughts, memories and dreams of mankind are integrated through a poetics of house and dwelling. For Bachelard, this primary state of being is poetically represented as intimacy associated with 'the house we were born in' (14) – it is not the literal house of our infancy but a geometric-oneiric structure of childhood reverie and it configures being in an ontic phase that precedes thrown experience. Inside this house is to be somewhere in the ontological sense of coming into being, 'for our house is our corner of the world' (4). Bachelard argues that poets and philosophers who pay too little attention to the 'humble home' cannot shape a comprehensive metaphysical structure through which to test and understand being. In order to understand the 'I and the non-I' close attention must be paid to the 'values of inhabited space' (5). Bachelard suggests that poetic images attending most assiduously to the conflicts of habitation are set in and against the external reach of the cosmos. In her discussion of the 'sanctuary topos' in *Landscape in Children's Literature* (2011), Carroll confirms the extensive reach of the humble home when she observes that 'The home is sanctified because it reflects, on a microcosmic level, the world as a whole' (Carroll [2011] 2014: 19). *The Ice Palace* emphasizes the tensions implicit in such contrasts of scale through its juxtaposition of cottage and ice palace; and the palace mimics the humble conditions of Bachelard's dwelling through its profusion of intensely interior rooms. As will become clear though, the childly conditions of reverie demand the possibility of leaving behind the home that welcomes us into being.

Although details of the girls' cottages are sparse in comparison to the meticulous intricacy of the poetic palace, Unn draws her snug cottage into the palace via memories of warm clothing: 'She has to admit she was a little chilled and shivering, in spite of the warm coat Auntie had given her' (Vesaas [1963] 2009: 50). Warmth is a constant feature of Bachelard's homely somewhere, as it is of *The Ice Palace*; when Siss first visits Unn she is welcomed 'into the warm' by Auntie (17). Unn's flight away from warmth is also charted as she shifts into nowhere and shivers with cold (52). When Unn eventually reaches a space beyond nowhere it is a space beyond childhood reverie. Consequently, Unn's thoughts begin to scatter and she feels neither cold nor warmth: 'She was not cold either. She was not comfortable, she was strangely paralysed, but she did not feel cold' (59). For Bachelard, Unn has moved beyond the possibility of being because she has lost touch with the warming associations of reverie. However, I must stress that unbeing (death) is not the same as being nowhere. Bachelard's metaphysics of homely being is altogether ambivalent about the possibility of nowhere, though he does allow for tensions thrown up by nowhere and somewhere. Bachelard's explication of the poetic image adheres to his insistence of the ontic quality of dwellings, of which vulnerability is a crucial aspect. Bachelard identifies poetic images that oscillate between the real and unreal, such as those offered up by an ice palace that is at once 'enchanted world' (47) and a natural phenomenon engaged in the flux of ice and water. Such oscillation results in fissures – fissures that invite Unn inside – and it is in such mutable crevices and cracks that vulnerability subsists. Just as the palace shares humble rooms and pockets of warmth with Bachelard's ontic dwelling, so it shares values of living beings:

> The image is created through co-operation between real and unreal. To use the implements of dialectical logic for studying, not this alternative, but this fusion, of opposites, would be quite useless, for they would produce the anatomy of a living thing. But if a house is a living value, it must integrate an element of unreality. All values must remain vulnerable, and those that do not are dead.
> (Bachelard [1960] 1971: 59)

Bachelard's dialectical positioning is not reductive, as he establishes here, rather he hints at a sort of Deleuzian dynamic structure. Moreover, in their vulnerability, Bachelard's somewhere spaces of homely warmth must always be susceptible to nowhere, as the (in)hospitable aspects of the ice palace suggest. Taking this a step further then, I suggest that recognition of nowhere and somewhere as living values can be found in Bachelard's poetics. His final point is crucial here too, for it helps to underscore the fact that, although Unn is never found, nowhere is not a figure for her death; to be nowhere is not simply to be dead. Nowhere has ontic qualities – explored extensively in children's literature, as we shall see – that confirm it as a living value of being in its proximal relation to somewhere. Before ever she reaches that final chamber of her death, Unn makes a metaphysical move from somewhere to nowhere – as tracked by Bachelard in *The Poetics of Space* – and it is a move that proves to be a foundational component of the metaphysics of children's literature.

The ontic framework I have started to identify for nowhere is crucial to recognizing it as a metaphysical feature of children's books, so it is worth taking a moment to pull together elements of the framework in play thus far. Nowhere operates at extreme reaches of the experiential world, also taking on childly features of forward progress and futurity. Deleuzian fluidity points to persistent tensions and movements in nowhere, which reveal that it intensely and repeatedly contains the possibility of somewhere and elsewhere. Nowhere is to be encountered here and now (thus the extremity of nowhere can be localized) and incorporates darker aspects of utopian world building; it cannot be avoided for it is an object of encounter in experiential being. This is where Deleuzian dynamism connects with Bachelard's poetics, for nowhere is within the oneiric structures of childly reverie. Nowhere has interior qualities pertaining to the edifices of somewhere, thus our experience of nowhere involves a process of ontological edification. Nowhere contains aspects of the warmth and humble homeliness of somewhere, yet it always pushes experience too far for comfort. In this sense, to be nowhere is to be discomforted, but always with the possibility of return to somewhere warm (or progress to elsewhere) in terms of childly reverie. All of this confirms that nowhere can indeed be considered a conceptual entity with spatio-temporal conditions; it is an object to be encountered in the world and it is of particular relevance to childly experience. In the following section, the workings of this 'nowhere model' intersect with my discussion of historical utopian threads carried through to a modern children's literature that explores the conditions of belonging.

Belonging not where

Conceptually and semantically, 'nowhere' is manifest as an idea in children's books across a range of forms and genres. Nowhere is embedded in discourse outside the philosophical remit of this book and a general preoccupation with nowhere in the field is suggested by a recent proliferation of 'nowhere' titles, such as *The Nowhere Box* (2013) by Sam Zuppardi; *North of Nowhere* (2013) by Liz Kessler; *The Middle of Nowhere* (2013) by Geraldine McCaughrean; *The Nowhere Emporium* (2015) by Ross MacKenzie; *Welcome to Nowhere* (2017) by Elizabeth Laird; *Olga and the Smelly Thing from Nowhere* by Elise Gravel (2017); *The Nowhere Girls* (2017) by Amy Reed; *Nowhere Boy* (2018) by Katherine Marsh; or *The Nowhere* by Chris Gill (2019). There are many more picturebooks and novels that deal with nowhere less overtly, between the covers, but this abundance of nowhere titles efficiently illustrates the idea that we might be dealing with a 'nowhere phenomenon'. These examples include a picturebook, graphic novel, junior fiction and young adult literature, and nowhere is conceived in numerous ways. Titular usage of nowhere points variously to secondary worlds of fantasy; geographically extreme settings of wilderness, wasteland or border crossings; while also presaging themes of immigration or migration, displacement, disorientation, loneliness, isolation, ostracization, loss and ennui. While not all of these titles engage with the metaphysical conditions of nowhere outlined thus far, I suggest that they are all shaped on some level by a long-standing metaphysical engagement with nowhere in books for young people.

The metaphysical roots of nowhere in children's literature reach back at least to the sixteenth century and in suggesting this I draw together the influence of Thomas More's neologism in *Utopia* (1516) and Deleuze's ontic articulation of *nowhere-here-and-now* (via Butler's *Erewhon*). Perhaps the best-known literary use of 'nowhere' is in More's coinage of 'utopia', taken from the Greek *ou-topos* meaning 'no place' (or nowhere). As Peter Liebregts observes, 'The word "utopia" has become one of the best-known puns in literary history ever since Thomas More designated his vision of an ideal non-existent place ... as such playing on the Greek for *ou*, "non-" and *eu*, "good"' (2010: 1). Pointing in two directions, More's pun intimates the unfeasibility of ideal worlds, while investing in political ideals through the process of utopian world building. More's nowhere island is built on tensions inherent in impossible possibilities and as Deleuze demonstrates, these fault lines result in dynamic potential; utopia (nowhere) is something that might happen in the right (good) conditions. Essentially, utopia is a modal proposition with the forward potential of Beauvais's mighty child. Although More's *Utopia* is by no means directed to a child audience, its *mighty potential* – in part for trying out progressive systems of education – was recognized by some of the most influential practitioners in the early development of children's literature, as Matthew Grenby establishes in his discussion of Thomas Spence and utopian radicalism (2016).[4]

Grenby demonstrates that Spence's 'understanding of education's potential was inspired at least in part by his exposure ... to a surprisingly radical children's literature' (2016: 131), including works produced by John Newbery, such as *The Lilliputian Magazine* (1751–2). A crux of Grenby's argument is that Newbery perceived children's literature as an especially useful vehicle for utopian politics, which would have appealed to Spence's ambitions for educational reform. In bringing together Newbery and Spence, Grenby 'highlights the remarkable radicalism of mid-eighteenth-century children's literature, and ... emphasises how important education was as a strand of Spence's utopian thinking' (142). Grenby not only establishes commonalities in their utopian vision but also distinguishes a crucial difference of perspective:

In Newbery's text the Golden Age, celebrated by 'poets and historians', was in the past, but its values could be recaptured. In Spence's, a past Golden Age, imagined by 'poets' and 'prophets', was a mere fiction, but a new, real Golden Age could actually be brought into being.

(140)[5]

Where Newbery seeks to 'recapture' the past through utopian thinking, in *The Rights of Infants* (1797) Spence conceives of utopia as a progressive tool that can *bring things into being*, in line with my earlier point about the mighty potential of utopian nowhere. Grenby suggests that both Newbery and Spence are engaged in contemporary politics – of the 'here and now' – yet Spence's utopia also belongs in the nowhere of potential futurity, anticipating the Deleuzian framing of a nowhere that comes into view as an object of ontological engagement. While it is not within the remit of this chapter to provide a history of utopian children's literature, it is essential to determine the roots of utopian projects, which have tenacity in the field and provide a bearing on the ontic conditions of nowhere.

In terms identified by Bradford et al. in *New World Orders*, Spence might be considered an early proponent of 'transformative utopianism' (2008: 2). Their concept is called on to 'suggest that utopian and dystopian tropes carry out important social, cultural, and political work by challenging and reformulating ideas about power and identity, community, the body, spatio-temporal change, and ecology' (2) and is deployed in order to move beyond limiting and static discussions of utopia. Spence's utopian vision has been taken as an 'early step toward the UN Convention on the Rights of the Child' (Grenby 2016: 140) and whatever the sociopolitical accuracy of this claim,[6] transformative potential is central to Spence's (re)construction of childhood. I seek to pull from this a conception of nowhere that comes into being through and beyond Spence's pamphlet. Although a driving force of transformative utopianism is its engagement with social practices, often through a response to seismic historical events (Bradford et al. 2008: 6), I suggest that the nowhere aspect of utopian world building is also of metaphysical consequence.

The Rights of Infants is fashioned as a 'Dialogue between the Aristocracy and a Mother of Children' in which a 'Woman' argues that the rights of 'every species of young … extend to a full participation of the fruits of the earth' (Spence [1797] 1982: 114). Spence places the infant child in a biosphere of natural sustenance in which humans exist alongside non-humans and contend that they should have free access to the world in which they exist, in the same manner as wolves or otters. Spence builds a case determined by the ontological condition of species, which (like Bachelard) recognizes that being is contingent on the nourishment of dwelling spaces, as is clear in the mother's furious cross-examination of the Aristocracy: 'Villains! Why do you ask that aggravating question? Have not the foxes holes, and the birds of the air nests, and shall the children of men have not where to lay their heads?' (114). In this final phrase, the mother invokes Bachelard's somewhere spaces of homely warmth – fox holes and bird nests – thereby emphasizing their proximity and vulnerability to nowhere, as human children have *not where* to lay their heads. The flourish of Spence's utopian revelation is yet to come in which 'lisping Infants shall tam'd tygers lead: / With deadly asps shall sportive sucklings play. … Then, Mortals, join to hail great Nature's plan, / That fully gives to Babes those Rights it gives to Man' (121). Significantly though, the denouement is foregrounded by the negative space in which the infant is denied the dwelling grounds of human being and is left to abide nowhere. Nowhere becomes an element of worldly encounter from infancy and thus it appears that reaching somewhere (those Rights it gives to Man) is contingent on what it means to be nowhere. Spence's utopia is much more than the product of idealistic dreaming and the spatio-temporal tensions of here–now are evident in the dynamics of his pre-utopian nowhere. Nowhere is a key element of Spence's transformative utopianism and it is evident – via nowhere – that More's neologism has an ontic basis for thinking through and restructuring the metaphysical conditions of being somewhere.

The beasts populating *The Rights of Infants* are enlisted by Spence to serve an anthropocentric agenda of human rights, yet a residual investment in non-human being and nowhere as an ontic category are central to his agenda. In looking back to the early culture of childhood and utopian thinking on which Spence draws, I suggest that nowhere takes its place as a metaphysical component of children's literature and that lines can be drawn from these early manifestations of nowhere to its expression in contemporary children's books. Indeed, consideration of the nowhere lands contested in *Fox*, Brooks and Wild's allegorical picturebook, indicates that (non-human) being nowhere is intrinsic to its ontological function. The fabular time–space of this tale of survival and companionship points to enduring themes, which tap into this ontic seam of being nowhere. Brooks's rugged and scratchy illustrations for *Fox* envision a world that is as hostile and potentially cruel as the creatures attempting to endure it. The external world confronts the reader/viewer first in this picturebook, as hot-red endpapers establish space as a relentless whereness[7] that appears challenging to any life form that might exist within it. At this stage, the burning scrubland could be anywhere – nowhere or somewhere – and it is not clear whether it exists in relationship to any other life form. This is a picturebook that deals with the rudiments of being and opens out into a world without strata, as Deleuze and Guattari express it in *A Thousand Plateaus*. It is a world of pure exteriority without milieu and its endpapers offer up story stuff without the structures and beings that might inhabit it.

It is perhaps not surprising that the first words of narration in *Fox* serve to manage this daunting exteriority, anticipating the workings of Bachelard's dwelling within: 'Through the charred forest, over hot ash, runs Dog, with a bird clamped in his big, gentle mouth. He takes her to his cave above the river, and there he tries to tend her burnt wing' (Wild and Brooks 2000: 4).[8] Dog's immediate action on finding the wounded bird is to provide shelter for her. Thus, Dog's cave is established as the sort of humble dwelling demanded by Bachelard's metaphysical system. It is also significant that the cave is occupied space and as such it becomes a *somewhere*, since in Bachelard's terms it is able to sustain *being within*. In order to bring Magpie into being, Dog must carry her into the safety of an interior space. The cave can also be seen in terms of territory, which is designated *somewhere* by Dog and Magpie's presence within. In their discussion of territorialities, Deleuze and Guattari suggest that the milieus of exteriority and interiority are modified by *territorial signs* (indexes), whereby 'the animal world … is constituted, marked off by signs that divide it into zones (of shelter, hunting, neutrality, etc.)'. However, they explain that such indices are 'inseparable from a double movement', because 'the associated milieu always confronts a milieu of exteriority with which the animal is engaged and in which it takes necessary risks' ([1980] 2013: 63). Risk taking is essential to lived experience and can be understood in terms of movement – or taking '*a line of flight*' (63) – between interior and exterior milieus. Dog, Magpie and eventually Fox undertake such movements and are exposed to risk as they struggle to survive in the mutable terrain beyond Dog's cave. The idea of indices managing the movement of beings is useful, as it suggests that ontic space is marked at different levels, or strata of being – and somewhere and nowhere can be conceived of as indices of experiential movement in space.

Dog, Magpie and Fox are each in danger of merging into their milieu at various points in this disquieting fable. For example, soon after being rescued by Dog, 'Magpie drags her body into the shadow of the rocks, until she feels herself melting into blackness' (Wild and Brooks 2000: 4). This near disintegration implies that Magpie cannot come into *animal-being* until she encounters the fullness of being somewhere and nowhere. Deleuze and Guattari describe a sort of ontological crisis, wherein

A second kind of line of flight arises when the associated milieu is rocked by blows from the exterior, forcing the animal to abandon it and strike up an association with new portions of exteriority, this time leaning on its interior milieus like fragile crutches.

(63)

Magpie's burnt feathers are a reminder of just such a line of flight, forcing her to abandon the forest that – we must assume – was once her dwelling place, her milieu of shelter. When Dog proffers his cave, Magpie is not yet ready to receive it as the dwelling space of being-within and thus Dog's home is no more than 'a fragile crutch' against which Magpie is propped. In order to move past grief for her lost wings, Magpie will need to find new ways of moving around her interior and exterior milieus and this is the gift that Dog offers her, a gift that eventually will lead her into the extremes of nowhere.

Although he is 'blind in one eye', Dog declares that 'life is still good' and this ontic positivity inheres in his ability to make the most of places – interior and exterior – that surround him. He is engaged in ontological edification and as a result he is able *to be somewhere* fully. The goodness Dog recognizes in life also points to a Levinasian understanding of *being-for-the-other*, bringing metaphysical ethics into the spatial frame of being somewhere and nowhere. Levinas confirms that 'The free man is dedicated to his fellow; no one can save himself without others' (66), and he explores this in terms of interiority and homeland. This process can be seen at work in *Fox*, as Dog makes space for Magpie, causing them to engage anew with their interior and exterior milieus. Drawing on a biblical expression of hospitality and 'the homesickness that can be surmounted by the edification of a house and possession of land', Levinas declares that 'no one is at home' and thus interiority requires a habitation of strange lands with and for the other ([1972] 2006: 66). It is not that Levinas denies Bachelard's metaphysical emphasis on dwelling within, but his ethical stance insists on an ontic abode that is *with*-in. When Dog and Magpie 'fly' into their exterior milieu, it is because Dog has recognized himself *in and with* Magpie. Hopping onto Dog's back, Magpie sees 'something else' reflected back at her: '"I see a strange new creature!" she says. "That is us", says Dog' (Wild and Brooks 2000: 6 – Figure 4.1). Dog's care for and fusion with Magpie extends their frame of being in spatial terms and together they are able to explore their external milieu, racing 'through the scrub, past clumps of straggly trees, past bushes and rocks, and into blueness' (8). Perched on Dog's back, 'Magpie feels the wind streaming though her feathers, and she rejoices. "Fly, Dog, Fly! I will be your missing eye, and you will be my wings"' (9). Brooks's earthy tones infuse

Figure 4.1 A 'strange new creature' reflects Levinasian dwelling *with*-in (Wild and Brooks 2000: 6–7).

the creatures, emphasizing the idea that Dog and Magpie are coming into being-animal through this line of flight into a *new portion of exteriority*, as well as through each other.

This shared experience of territorial indexing allows Dog and Magpie to be somewhere hostile and somewhere safe, and it is not until Fox appears that nowhere comes into being. Dog welcomes Fox, offering food and shelter from the outset, while Magpie 'shrinks away' (13) for fear of 'his smell that seems to fill the cave – a smell of rage and envy and loneliness' (14). In his excluded state – perpetuated by Magpie's rejection – Fox challenges the safe interiority of the cave. If Dog and Magpie seem to exist securely in (and outside of) their cave dwelling, Fox's arrival is a reminder that the house as a living value is contingent on Bachelard's vulnerability. Magpie recognizes that Fox '"belongs nowhere"' (16) and her warning to Dog foreshadows her own journey into the territories of nowhere. Dog retorts that Fox is '"all right"' and when he tells Magpie to *let Fox be*, it seems that the picturebook's ontological concerns are confirmed (16).

Magpie has not fully settled into being though, and Fox senses this, tempting Magpie away from Dog and their interior milieu with the promise that he will make her '"truly fly"' (18). Brook's burning, abrasive oils bring nowhere visually into expansive focus, evoking the malign sprawl of the endpapers and anticipating the inevitable danger to come. It is soon evident that Fox does not intend to devour Magpie – as predation might dictate – for this tale is about who belongs where (somewhere and nowhere) and with whom (being for the other). As Vesaas and Bachelard have demonstrated, all beings belong nowhere some of the time and, 'in the stillness' (25), this is Magpie's moment to be nowhere; this is her *now in the where*.

As Fox turns away from Magpie, abandoning the injured bird to the dusty plains of the 'hot red desert' (22), he makes an ontological pronouncement bereft of Levinasian fellowship: '"Now you and Dog will know what it is like to be truly alone"' (25). Yet, Fox is not a harbinger of death; Magpie was right when first she recognized his state of 'belonging nowhere'. Nowhere is somewhere close to non-being, but as I have established, nowhere is not synonymous with non-being. Nowhere is at an extreme reach of being – and Fox has delivered Magpie to this extreme – so she recognizes that she could yield to the heat: 'She can feel herself burning into nothingness. It would be so easy just to die here in the desert' (27). This modal proposition – it *would be* so easy just to die – is not to be realized though, for it is only one of several possibilities leading away from her being in nowhere. As it turns out, the dark sanctuary of Dog and his cave exerts enough drag on Magpie to draw her back to its homely interiority. This is echoed by the silent balm and perspectival pull of Brooks's illustration, which reflects Magpie's thoughts 'of Dog waking to find her gone' (28). Finally, Magpie has come to see Dog beyond herself and is able to see him as a being that extends outside of his care for her. As Levinas perceives it, 'I am responsible for them without reposing in their responsibility to me which would allow them to substitute themselves for me, because even for their responsibility I am, in the last analysis and from the beginning, responsible' ([1972] 2006: 68). Magpie's broken wing no longer obscures Dog and thus Magpie responds to him and the shelter he provides in their ontic condition of being somewhere that she needs to be. Still, Magpie must endure the scorching conditions of her encounter with nowhere as: '"Slowly, jiggety-hop, she begins the long journey home"' (30). Nowhere must be encountered truly if it is to lead back to somewhere safe; back to Dog and his cave in the first dwelling of *being within*.

So concludes the fabular terrain of *Fox*, in which nowhere is offered up as a metaphysical condition of being, and being for others is validated as a condition of being somewhere. Wild's fable serves as a vessel for getting at deep truths of being in the world. The sparsity of her prose allows for a confrontation with nowhere that is matched by the stark honesty of texture and tone in Brooks's images. Once again, the formal conditions of the picturebook are exploited in the service of metaphysical exploration and fabular simplicity is exposed as a mechanism for deep digging into what it means to be nowhere. It is not surprising then that the challenging reach of not where (to be) is often approached through the lens of migration – and *Fox* can be read as a migratory fable as the Levinasian implications of homeland suggest. Moreover, several authors pursuing this migratory thread take up a fabular and visual approach, including Tan's *The Arrival* (2006); *I Am Thomas* (2011) by Libby Gleeson and Armin Greder; *The Unforgotten Coat* (2011) by Frank Cottrell Boyce; and *King of the Sky* (2017) by Nicola Davies and Laura Carlin.

The Arrival, Tan's wordless graphic novel about migration, is typical of many children's books that imbue this experience with ontological weight. In the fabular and ontic terms of these books, the migrant experiences the world as a displaced nowhere, which has the potential to overwhelm other indices of being (somewhere, anywhere, elsewhere). There is a risk attached to nowhere, as we witnessed in *Fox* and as articulated by Deleuze and Guattari. Although Tan's complex visual text is longer than most fables, it utilizes fabular techniques to convey symbolically the experience of many via the every-person's journey. Endpapers confirm the persistent and shared nature of an experience that reaches into the core of being human, as sixty faces stare out at the reader (directing their gaze somewhere) or refuse eye contact (directing their gaze nowhere). Through stylized passport photographs, each portrait bears witness to one man's story of being in the nowhere and coming back into the somewhere – but not the somewhere from whence he set out.

The Arrival opens with an affirmation of the dwelling space of home, family and the somewhere of being within, via a series of nine vignettes depicting domestic and familial objects: a family photograph; a mantle clock; an origami bird (Figure 4.2).[9]

However, these damaged objects also point to the vulnerability of house as a living value, for the teapot is cracked; a child's family drawing is crumpled; a cooking pot is empty. Furthermore, it appears that somewhere is soon to be left behind, or put at risk, as suggested by a packing case that is almost full and a hat hung on a peg. What ensues is a father's journey into nowhere in its unknown aspect, as he leaves behind his family and ventures into a world of Tan's imagining. In common with utopian explorers, Tan's migrant boards a ship

Figure 4.2 The thingness of objects is replete with nowhere (Tan [2006] 2007: 3).

and finds himself in a new world, overwhelming in scale and indecipherably daunting. Tan conveys the alienating, frightening and sorrowful aspects of a place so far from somewhere within. However, his nowhere is also beautifully rendered in its detailed strangeness and gradually the migrant finds a way of being in this new place – a way of being that brings him back to a dwelling within, as he is reunited with his family. The migrant experience reveals that being nowhere is integral to being somewhere and, as such, tales of dis-location have much to reveal about the ontological conditions of being human. Tan resists interpreting the symbolic structure of his own work, explaining that he is 'more attracted to a kind of intuitive resonance or poetry we can enjoy when looking at pictures, and "understanding" what we see without necessarily being able to articulate it' (Tan n.d. c.). Tan's nowhere world in *The Arrival* is resonant with the unarticulated poetic space – of being somewhere and nowhere – of the sort identified by Bachelard as poetic reverie and encountered vividly in moments of childly world building.

Tan acknowledges that belonging is a common theme in his work and that 'the "problem" of belonging is perhaps more of a basic existential question that everybody deals with from time to time, if not on a regular basis' (Tan n.d. c.). I tease this out further to suggest that Tan's rendition of *be-longing* collapses into *longing-to-be*, as his migrant encounters nowhere. A similar ontic strand wends its way through *King of the Sky*, wherein a young boy is stranded in streets 'that smelled of mutton soup and coal dust' and where 'no one spoke my language'; he is somewhere quite specific and yet he finds himself nowhere, because 'All of it told me this is not where you belong' (Davies and Carlin [2017] 2018: 7). Moreover, although nowhere is rendered strange and distant in these migrant narratives, the experience is also familiar, recognizable and relevant to what it means to be in the world now. This visual and verbal transformation of nowhere into the Erewhon of here-and-now can also be seen at work in *The Unforgotten Coat* – in which photographs of a somewhere that could be Mongolia are revealed as being from nowhere at all, or from anywhere that is not Mongolia. Images that first appear to be 'authentically Mongolian' are destabilized in a narrative that problematizes exclusive and discriminatory notions of origin, belonging and home. When Chingis shouts for his vanished brother, 'the voice seemed to come from nowhere. Or from everywhere' (Cottrell Boyce [2011] 2012: 91), thus foreshadowing the threat of deportation hanging over two immigrant brothers who understand fully the consequences of *being nowhere shut in*. Each of these tales expresses the ontological encounter with nowhere in terms that are vividly expressed through gaps in word and image and via a soulful reverie of childly might that pushes at the conditions of being-somewhere-being-nowhere.

I Am Thomas uses migration as a mechanism for hope but is not concerned with ontic conditions of the migrant experience. It deals primarily with non-conformity and its message is conveyed through a sparse verbal and exacting pictorial narrative. This parable about the conditions of being in a restrictive society delivers a dystopian vision of the regimented demands of authoritarianism, which ultimately it rejects through the promise of a utopian nowhere. Gleeson and Greder present a relatively bleak and darkly parodic view of a society that eschews individuality. Bold typeface screams its message: 'do as we say, think like us, be like us' (Gleeson and Greder 2011: 12), which Thomas seeks to ignore 'in the shelter of my headphones' (8). Charcoal images of stern, angry or sad people confront the reader alongside Thomas, as eyes glare out from the page in a visual form of direct address. Body gesture and facial expression are used to reinforce the repetitive barrage of verbal insistence that Thomas grow up and into hegemonic institutions – army, church, government – that will shape him to their ideological vision. Running alongside this centrally insistent narrative though is a series of colour vignettes, which suggest that Thomas dreams of escape to someplace else. This counter-narrative is implemented from the title page and leaves a trail of iconic images throughout the picturebook suggestive of travel or even running away: a toy bus, a map, a torch (and so on). This narrative thread is not acknowledged by the verbal text and so the reader is left to infer the direction of Thomas's journey to an unidentified nowhere. It is significant that on the penultimate spread, Thomas clutches the small yellow toy bus of his early childhood. He looks forward and over the page-turn to a full-scale, colour-saturated bus ready to take him into his future. Thomas carries in his hand a wrapped object that could be his childhood toy, a childly thing that will help him to make sense of the nowhere lands *wherever they might be*. Moreover, it is the modal thrust of possibility that brings nowhere into play here and it allows for a re-evaluation of the words that open the book. 'I am not the child I once was' is not a denial of childhood itself (I am no longer a child); rather it is an affirmation of the child he *might* be. Thomas carries within him the poetic conditions of childhood reverie, clutched tightly in his hand as he boards a bus into his future into the mighty potential of nowhere. In embracing the possibility of nowhere, Thomas is now the child who might be somewhere else.

As these examples of contemporary migrant narratives suggest, the fables, parables, and allegorical storytelling of children's literature offer an ontic template for thinking through the conditions of being, elements of which Spence draws on in his utopian visions. Indeed, there is an ontological thread here, that loops back to embryonic forms of utopia, through fable as a rhizomatic form that sends out connective and overlapping shoots – a threading through of literary forms that starts to map a nowhere in the childly realms of junior fiction. Furthermore, this mapping of experiential indices indicates that the fable is not (always) quite the monolithic form of domestication and taming that Derrida objects to in

The Animal That Therefore I Am.[10] Indeed, given the momentum of a structure that moves somewhere-nowhere-somewhere, the fable can be considered a metaphysically progressive form in its utopian aspect. As I have established, this has clear benefits for writers seeking a form of expression for the migratory passage of human being and exploring the ontic conditions of belonging and dislocation, while not dispensing with its political aspect. Retaining a focus on this propensity for movement around the nowhere index, I now explore the local conditions of a utopian drive into the metaphysical structure of children's literature.

Here-and-now

In *The Soul of Man Under Socialism* (1891) Oscar Wilde makes a typically perceptive (even acerbic) aside about utopian mapping during his socialist discourse on the importance of Individualism. While reflecting on the role of the machine in future worlds, he pauses to ask:

> Is this Utopian? A map of the world that does not include Utopia is not worth even glancing at, for it leaves out the one country at which Humanity is always landing. And when Humanity lands there, it looks out, and, seeing a better country, sets sail. Progress is the realisation of Utopias.
> ([1891] 1909: 40)

Wilde implies here that he is less invested in 'mechanical slavery' (39) than he might have appeared to be (earlier in the essay) and in this particular passage he sows doubt on the nature of progress instilled by 'scientific men'.[11] Wilde suggests that utopia quite literally gets humanity nowhere if we do not pause to understand the nowhere with which we are dealing. Constantly sailing from one utopian island – relentlessly moving from one present to another future – is not progress; ignoring the present in order to create a better future will not prevent 'crowding round the doors of loathsome shelters' (5). Of course, Wilde is invested in a utopian scheme himself in this pamphlet, but he recognizes the importance of the here-and-now in effecting social change, so a globe charting an endless succession of utopias spins pointlessly. If human beings are to sail to nowhere, they must sail back to a somewhere with nowhere encountered as an intrinsic part of being human – and this is the point at which Wilde's social project tips into an ontological concern with humanity. In this section, I demonstrate that the here-and-now facet of utopian venture – which can be seen as a metaphysical project embedded in sociopolitical conditions of the here-and-now – accommodates local, contained, or pedestrian experiences of being human.

The nowhere islands of children's literature variously navigate towards and steer away from the political conditions of early utopian voyages – though they all maintain a Deleuzian engagement with Erewhon and an underlying metaphysical concern with the conditions and boundaries of reality. Newbery's interest in utopian dreaming has already foregrounded Jonathan Swift's *Gulliver's Travels* (1726) as an ur-text of children's literature. Swift's satiric turn to nowhere – as Lemuel Gulliver travels to the Land of the Houyhnhnms – has extensive influence in the field and many writers for children have exploited the political and ideological potential of such utopian visions. The social commitment of Edith Nesbit's work has long been recognized, for example, and Suzanne Rahn points out that *The Story of the Amulet* (1906) can be considered a search for utopia in the guise of an amulet (Rahn 1985: 126). Rahn also confirms that Nesbit's socialist vision is influenced by William Morris's *News from Nowhere* (1890) and H. G. Wells's *A Modern Utopia* (1905), inspirations that become clear when the four siblings travel to a future version of the London streets they inhabit (Rahn 1985: 133). Via a grumpy Psammead, Nesbit distinguishes between 'prophetic vision' and 'dream' as the children try to understand the status of an encounter that leads them from the 'sorry present' to a distant future in which human worry has been alleviated ([1906] 1996: 247). The Psammead's distinction seems focused on the difference between socialist potential for change in a vision of a possible future and a dream imbued with psychological drama. I suggest that this prophetic vision can also be seen in ontic terms that drill down into here-and-now through this journey into a futuristic nowhere.

The children walk out of the British Museum into 'the sudden glory of sunlight and blue sky' (231). The language here evokes a spiritual awakening of sorts, but is more in tune with the visionary nature of what they are about to discover. The utopian scene is well lit in order that the children can observe the space and people around them, causing Nesbit to comment: 'I hope they did not stare' (232). This close attention allows them to perceive something fundamental about the people in this nowhere space: 'It was the expression of their faces that made them worth looking at. The children could not tell at first what it was. "I know," said Anthea suddenly. "They're not worried; that's what it is"' (232). The children are drawn immediately to this (ostensibly) carefree domain and are fascinated by the inhabitants' lack of concern. In spite of this, as they find out more about the conditions of this world the children begin to react 'doubtfully' (235) and 'uneasily' (238). Their misgivings are not voiced directly, but their discomfort can be explained by the ontic conditions of their experience. The strangeness of Nesbit's utopia is confirmed by a population that is not fully human, in that they are not beset by ontological conditions of being human in the world. The (non-human) beings of Nesbit's utopia cannot *be there* in Heideggerian terms, because Da-sein is contingent on care, an ontological aspect of being that runs far deeper than 'worries' or 'troubles' (Heidegger [1927] 1996: 183). Care is a fundamental and inescapable aspect of Da-sein, such that it marks out human being at the level of daily routines in which we care about and for the mundane aspects of life. Consequently, the children's engagement with the conditions of nowhere allows self-reflexive consideration of what it means to be in the world of their own experience, because nowhere brings into focus the care-ful state of being human.

This ontological freight works against the socialist facet of Nesbit's project to some extent – in that the ideal conditions it imagines are impossible on metaphysical grounds – but paradoxically the children's reaction to utopian London gives it the sort of grounding in (ontic) reality it needs to become possible in the future. Through the children's recognition of what it means to be human, the utopian vision is given potential at the level of childly might. On encountering this vision of worry-free life, the children wish that they could live in this nowhere future, and the very act of wishing – on which so much of the Psammead series hinges – is contingent on care; as Heidegger observes, 'Ontologically, wishing presupposes care' (182). The children's wish is not granted in this instance, and they come to see that this society is not as ideal as first they perceived it to be. Indeed, Nesbit cannot sustain the worry-freeness of her utopian idyll, for the children soon encounter a boy concerned about his recent expulsion from school and the ontic reality of being human bursts the banks of utopian invention. Nesbit sends her children to a future that ostensibly transforms the London with which they are familiar, only to discover that their journey actually maps the ontic contours of their own cityscape.

Another utopian vision at the 'golden' heartland of children's literature is provided by Kenneth Grahame's *The Wind in the Willows* (1908), (in part) a river-land tale that oars its way back to Homeric voyages, bringing with it a cargo from the island adventuring of Daniel Defoe's *Robinson Crusoe* (1719), R. M. Ballantyne's *The Coral Island* (1858) and Richard Jefferies's *Bevis* (1882). These are only a few of the antecedents to Grahame's novel that tap into a utopian vein of adventure or escape to a nowhere space, and his tale also anticipates the Lakeland world building of Arthur Ransome's *Swallows and Amazons* (1930), or the anthropomorphized isolation of *Abel's Island* (1976) by William Steig. In his discussion of the influence of More's *Utopia*, Terry Eagleton describes *Robinson Crusoe* as one of those 'more austere utopias, in which everything is odourless and antiseptic, intolerably streamlined and sensible' (Eagleton 2015: n.p.). Yet by the time the Robinsonade reaches *The Wind in the Willows*, austerity has made way for mysticism in the novel's rural idylls and its poetic struggle between 'loyalty to home and convention, and the temptations of adventure', as Peter Hunt puts it (2018: 79). Conceived from the metaphysical perspective of this chapter, nowhere and somewhere become poetic sites of struggle, thus Grahame's masterpiece of reverie provides 'experiences in concrete metaphysics', for 'poetic reverie gives us the world of worlds' (Bachelard [1960] 1971: 13).

The Wind in the Willows is awash with nowhere territories of varying shades, which inhabitants of the riverbank – itself a nowhere space of utopian dreaming – fall prey to periodically. The metaphysical importance of Bachelard's being within is expressed poignantly by Mole in 'Dulce Domum' as he recognizes 'the special value of some such anchorage in one's existence' (Grahame [1908] 2010: 59). Identifying the 'caressing appeals' thrown out by his long-departed home, Mole encounters the dread feeling of being nowhere, 'alone in the road, his heart torn asunder' as Rat ignores Mole's plea to return to 'the home he had made for himself' (50–1). Mole echoes Bachelard's observation that 'our house is our corner of the world' in this moment of ontic edification and finds ontological comfort in the knowledge that home awaits him, wherever else he might be – being within is within Mole. This restless tension arises again in 'Wayfarers All', as Rat is seduced by the potential for southward travel beyond 'his simple horizon hitherto, his Mountains of the Moon, his limit beyond which lay nothing he had cared to see or know' (96).[12] Until his conversation with the wayfarer, Rat has been content with dwelling spaces marked by home horizons, but a psychological and ontological shift takes place in which the indices of his existence are mapped differently: 'to-day, the unseen was everything, the unknown the only real fact of life. On this side of the hills was now the real blank' (96). Rat's changing perspective of home is expressed topographically in a sustained passage of metaphysical reflection on the status of those once familiar hills. The somewhere space of home has become 'the real blank' of nowhere, confirming that the nowhere index can mark out local territories, as well as distant territories of the unknown. Rat's encounter with nowhere is expressed partly in terms of psychological trauma, yet when it comes to explaining his experience to Mole, ontic language comes into play: 'he found it difficult to account for what had seemed, some hours ago, the inevitable and only thing'

(104). The substantial *thingness* of the shifting indices locating somewhere and nowhere is evident here and Rat recognizes the fundamental status of an encounter that he finally works out through the concrete practices of poetic reverie, 'alternately scribbling and sucking the top of his pencil' (105).

Tracking the utopian conditions of being nowhere into the twenty-first century allows me to reveal how it works within a different geopolitical framework. An alternative and insular utopian vision[13] is provided by Ellis's *Outside In*, in which an unidentified Canadian cityscape is defamiliarized through an ideological and metaphysical challenge to material culture. The novel opens up an Arcadian space inhabited by 'Underlanders' who have carved out an alternative existence – albeit fragile and unstable – beneath the city's reservoir and beyond the reach of civic authorities. According to the thrust of institutional hegemony, delineated through Althusser's Ideological State Apparatus,[14] Blossom and her adoptive family could be defined as homeless (by institutional norms). However, the utopian vision of the novel allows for the ontic necessity of being-within a dwelling place, as confirmed by the topography of its cityscape. The city is drawn into the novel's utopian vision in terms identified by Michel de Certeau in *The Practice of Everyday Life* (1980) and in particular his notion of 'Walking in the City'. Certeau observes that conceptually the city is 'founded by a utopian and urbanistic discourse' ([1980] 1988: 94), thus his starting point for considering everyday encounters with the city is pertinent to the concerns of this chapter.

Pedestrian navigation is crucial to a novel that shapes its utopia within the secret spaces of a here-and-now city, with attention being drawn constantly to direction and location. Certeau contends that walking the city is the only way to make it unfold and come into being at the level of everyday experience: 'The ordinary practitioners of the city live "down below", below the thresholds at which visibility begins. They walk – an elementary form of this experience of the city' (93). Certeau's walkers are *Wandersmänner*, who do not seek to view the whole of the city from on high, or by looking down on it, from a totalizing perspective (92–3). Rather, the networks carved out by the movement of walkers tell manifold stories, 'shaped out of fragments of trajectories and alterations of spaces: in relation to representations, it remains daily and indefinitely other' (93). Walking the city thus allows for an alternative composition of space and these other trajectories have a subversive (political) and metaphysical potential.

Outside In is focalized through 13-year-old Lynn and maps out her friendship with Blossom, the Underlander who mysteriously vanishes – on foot – after performing the Heimlich manoeuvre on Lynn at a bus stop. Blossom saves Lynn's life while she awaits an overdue bus, and the encounter changes the direction of Lynn's relationship with the streets of her neighbourhood; she comes to realize that 'there was a shadow grid underneath the official grid of the city' (Ellis [2014] 2016: 59). From the outset, their relationship is topographically demarcated, and Lynn is forced to reassess the situated whereness of the city she thought she knew: 'They set off, Blossom taking the lead. The route involved back alleys and cut-throughs. After about three turns, Lynn was completely turned around. What were the mountains doing *there*?' (46). The mountain vista appears to have relocated, but actually it is Lynn herself who is 'turned around' here, suggesting an ontological revelation or shift at the level of being. This re-mapping of the city moves mountains metaphorically and literally, and the whereness involved in this process overlays somewhere with nowhere in a moment of metaphysical revelation and uncertainty. As Lynn tries to grasp the strangeness of her new friend, her first instinct is to attribute her eccentricity to (dis)location: '"Blossom, are you from somewhere else?"', and Blossom replies: '"No. Here"' (47). Blossom's response is only a letter short of nowhere, yet she insists on a situated existence that has a relationship with Lynn's own sense of the city being somewhere that she could once map, but which now evades the whereness of cartographic certainty. Nowhere is thus configured on a number of levels in *Outside In*: it is a spatial entity that Lynn confronts through her relationship with Blossom; as an entity to be encountered it has ontological impact on the status of human being, so that Lynn finds herself nowhere; it manifests as a utopian here-and-now through the Arcadian living conditions of Blossom's family.

Blossom walks the city differently from Lynn, thus identifying the life-story she tells through her movements as 'indefinitely other' in Certeau's terms: 'Blossom's style of walking favoured back alleys and hidden features. The backwards house, the bubble-blowing equipment nailed to a telephone pole, the little free library. … Lynn felt like a tourist in an unknown city' (49). Certeau values walking as a form of unconscious storytelling and something of Blossom's life-story and unconventional upbringing is expressed through her 'style of walking'; the narrative evolves through the steps taken by its *Wandersmänner*. Citizens – as Blossom refers to Lynn and other official residents of the city – and Underlanders bring into being a mutable city space that is either nowhere or somewhere, depending on how it is traversed. Blossom's pedestrian navigation of this alternative cityscape is assertive and creative, challenging Lynn's sense of how the world works; yet it also reveals the proximity of Blossom's homelessness and her challenge to official life. Certeau asserts that 'To walk is to lack a place. It is the indefinite process of being absent and in search of a proper' ([1980]

1988: 103). The city is 'an immense social experience of lacking a place' and as pedestrian traffic moves in search of place the city becomes 'a universe of rented spaces haunted by a nowhere' (103). In this novel, the *perambulatory function* of Blossom and her family is to bring into being the hidden sites of the city; crucially the Underlanders bring about nowhere. Nowhere haunts city spaces, thus rendering it an entity ready for ontic encounter.

When first Blossom disappears, she confesses to Lynn that she was 'being invisible' (Ellis [2014] 2016: 44) and later Lynn wonders whether Blossom and her family 'really exist' (95). However, it is soon clear that the Underlanders' existence is never in doubt. Essentially, they generate nowhere in order that Lynn (a citizen of the city) can encounter it as a necessary condition of being human. When Lynn betrays Blossom and tells her own unreliable mother about their existence, the Underlanders disappear and Lynn is forced to confront nowhere. She goes in search of her friends, desperately seeking out the Underlanders in what was once their dwelling place: 'It was the emptiest place she had ever been, with no objects, no people, no story, no messages, nothing to show that it had been a home' (172–3). This nowhere space of abandoned habitation throws Lynn into ontological crisis as she tries and fails to imagine a world that once was 'back into being' (173). As a consequence, Lynn discovers that 'Not herself was exactly who she was' (174). It is only once Lynn accepts the ontic possibility of nowhere that Blossom locates her – not the other way round – and together they travel on a bus to the new somewhere of Blossom's home.

Outside In is committed metaphysically to exploring the underbelly of the city through a nowhere that disturbs and haunts Lynn's reality. However, its utopian vision also has a sociopolitical dimension that locates it in the here-and-now of twenty-first-century concerns. In various ways, the novel picks at the persistent ideology of nuclear families in a modern society that never sustained them and offers an alternative through the Underlanders' collective of abandoned children and lonely people. The Underlanders exist on the waste of a capitalist society and (tellingly) Blossom asks, 'Why do citizen make bicycles that go nowhere?' (66). The question underlying this is how people can be discarded as easily as bicycles on city streets. They also seek to subvert official life through what might be described as an ecocritical manifesto:

> Underlanders rearrange the world. We reorder things. We collect recycling and take it back to where it is useful. We pull up weeds and put them in the compost where they turn into dirt to grow more things. And sometimes we just fancy things up.
>
> (101)

The ecological agenda is obvious, but it serves as more than a political statement in the wider context of Ellis's novel. The utopian vision offered up by *Outside In* involves an alternative way of living, being and moving through a childhood space that we thought we knew. Its metaphysical dimension questions the conditions of reality when it rearranges the world in tune with its environmental concerns. It is an exploration of what it means to live and city-walk the spaces of being-within childhood and to reorder them via a nowhere that encompasses change. This is a utopia for the here-and-now that turns the conditions of human being outside in, so that we can experience Da-sein from another position.

Certeau observes of the metaphoric fabric of childhood negations with space: 'To practice space is thus to repeat the joyful and silent experience of childhood; it is, in a place, *to be other and to move toward the other* ([1980] 1988: 110). With echoes of ontological exchange here, he perceives this childhood exploration of space as an insular process that interrogates the 'relationship of oneself to oneself' (110). This is precisely what Lynn discovers when she goes in search of Blossom on the underside of the city she thought she knew – all along the search was for herself and a nowhere that confronts her with Da-sein. In the next section, my exploration of nowhere shifts from the individual and local to an engagement with the remotest poles of human being in the world. This does not involve a departure from the nowhere conditions of childhood though, for as Certeau observes, 'The childhood experience that determines spatial practices later develops its effects, proliferates, floods private and public spaces, undoes their readable surfaces, and creates within the planned city a "metaphorical" or mobile city' (110). Let us discover what might happen when we set sail from childhood with maps that inevitably – given a childness that proliferates unpredictably – contain no readable surfaces.

Poles of inaccessibility

> The literary north is barren, dismal and desolate. Here we are dealing with words of indefinite meaning into which each of us reads what significance he chooses.
> (Stefansson 1921: 20)

Vilhjalmur Stefansson makes a case for the *Pole of Inaccessibility* in *The Friendly Arctic* (1921), a concept that allows the explorer and philosopher to challenge historic, contemporary and persistent ideas about the 'inhospitable' north – indeed he makes *somewhere* of a relentlessly idealized *nowhere* in his significant challenge to the Arctic north of imperialist, literary and popular imagination.[15] Stefansson argues that previous attempts to reach the North Pole had occluded a region of the Arctic that represents a particular exploratory challenge, an area that had been dismissed as *nowhere of concern* to explorers and those who backed them in periods of 'rising imperial competition' (Bravo 2019: 133). Stefansson offers a new approach to polar exploration through his concept of inaccessible polar regions. His Pole of Inaccessibility encompasses an area of the Arctic that is 'hardest to get at' (Stefansson 1921: 10) – acknowledging that 'hardest' relies on a complex system of variables, which render its position and qualities changeable. Stefansson's meticulous approach to Arctic exploration would not involve a race of imperialist or heroic significance, but rather an embrace of the region and its indigenous populations, flora and fauna. Stefansson maintains that his pole *could be accessible*, if established pictures that present it as 'a lifeless waste of eternal silence' are challenged: 'we have to unlearn before we can read in a true light any story of arctic exploration' (Stefansson 1921: 7). Stefansson provides a detailed account of a region abundant with plant and animal life that sustains adjacent Inuit communities. In so doing, Michael Bravo suggests that Stefansson shapes 'a cosmology in which living with animals was a form of mutual dependence between humans, animals and spirits' (Bravo 2019: 203). Stefansson's cosmology has much in common with Leopold's biosphere and his radical views on the American wilderness,[16] and they each proffer a political, sociological and metaphysical challenge to systems that ignore non-human being. The fierce conviction of Stefansson's revisionist eco-criticism comes across in a deflation of exploratory hubris:

> 'Barren Ground' is a libelous name by which the open land of the north is often described. This name is better adapted for creating the impression that those who travel in the North are intrepid adventurers than it is for conveying to the reader a true picture of the country.
>
> (Stefansson 1921: 16)

Like Leopold, Stefansson is concerned with bringing into being a particular geographical area comprising its own topography and political terrain. Moreover, as the tensions at work in this passage suggest, Stefansson's concept has broader metaphysical relevance – outside of the Arctic – which I draw on in this section. The Pole of Inaccessibility pertains to the overlap and distance between being somewhere (something) and nowhere (nothing). Inaccessible climates and terrains are only ever relatively inaccessible; they are never entirely barren. As can be inferred from Stefansson's polemic, the middle of nowhere often turns out to be somewhere; and from the ontic perspective of children's literature the *turns out to be* is crucial. The Pole of Inaccessibility is conceptually apposite for discussion of *nowhere in extremis*, which – as my exploration of *The Ice Palace* reveals – is an important facet of nowhere realms. Poles of inaccessibility are identified across a range of children's books, including the nonsense poetry of Edward Lear and Lewis Carroll; Lindsay's *The Magic Pudding*; Steig's *Abel's Island*; and *The White Darkness* (2005) by Geraldine McCaughrean.

Bravo proposes that the Pole of Inaccessibility was rendered a redundant concept in the face of changing technologies and growing international tensions in the twentieth century, and he wonders whether Stefansson's account of subsisting on indigenous wildlife amounted to utopian world building, 'to challenge the dominant imperial values of his age' (2019: 203). Bravo is somewhat suspicious of the utopian turn in Stefansson's writing, yet *The Friendly Arctic* is the sort of transformative utopia advocated by Wilde, Bradford et al. – his writing is certainly grounded in the here-and-now and if his ideas have utopian traits, they are ideas of mighty potential. Bravo does go on to recognize that Stefansson's term 'would be an apt description of the gendering of polar fieldwork' (2019: 215), hinting that it is not quite the 'pole of diminished significance' (207) attributed to it by the direction and history of polar endeavour in the twentieth century. The droll tone of Stefansson's writing, upon which Bravo remarks, also brings it into the remit of satire. Bravo observes that 'While the poles could serve to inspire, they were also ripe for satire and political dissent' (147). Bravo explores a range of satirical responses from the early modern period through to the nineteenth and twentieth centuries – including those from George Cruikshank and A. A. Milne – behind which 'grew a realization that the struggle to sail, saw and pull large ships across the surface of large fields of ice revealed the absurdity of the human condition being unable to escape the limitations of inhabiting the surface of the Earth' (148). Satirists evidently tapped into the metaphysical remit of attempts on the North Pole, hence I draw into this discussion purveyors of nonsense in the nineteenth century who have made a significant contribution to the nowhere conditions of children's literature.

For example, in Lear's *A Book of Nonsense* (1846), characters journey by train, boat and balloon, befitting an era of exploratory zeal. Lear's nonsense rhymes frequently intimate the ultimate failure or pointlessness of voyages that never get underway, as demonstrated in this example:

> There was a Young Lady of Portugal,
> Whose ideas were excessively nautical;

She climbed up a tree, to examine the sea,
But declared she would never leave Portugal.

(Lear [1846] 1992: 18)

The limerick reveals as much about the thwarted traveller as it does the venture itself and, in the context of the wider satiric climate sketched above, it is difficult not to see in them the hubristic claims of explorers, or failed attempts on the North Pole (such as Edward Parry's 1827 polar expedition). Of particular significance here, the Young Lady of Portugal ultimately goes nowhere due to her earthbound human plight. In Heideggerian terms Da-sein thwarts the Young Lady in a sort of being-there stasis in which the ambition to be somewhere remains comically nowhere. In 'The Jumblies' (1871) warnings of danger are ignored and the Jumblies sail away from 'the lands where the Jumblies live', which are 'Far and few, far and few' (Lear [1846] 1992: 79). This suggests that Bachelard's being-within is time and space limited and that voyaging to poles of inaccessibility is a necessary and inevitably arduous condition of being in the world. Spinning in a sieve serves figuratively to suggest the directive pull involved in travelling somewhere but getting nowhere. The apparent impossibility of the Jumblies' endeavour should not rule it out though, for to be human is to deal with being thrown in the world. The nowhere encounter with 'the Lakes, and the Torrible Zone, / And the hills of the Chankly Bore' (82) is challenging due to relative inaccessibility, nonetheless it allows the Jumblies to grow happy and tall. In this context 'nowhere' is understood partly as a nonsense or fantasy place that does not exist in consensus reality, yet it accrues metaphysical consequence for human being through the riskiness involved in Deleuze and Guattari's taking line of flight. The Jumblies' testing passage through territorial indices of somewhere (the land where the Jumblies live) to nowhere (the Chankly Bore) requires them to confront a milieu of exteriority that benefits them at a fundamental level of existence. In line with the mighty potential of such excursions, it encourages 'every one' (other beings or Jumblies) to follow suit: 'And every one said, "If only we live, / We too will go to sea in a Sieve"' (82). *If only we live* points to the ontological concerns of Lear's song, which suggest that reaching for the inaccessible is a condition of being alive – and that never to attempt the poles of nowhere lands is to be less than alive.

A similar commitment to the extreme reaches of nowhere inheres in Carroll's *The Hunting of the Snark* (1876), alongside a rich seam of parody and satire (mostly outside the remit of this discussion). The difficulty of securing precise locations on ambitious, arduous and nonsensical expeditions (literary and actual) is expressed in various ways in Carroll's poem – and the ontological slipperiness of geographical regions comes into play. The satiric edge of *The Hunting of the Snark* exposes the tendency for children's books to impose order on a world that is otherwise chaotic – a role often taken up by cartographic attempts to map regions constantly in flux. Sinéad Moriarty suggests in 'Unstable Space: Mapping the Antarctic for Children in "Heroic Era" Antarctic Literature' (2017) that 'while maps can play a productive role in Antarctic children's texts, they also risk fundamentally misrepresenting the nature of the landscape they depict' (Moriarty 2017: 58).[17] Moriarty detects a misplaced authority and imperial agenda in recent books on Antarctic exploration for children (published between 1997 and 2014) that nowhere regions of children's literature implicitly question and counteract. Moriarty observes that 'Antarctica is the continent cartography created. The inhospitable climate and the dangers posed by pack ice to vessels entering Antarctic waters ensured that the continent remained a blank spot on world maps well into the late nineteenth century' (57). It is this blank spot that interests Carroll as he navigates inaccessible poles in *The Hunting of the Snark*, and it proves central to the ontic structures of nowhere in children's literature more widely.

A challenge to the misplaced authority of exploratory undertakings is evident in Carroll's preface on the conditions of nonsense: 'They knew it was not of the slightest use to appeal to the Bellman about it – he would only refer to his Naval Code, and read out in pathetic tones Admiralty Instructions which none of them had ever been able to understand' (Carroll [1876] 2000: viii). Such pointed satirical targets would likely have been savoured in an era when the British state insisted that 'polar exploration should fly the flag of nationalism and take itself seriously, by being empirical, disciplined and serious in its pursuit of science' (Bravo 2019: 157). Martin Gardner confirms that many contemporary readers 'supposed that the ballad was a satire on an arctic voyage, the Snark a symbol of the North Pole', though he adds that 'there is little to recommend this theory' beyond topical interest (Carroll [1876] 2006: xxxiv). Indeed, such literal readings of the poem's symbolic coding overlook its refusal of any such geological specificity and miss Carroll's oscillating ontic move between location and dislocation. For example, Nelson's rousing signal prior to the Battle of Trafalgar in 1805 is undercut as the Bellman prepares his crew for the hunt: '"But the Snark is at hand, let me tell you again! / 'Tis your glorious duty to seek it! … For England expects – I forbear to proceed: / 'Tis a maxim tremendous, but trite"' (Carroll [1876] 2000: 17–18). The pomposity of the Bellman's speech is foregrounded by the metafictive contradiction of the final phrase, and thus the heroics of naval warfare are pilloried. The hollow grandiosity of the language knowingly disguises the fact that the Bellman is leading his valiant crew to an unknown destination for an indeterminable goal. The metaphysical concern of the poem is also (dis)located here, suggesting that the condition of human being is to search for the unknowable in the unknown – and the metaphysical remit of nowhere allows for this search.

Maritime exploration had long been supported by scientific calculation and cartographic symbolism, so it is not surprising that a sort of cartographic propaganda also traced the race to the poles. The crew's map in *The Hunting of the Snark* involves a renowned piece of cartographic satire and it usefully articulates the conceptual vagueness of Stefansson's Pole of Inaccessibility:

> 'What's the good of Mercator's North Poles and Equators,
> Tropics, Zones, and Meridian Lines?'
> So the Bellman would cry: and the crew would reply
> 'They are merely conventional signs!'
> 'Other maps are such shapes, with their islands and capes!
> But we've got our brave Captain to thank'
> (So the crew would protest) 'that he's bought us the best –
> A perfect and absolute blank!'
>
> (Carroll 2000: 7)

Carroll's 'absolute blank' reflects the failure of real expeditions to reach their destination or to bring back promised cargo. Moreover, the visual emptiness of the 1876 Ocean Chart (Figure 4.3) anticipates the nowhere realms of the Boojum. Gardner observes that the Boojum 'means nothing at all. It is the void, the great blank emptiness out of which we miraculously emerged; by which we will ultimately be devoured; through which the absurd galaxies spiral and drift endlessly on their nonsense voyages from nowhere to nowhere (Carroll [1876] 2006: xxxix). In the perfection of its blankness, the chart itself is a Boojum, as its own obscure origins might imply – though I would suggest that Carroll's chart allows for somewhere in its nowhere.[18]

The Ocean Chart speaks to the impossibility of ever representing mutable terrain and, more specifically, points to a paradox recognized by Stefansson. The Pole of Inaccessibility is only inaccessible relative to the local knowledge, methods and resources used to reach it – and after all the Bellman's crew is able to land: 'he landed his crew with care' (Carroll 2000: 1). In Stefansson's relativity inheres a variable that cannot be mapped with the sort of precision we might

166　　　　　　　　*Metaphysics of Children's Literature*

Figure 4.3 Ocean Chart from the 1876 edition of *The Hunting of the Snark* (Carroll [1876] 2006: 28).

expect of cartography – and Carroll's chart (in combination with the Pole of Inaccessibility) suggests that we are wrong to expect it, as Moriarty and Bravo also indicate. Stefansson does locate a particular Arctic region of interest in what he terms his 'fourth stage' of exploration,[19] but he explains: 'any discoveries which might be made through the application of this method were secondary to the establishment of the method itself' (Stefansson 1921: 6). He thereby confirms that the purpose of his expedition does not involve a mappable pole, suggesting that the philosophy behind it involves *nowhere in search of a somewhere*. It seems to me that Carroll's map recognizes this sort of metaphysical manoeuvre – hence his Ocean Chart points to the ontic foundation of nowhere in children's books, marking out nowhere as an entity worth recording on a map.

Carroll's 'Agony in Eight Fits' can be considered a purposefully episodic expedition, drawn out by the chaos and nonsensical ambition of a crew who have no comprehension of their quarry and only a vague sense of where they might locate a Snark. There is a desperate urgency and commitment to their voyage though, which echoes the metaphysical task of making sense of a world that is largely nonsensical. Carroll's investment in nowhere also expresses something of the metaphysical structure that Bachelard envisions in *The Poetics of Reverie*. When it comes to finding the creature they know nothing about, the Butcher and the Beaver fix on the very same place: 'a spot unfrequented by man, / A dismal and desolate valley' (Carroll 2000: 21). They survive this nowhere territory, which is marked as such by the fact that it takes them to an instance of childhood reverie: When 'a scream, shrill and high, rent the shuddering sky', the Beaver 'turned pale' and the Butcher, feeling queer, 'thought of his childhood left far far behind' (22). Momentarily the Butcher moves into that 'blissful and innocent state', suggesting (in line with Bachelard) that childhood remains a source of metaphysical understanding – even if in this case it is realized by a scream that 'recalled to his mind / A pencil that squeaks on a slate!' (22) Their encounter with nowhere has the positive outcome of cementing a lifelong and unlikely friendship; previously the Beaver had feared the Butcher, who confessed on embarking that he 'could only kill Beavers' (4). Having encountered nowhere, in the mighty context of childhood reverie, the potential is forged for a future that is more certain than their current voyage; as confirmed at the end of the fit, 'In winter or summer, 'twas always the same – / You could never meet either alone' (26). Ultimately, it is the Baker – 'their hero unnamed' (34) who moves beyond nowhere and discovers (like Unn in *The Ice Palace*) that we can be nowhere shut in; the Snark, revealed as a Boojum, reduces him to the nothing he has dreaded all along. In common with Vesaas and Bachelard, Carroll recognizes that nowhere carries intimations of death in the vulnerability of its fissures, while also confirming that death is never nowhere. Nowhere is revealed as an ontic structure relevant to the condition of being human, as well as functioning as an index of territorial milieu that can be identified in its own right as a Pole of Inaccessibility.

The nonsense realms of Carroll and Lear provide an important foundation for the metaphysical groundwork of children's literature and its influence can be traced in the nonsense of other practitioners. For example, Mervyn Peake's investment in the metaphysical conditions of travel find an outlet in two of his nonsense works for children: *Captain Slaughterboard Drops Anchor* (1939) and *Letters from a Lost Uncle* (1948). Lindsay draws on Australian social history and culture in *The Magic Pudding*, but he also inherits the lambasting sprit of nonsense expeditions in the 'Adventures of Bunyip Bluegum and His Friends Bill Barnacle and Sam Sawnoff'. Lindsay's adventure was apparently inspired by 'a passage about a ridiculous dinner' in Carroll's *Through the Looking-Glass* (1871),[20] so his familiarity with Carroll's work is well established. Nonetheless, it is the book's structural and thematic indebtedness to the picaresque and nonsense journeys that lends it a certain Snarkian force and gives it a footing in the conditions of nowhere. When Sam and Bill recount the tale of how they came to own their remarkable Puddin', they '"Let her go for a song"' (Lindsay [1918] 1995: 23) and launch into a ballad about rounding the Horn aboard the *Saucy Sausage*. Their ship 'strikes on the ice', stranding them in the middle of an Antarctic nowhere with 'Curry and Rice', the ship's cook (24). It is hard to say exactly where Sam and Bill are marooned, but the Cape Horn is notorious for the sort of icebergs and high winds (running off the Andes Mountains and the Antarctic Peninsula) that sink their ship. Their eventual escape on a chicken coop bound for Tierra del Fuego confirms the general vicinity of their stranded isolation, but here another Pole of Inaccessibility enters the horizon:

> For Sam an' me an' the cook, yer see,
> We climbs on a lump of ice,
> And there in the sleet we suffered a treat
> For several months from frozen feet,
> With nothin' at all but ice to eat,
> And ice does not suffice.
>
> (24)

The duration of the pair's plight is exaggerated here, as is their starvation – in contrast with Curry and Rice, who has been subsisting secretly on 'a big plum-duff an' a rump-steak hot' (25). The iceberg can be identified as an inaccessible pole in Stefansson's terms, because the territory is *ostensibly* ill-equipped to sustain human life. When Sam and Bill locate food unexpectedly, a reminder is provided that the Pole of Inaccessibility is only relatively inaccessible. Of course, the discovery of food in a nonsense poem is unlikely to be conventional and Lindsay's dark satire is certainly creative in the direction of its 'foraging'. This episode caricatures not only the 'heroic-era' narratives of Antarctic exploration[21] but also earlier and more notorious (murderous) ventures, such as the ill-fated 1629 voyage of the *Batavia*.[22] A 'missing' verse implies that Sam and Bill have murdered the cook for the sake of his Puddin', a suggestion that the Puddin' corroborates through his version of events. As might be expected of a nowhere location, much is slippery and unaccounted for in this ethically elliptical episode of the Puddin's origin. Nowhere is shifting and imprecise, yet the encounter proves significant (as ever). The acquisition of the Puddin' on an iceberg drives the plot and allows the protagonists to move from a hostile nowhere territory to a welcoming somewhere in which they can thrive. The story closes with a celebration of being-within a dwelling place, the friends having built themselves a 'snug tree-house' complete with 'a little Puddin' paddock', where they can live together: ' "For the homeward-bounder's chorus, which he roars across the foam, / Is all about chucking a sailor's life, / And settling down at home" ' (171). *The Magic Pudding* follows the return home from adventure or cessation of trials common to songs or ballad forms of the earliest origin. Certainly it has something of the *eucatastrophe*, or 'joyous turn' (Tolkien 1947: 81), on which Tolkien insists in 'On Fairy-Stories', and this sort of fairy-tale elation also has metaphysical aspects. However, the companionable and emphatic snugness of settling into the tree house are ontic qualities of being somewhere. Set against the indeterminate isolation of a frozen nowhere, the metaphysical mechanisms identified by Bachelard, Deleuze and Guattari come back into focus. Lindsay's iceberg and tree house can be considered ontic indices of being nowhere and somewhere, and consequently *The Magic Pudding* is embedded in the workings of a modern children's literature that recognizes the ontic significance of poles of inaccessibility.

The Magic Pudding's ontic commitment to the conditions of being nowhere demonstrates an affinity with nineteenth-century nonsense, but it extends beyond the conditions of nonsense as I have started to suggest. In *Abel's Island*, whimsical aspects of Lear's nonsense remain, fused with the reflective anthropomorphism of Potter's *Tales*, or Grahame's *The Wind in the Willows*. Steig's illustrated chapter book is interesting for its scaling down of nowhere in extremis, so that the young implied reader is embraced in this humorous rendition of being nowhere. Steig achieves this via miniaturization and, as Bachelard discloses, 'Miniature is one of the refuges of greatness' (Bachelard [1958] 1994: 155), lending a metaphysical magnifying glass to external entities. Steig's eponymous protagonist is a mouse and, thus, the reach of his encounter with nowhere is relative to his size and experience of the world. Much of the book's droll humour comes from the knowledge that Abel is never really far from home, but for a mouse of limited world experience he is nowhere in extremis, relative to the miniature conditions of his being. While picnicking, 'some distance from the town where they lived' (Steig 1977: 3), newlyweds Amanda and Abel are forced to shelter from a storm. Abel impetuously chases after the gauzy softness of Amanda's scarf – and indeed it is this comforting texture that Abel later holds to him for the familiar reassurance of being-within – as it is whipped from Amanda by the same ferocious wind that sends Abel into a swelling stream, over a waterfall and eventually to his marooned state. Abel has reached a Pole of Inaccessibility that he must contend with before he can be reunited with Amanda and the home they share.

In common with other nowhere encounters, Abel is disorientated early on and thus this becomes a tale of recovering ontological bearings: 'he was being knocked about in a world that had lost its manners, in a direction, as far as he could tell, not north, south, east, or west' (8–10). Abel is not certain of *where* he has landed, though he is able to recognize the topographical features of an island, and thus whereness is established as an ontic trope. The vagueness of language used here is revealing: 'he was now where he was, on his boat at the top of a tree, on an island, in whatever river this was' (16). Abel recognizes that he has been dislocated and the expression of nowhere is clear in the uncertainty of *now where he was*. Only a few lines later, Abel identifies nowhere and sets it in contrast to the *familiar home* he has left behind: 'Ah, cherry birch! One of his favorite flavors. The familiar taste made him feel a little more at home on his roost in the middle of nowhere' (16). Through this sensual experience of familiarity, nowhere and somewhere are set against each other. The narrative thrust of the tale is thereby established and it is clear that (in part) Abel's journey will involve an ontological acceptance of being nowhere in order to reach home. Initially Abel is resistant to being nowhere, distancing himself from the creatures and surrounding landscape. He refuses to communicate with the local birds, because 'They were wild, and he civilized' (28) and observes that 'the river was where it ought to be; [he] wasn't' (31–2); ultimately, 'he was fed up with the stupid, pointless island' (29). This is the sort of combative posturing that Stefansson identifies as destructive and Abel will need to communicate with nowhere if he is to escape it.

In time, Abel starts to see that being nowhere has more relevance for him than he realized: 'By the end of the month of August he knew he was an inhabitant of the island, whether he liked it or not' (42). Here a move is made towards a biospheric view of being in the world and Abel recognizes that Da-sein is never a matter of choice. Abel discovers that the island is not barren after all and that being is rather more complex than his hitherto sheltered existence had led him to believe: 'Living in the heart of nature, he began to realize how much was going on in the seeming stillness' (54). ... 'Plants grew and bore fruit, branches proliferated, buds became flowers, clouds formed in ever-new ways and patterns, colours changed. He felt a strong need to participate in the designing and arranging of things' (54). Abel finally embraces the fullness of being and conceives himself as part of a wider process. He goes through an ontological epiphany in which he recognizes that the very fact of being is worth celebration: 'How vividly actual and therefore marvellous!' (76). This is the point at which Abel appreciates the Pole of Inaccessibility on its own terms and his nowhere island becomes a somewhere of significance as he leaves it behind: 'He saw it for the first time from a far perspective, embracing its wholeness. No wonder he loved it; it was beautiful' (107–8). The ecocritical strand of *Abel's Island* makes of this nowhere space a utopia and – for one small, conceited mouse – the metaphysical conditions of being are exposed and examined under the powerful gaze of miniature's microscope.

McCaughrean is a writer who frequently engages with nowhere in extremis – her work is saturated in nowhere and much of her writing instinctively reaches for the metaphysical seams in which poles of inaccessibility are entrenched. *Stop the Train* (2001) is set in the Oklahoma prairies of 1893 and settlers are arriving to stake their 'claim to a future' in 'map-born towns' (McCaughrean [2001] 2007: 3–4). Immediately it is apparent that for Cissey Sissney and her family, nowhere is going to be rather more than an encounter; or at least that the novel will dig down into the conditions of nowhere before moving on. The second chapter is entitled 'Nowhere', and when Cissy peers at her new home for the first time she has 'a strong inclination to stay in the luggage rack' for she realizes that 'Florence did not exist' (6). Certainly this is a novel about how places come into being out of ostensibly barren landscapes; 'This was Nowhere, in the State of Nowhere. An empty space waiting to be filled' (7). However, this is also a tale of ontic encounter and of faith in the temporary status of nowhere. Cissy recognizes early on that the evolution of Florence is connected with her own potential to be and to come into Da-sein. When her father encourages the children to imagine Florence into being, Cissy instinctively uses herself as a measure of the town's potential to be somewhere: 'What am *I*, Poppy?' called Cissy, feeling her heels rise off the ground with excitement. 'What's going to be here, where I'm standing?' (9). There is a childly emphasis on future possibility growing out of a nowhere that is also vulnerable to failure – a vulnerability that inheres in ontological edification for Bachelard. Cissy's parents characterize the competing concerns of being-within somewhere (mother) and of taking the risks involved in a line of flight to nowhere (father) – and Cissy visualizes the difference in physical terms. She recognizes the concrete weight of ontological concern: 'it was a scary feeling, to think of her parents pulling against one another – as though the legs on one body had set off to walk in two different directions' (15). Cissy knows instinctively that to be human is to encounter nowhere in order to be somewhere and that her mother's emphatic denial of nowhere could have troubling repercussions. Finally, it is Cissy and her friends who must confront the risk of nowhere in order to make the train stop at their town.

Having staked out a claim for nowhere in *Stop the Train* and made nowhere relatively accessible, McCaughrean spins the globe in later novels to access nowhere from a different direction. *The White Darkness* is set in the context of Antarctic exploration, nonetheless McCaughrean explores the sort of Arctic territory dislocated by Stefansson's Pole of Inaccessibility. This novel can be seen as a fictional companion to *The Friendly Arctic*, for it is invested in a multilayered approach to a spatial encounter that can never be fixed by coordinates. Obviously their projects differ in emphasis, since McCaughrean is more interested in exploring the conditions of being human than she is in arguing for a particular approach to Arctic exploration.

The White Darkness provides a sophisticated encounter with nowhere, moving into the realms of young adult fiction with its teenage protagonist Symone (better known as Sym). However, its poetics of nowhere is located within a framework of children's literature that draws on Oscar Wilde's 'The Happy Prince' (1888), J. M. Barrie's *Peter and Wendy* (1911) and Enid Blyton's *The Famous Five* series (1942–63). These ongoing references contribute to a sense that Sym's journey into nowhere is a complex process of assemblage, which does not discard childhood experience. Her Antarctic encounter is not purely a metaphor for growing out of childhood into adulthood – though nowhere can be conceived figuratively in this way (as revealed in the next section) and it is echoed in Sym's struggle to perceive herself as a sexual being. Emphatically though, nowhere in extremis is not to be understood as a liminal marker of developmental growth and it would lose its ontic potential if this were the case. Nowhere can be experienced at any point of human being, yet it has a childly aspect in its potential for forward movement and Sym draws on this in her own encounter with being nowhere – an encounter that forces her to reach back into earlier moments of childhood trauma and grief.

This beautifully strange novel is about loss, obsession and coming into being by travelling to an ever-shifting Antarctica. Fourteen-year-old Sym knows a great deal about polar exploration and, consequently, this novel is informed by an extensive intertextual network of materials related to Antarctic endeavour. As she confesses on the first page, Sym is in love with Titus Oates, an explorer who has been dead for ninety years but who remains alive inside her head. Sym's relationship with Oates becomes real while her father is dying – a father whom she believes never liked her (McCaughrean [2005] 2006: 12–14). When the opportunity arises to visit the Antarctic with her Uncle Victor – a trip that Victor has engineered for sinister reasons – Sym is thrown into an experience over which she has little control initially. Sym's voyage into the white darkness of the Antarctic is an exploration of grief and the influence of psychosomatic manifestation on external reality. However, there is a metaphysical undertow to the never-still icebergs of Sym's journey and her navigation of the Pole of Inaccessibility. The novel's dark humour also works (in part) through an ontic remit, since its precise use of language exposes an affinity with the works of nonsense explored earlier. For example, semantic irony is employed to signal the spurious motives of Sym's fellow travellers. When Sigurd (another young member of the party who has claimed to be in love with her) tells Sym that he'd 'always be there' for her, the Titus in her head questions Sigurd's motives through linguistic play:

> '*There*?' said Titus tartly. '*Where*?'
> 'There. It's an expression,' I explained.
> '*It's a geographical disposition*.'
> 'There. Here. Around. On hand. OK?'
> '*Ah!*' said Titus, enlightened. '*Lurking, you mean*'.
>
> (180)

Sym's adverbial joke with herself draws attention to the sort of semantic minutiae that can get lost in the enormity of self-expression. Adverbs often shrink into grander phrases, but there is something immediate about the adverbial link between entities and locations that Sym recognizes here. It also anticipates her later struggle to convey her encounter with Antarctica: 'Words can't cope. The space between the letters ought to make them elastic enough, but they aren't'

(250). Ultimately though, via the rhythms and layers of its poetic prose, the novel expounds an ontological awareness that whereness is crucial to being human.

McCaughrean configures nowhere as a site of multilayered investigation, encompassing theological, psychological and metaphysical concerns: 'God sketched Antarctica then rubbed most of it out again, in the hope a better idea would strike Him. In the centre is a blank whiteness where the planet isn't finished. It's the address for Nowhere' (53). Even if Sym's faith has been shaken in most aspects of her existence, she can be sure that nowhere exits – and it has an address; nowhere is a place that we can visit – if only we can locate it – and it is only relatively inaccessible. Indeed, nowhere exists as a geographical entity of human encounter and Sym recognizes that the encounter might not lead back to somewhere – like Unn she could very well lose the battle for being real (or sane, if the book's parallel concern with mental health is followed through). Sym recognizes that she must confront nowhere in order to come into being: 'Surely, if I was ever to set foot down there, even I might finally exist. Surely, in this Continent of Nothingness, anything – anyone – had to be hugely alive by comparison!' (53) Antarctica is thus set up as a nowhere site of intense and difficult ontological encounter but one that has the potential to offer up Da-sein.

Disorientation is once again marked out as a feature of this encounter, suggesting that poles locating a particular spot are redundant. Sym discovers that 'Vertical and horizontal lose all their meaning in a place without horizons' (114) and reiterates that 'We're in the middle of Nowhere. That's where we really are' (118). This is not a place that can be configured by maps, contradicting years of cartographic endeavour and embracing the variable conditions of Stefansson's Pole of Inaccessibility: 'Geographers can't map the chaos of the Shear Zone; it is always changing. This is where the Ice Shelf hinges against solid land, flexing, blistering, and gaping, like a scar that won't ever heal' (147). Sym also learns that reaching beyond nowhere in extremis is to contradict being itself and even to move past death: 'A few icefalls, then we'll be on the Polar Plateau. A white hole. Life in negative. Not just a lack of anything, but a space ready to devour existence itself' (197). Having visited nowhere, Sym must find a way to return from it because: ' "This is not a good place to be. There's nothing underneath us" ' (220). When eventually Sym is rescued from her descent into nowhere by the crew of an icebreaker her return to the world is painful: 'Coming back to life isn't something I'd wish on my worst enemy' (240). Being somewhere in the world is not easy, but through a process of metaphoric transfer McCaughrean finds poetry in the white darkness that is human being.

Nowhere encounters take McCaughrean to the extremities of human being, and through the mechanisms of her geo-historical fiction, she reaches beneath the surface of American prairies and Antarctic plateaus. Her ontological encounters with nowhere in extremis continue in the Australian outback of *The Middle of Nowhere* and the Hebridean sea stacs of *Where the World Ends* (2017). Her writing reveals that *nowhere is ever far enough* to escape the challenging conditions of being human. No matter how far people travel from the populated communities of civilization, they will be confronted with the stripped-back angst of Da-sein – to be there is to be human; and to be there in a modern world is to internalize the shrapnel of social structure. When Herbert Pinny moves his wife Mary and daughter Comity to 'the loneliest, most godforsaken patches of nowhere on the whole continent of Australia' (McCaughrean [2017] 2018: 22) it is inevitable that the social tensions they bring with them will be heightened. *The Middle of Nowhere* is also a work of utopian social world building though, so after an extreme period of loss and dislocation, Comity (by name and nature) brings nowhere into focus: 'After all, standing on a seabed in the Middle of Nowhere makes almost anything possible' (295). McCaughrean is not the only children's writer engaged with nowhere in extremis, but her repeated engagement with this particular region of being demonstrates its depth and poetic resilience.

The Pole of Inaccessibility has proved a useful tool in extrapolating the ontological conditions of nowhere at its farthest reach. Nowhere in extremis is geographically located in places that are relatively inaccessible to human beings, yet these places are within reach enough to throw up a nowhere encounter of relevance to being human. Identified as a Pole of Inaccessibility, nowhere is an entity of ontic encounter in its own right, yet simultaneously, nowhere in extremis is an aspect of being human that arises from this encounter. Having recognized that nowhere has local and extreme geographical reach, I now turn to works of children's literature that deal with nowhere of the middle ground. The metaphysical groundwork of such books deals with a more internalized *awareness of whereness*, conveyed through seemingly mundane and featureless facets of nowhere.

Nowhere for miles and miles

> We are adept ... at saying what we make of places – but we are far less good at saying what places make of us. For some time now it has seemed to me that the two questions we should ask of any strong landscape are these: firstly, what do

I know when I am in this place that I can know nowhere else? And then, vainly, what does this place know of me that I cannot know of myself?

(Macfarlane [2012] 2013: 27)

In *The Old Ways: A Journey on Foot* (2012) Macfarlane poses questions that offer a self-reflexive approach to the conditions of nowhere and, from his phrasing of these questions, arise central concerns of this chapter: as to how any space can be nowhere and as to the nature of nowhere's relationship with being human. In the context of the Macfarlane's ontologically directed questions, nowhere might be understood as a relative reflection of self and space. Conceivably, nowhere is a place that knows nothing of me, a place that cannot reveal anything to me that I do not already know. By contrast then, somewhere is a place that has a part of myself in its landscape, or that speaks to me of myself. Perhaps this is what Huckleberry Finn is getting at when he explains: 'All I wanted was to go somewheres; all I wanted was a change, I warn't particular' (Twain [1884] 2003: 50). Huck cannot be himself in the confines of Widow Douglas's home and makes his own journey to escape the stifling nowhere of her 'sivilizing' ways. While this becomes a larger journey, marking Huck and Jim's flight down the Mississippi river, it also maps a 'boy-life out on the Mississippi' through the means of narrative autobiography (Twain [1884] 2003: 13). In this section then, I focus on the intimate conditions of nowhere as an ontological function of coming into the region of somewhere. I demonstrate that mapping has a particular role to play in this process and suggest that (to some extent) this explains the proliferation of verbal and visual maps in children's books. In this particular recourse into the self-reflexive regions of nowhere, my project is not to explore the role of maps in books per se but to demonstrate some of the ways in which the process of mapping sheds light on hidden nowheres.

I am interested in those steps that lead from nowhere to somewhere (or vice versa) and the extent to which verbal and visual maps engage with a whereness that relates to awareness – that is, an ontological awareness of the outside world and, ultimately, ontic self-awareness. In his discussion of the role of 'Maps and Memorability' (1982), Arthur Schulman observes that 'Things appear to us with a spatiality, a "whereness", that we cannot ignore. Events, though they unfold over time, are said to take *place* ... even if we must *learn* to observe and record spatiality, and even if our spatial records are incomplete or flawed, there can be no question of the existence of an "awareness of whereness"' (Schulman [1982] 1983: 359). Schulman establishes the cognitive significance of this *awareness of whereness*, going on to argue that maps are valuable tools in the service of comprehension and memory. Bringing together Schulman and Macfarlane,

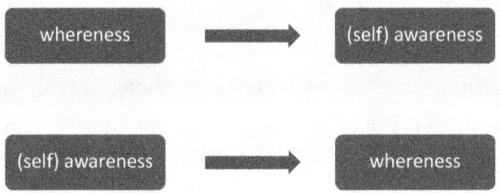

Figure 4.4 The whereness of self-awareness.

I have identified the reciprocal nature of a relationship from which arises the *whereness of self-awareness* (Figure 4.4).

Following from Schulman and Macfarlane, I recognize that maps can serve to orientate the reader in a process that simultaneously orientates subject and object. This is also suggested by the etymological adjustments in *orientation*, allowing for the bearing of self and thing.[23] This assumes that maps are actually in search of somewhere, but as the ontic realms of children's literature have demonstrated, somewhere frequently entails nowhere. Indeed, a number of children's books pursue the mapping of nowhere and this engagement suggests a relationship between awareness and self-awareness.

From the outset it is important to recognize that cartography is not an exact science. Mapmakers might manage a degree of accuracy in gauging somewhere, but as my discussion of conceptual vagueness reveals, whereness is difficult to measure with any precision. In *The Phantom Atlas* (2016) Edward Brooke-Hitching observes that inaccurate maps of non-existent places have enjoyed a 'remarkable durability' (2016: 9) and the first example he offers relates to the navigation of a nowhere island:

> Finally, they reached the given coordinates – and there they found nothing. Only open, unbroken water, as far as the eye could see. There was no trace of an island certified on countless navigational charts. The mariners were thorough and swept the area, taking extensive measurements and soundings, but to no avail. Bermeja, it turned out, was a phantom.
>
> (8)

In this cross-over between cartographic conviction and geographical absence, it is possible to trace the relationship between somewhere and nowhere. As discussed earlier, Grahame makes use of this ontic tension in 'Wayfarers All' when he calls attention to the Rat's ontological uncertainty through reference to the much mapped but non-existent Mountains of the Moon.[24] Carroll goes further in *The Hunting of the Snark* and suggests the impossibility of locating anywhere with any degree of certainty via *a perfect and absolute blank*. Such cartographic absences and anomalies point to a metaphysical facet of maps, which has drawn the attention of philosophical geographers. Varzi notes that the world mapped by geographers is full of 'ontological variety' (2001: 1) and that this world 'is philosophically interesting precisely in that many geographic entities exist in spatial reality (in the world "out there") while also depending for their existence on our social and cognitive practices' (2). It is inevitable that some of the metaphysical underpinnings Varzi recognizes in distinctions made by geographers are also at play in literary texts as writers seek to build worlds; consequently his observations can help to unearth the nowhere regions of children's books. For example, the distinction between *bona fide* and *fiat* boundaries will prove useful in identifying topographical (and thus literary) features of nowhere territories:

> On the one hand, there are entities like Australia, the island of Malta, or Lake Ontaio – entities whose boundaries correspond to some *bona fide* qualitative discontinuities (shorelines, water courses, etc.) in the underlying territory. On the other hand, we have Maryland and Pennsylvania, Saskatchewan, or the North Sea, whose boundaries are at least in part the result of human *fiat* and do not reflect any pre-existing physical differentiations.
>
> (7)

The mutable regions of nowhere in extremis have already demonstrated the challenges of dealing with topographical features, such as Antarctic ice-plateaus, so it is clear that ontological markers will prove useful in discussing the boundaries between somewhere and nowhere (involved in identifying the whereness of self-awareness).

Before looking more closely at children's books that deal expressly with nowhere, I examine a passage from Elizabeth Wein's *Codename Verity* (2012), which is invested in locating somewhere specific through a verbal mapping of regional topography. In Wein's novel about female Special Operations recruits during the Second World War it is important that the British Isles are rendered in terms of an open landscape with a natural splendour and history worth preserving, since it serves as a contrast to the confined space (also mapped through a coded series of confessions) of the Nazi prison in which the eponymous Verity is being held. This description of Maddie Brodat's solo flight delivers a sense of distance and space travelled:

> The Northumbrian coast is the most beautiful length of the whole trip. The sun still sets quite late in the north of England in August, and Maddie on fabric wings flew low over the long sands of Holy Island and saw seals gathered there.

... Maddie flew back following the 70-mile, 2000-year-old dragon's back of Hadrian's Wall, to Carlisle and then south through the Lakeland fells, along Lake Windermere. The soaring mountains rose around her and the poets' waters glittered beneath her in the valleys of memory – hosts of golden daffodils, *Swallows and Amazons*, Peter Rabbit.

(Wein 2012: 36)

The passage provides an impression of the British landscape over which Maddie flies. This gestalt map is rendered through precise landmarks, replete with historical detail and cultural references to literature that allow (via intertextual framing) an interpretative response that digs into its geographical surface. This is a heritage flight of sorts, invested in marking out a terrain that will soon be scarred by the ravages of war, for Maddie's flight takes place 'days before Britain declared war on Germany' and she must avoid 'the barrage balloons like silver ramparts protecting the sky around Newcastle' (35). If this is to be recognized as map-work, then the locations can be seen as nodal points, or cairns, that converge haphazardly to form an identifiable route. Returning to Varzi's ontological framework, this process of mapping could be described as *convergent vagueness*.

Varzi observes that 'vagueness is a pervasive phenomenon of human thought and language' and that 'conceptual vagueness is a feature that geography shares with many other disciplines' (2001: 9). An example will help to clarify his position here: 'It makes no sense to ask for the *lowest mountain* on Earth, or for the *shortest river*, or for the *smallest city*. It makes no sense because such concepts as "mountain", "river", and "village" do not have precise standards of application' (9). The lack of linguistic precision Varzi outlines here certainly shares ground with literary attempts to render the external world. Furthermore, Varzi argues that this vagueness is not just a question of semantics but that it amounts to an ontological indeterminacy (11). For instance, 'To say that there are no definite boundaries demarcating Mount Everest ... would then amount to treating Everest as a fuzzy object' (10); and the fuzziness of mountains is thus ontologically determined. Returning to Maddie's map of the Northern England, this vagueness should not be considered a hindrance to gaining a sense of whereness that encompasses both Maddie and the topographical features of her journey. Vagueness is an ontic quality of topographic mapping that leaves space for the reader to make connections between points of convergence, such as Hadrian's wall, seals on the Farne islands or Peter Rabbit. Maddie's flight purposefully renders the whereness of self-awareness, shaping protagonist as subject (and implied reader by association) through the mapped significance of its landscape. Consequently, this passage can be said to map ontological entities – someone and somewhere – through the process of convergent vagueness.

As can be inferred from this example of convergent vagueness though, any conceptual rendition of somewhere contains within it the potential for nowhere; mountains will always be fuzzy and can never be mapped with the accuracy that cartographers might suggest. Given that children's literature is committed to exploring emergent whereness and self-awareness, it is perhaps not surprising that a tradition of mapping the convergence of somewhere with nowhere extends back at least to Stevenson's *Kidnapped* (1886). Fictional maps in literature for children predate *Kidnapped*, but Ian Duncan points out that *Kidnapped* is the first to represent physical topography of consensus reality in support of its narrative: 'the inclusion of a map of real-world locations, plotting the course of the adventure across actual coasts, glens, and hillsides, is another of the innovations of *Kidnapped*' (Duncan in Stevenson [1886] 2014: xxi–xxii). Stevenson directs his reader to look at the visual map as Davie moves deep into the highlands and it is the relationship between actual and represented topography that interests me, a relationship forged through the combination of visual and verbal mapping. The heightened whereness of the Scottish highlands is intimately tied to human being as Stevenson mixes his pallet of historically real and imagined characters, so that credibility lies less in historical veracity than it does in topographical placement. Through direct address, Stevenson's reader is also instructed to locate the narrative via the map in a process of growing (self) awareness of whereness that will further be influenced by familiarity with the Scottish setting. As Christopher MacLachlan observes,

> Like most Scottish readers, I believe, I look at the map usually printed with the text of *Kidnapped* to find places I know, and I then picture the characters in the scenery I have seen myself. I assume of course that the map is not fiction, unlike the map in *Treasure Island*, though why I make that assumption might be debated.
> (MacLachlan n.d.)

The categorical distinction MacLachlan makes here between the ontological status of visual maps in *Treasure Island* (1883) and *Kidnapped* is interesting, since it is based on a whereness directly related to self-awareness. He suspects that his assumption and the distinction ensuing from it are debatable, a suspicion that might well arise from the ontological vagueness of geographical classification. Ontological vagueness confirms that the map in *Kidnapped* does not represent a topographically accurate Scotland and that it cannot stand in for geographical reality in any straightforward way. However, its landscape appears real to MacLachlan because his own autobiography is bound up in his experience of the topography it demarcates. For MacLachlan, *Kidnapped* takes place somewhere and he knows this because he can trace the adventure on a map of a landscape he recognizes. By comparison, the map in *Treasure Island* points nowhere for MacLachlan (and thus towards fantasy), since it is not a place that he recognizes or is known to him. MacLachlan appears to be investing in philosophical boundaries familiar to geographers, in which *Kidnapped* is marked by bona fide boundaries and *Treasure Island* by fiat boundaries. As Varzi observes though, 'even bona fide boundaries may involve vagueness of some sort, but only insofar as sometimes it is just not clear *what* the relevant bona fide boundary is. Consider the question "Just where, and how long, is the coastline of Britain?"' (2001: 13). Varzi's identification of vagueness in bona fide boundaries is further confirmation that the map in *Kidnapped* can have no straightforward relationship with physical features of the Highlands it appears to demarcate, yet this vagueness does not trouble MacLachlan's process of identification with its landscape. MacLachlan does not identify the nowhere in *Kidnapped*, because self-awareness identifies its whereness.

Recourse to Stevenson's prose in *Kidnapped* reveals that nowhere arises on a number of occasions though. For example, when Davie Balfour is shipwrecked he reflects on the sinking of the *Covenant*, thus: 'There was no sign of the brig, which must have lifted from the reef and sunk. The boat, too, was nowhere to be seen. There was never a sail upon the ocean; and in what I could see of the land was neither house nor man' (Stevenson [1886] 2014: 82). Davie's isolation is emphasized by the nowhere status of the ship, a status extended to the surrounding landscape by the associative mechanisms of pathetic fallacy. Boy, ship and landscape are connected by a narrative awareness of whereness, a whereness configured as being nowhere. This topographical marking of nowhere is the starting point for Davie's journey through the heather, in which (dis)location contributes to Davie's sense of self-doubt in relation to the slippery Alan Breck. Nowhere is thus an ontological feature of this fiat map, which overlays the bona fide, printed map of MacLachlan's reading experience. This metaphysical mapping lends a further layer of reality to the novel, yet it is a layer that can also be found at work in *Treasure Island* when the pirates hunting Jim in the Admiral Benbow declare that he is 'nowhere to be found' (Stevenson [1883] 1953: 52). I draw on this comparison to demonstrate that mapping does not separate these novels generically in the manner suggested (albeit doubtfully) by MacLachlan, for mapping the nowhere is not necessarily a marker for identifying fantasy in contrast to realism. Instead, I suggest that the mapping of nowhere helps to identify the shared ontological foundations of *Kidnapped* and *Treasure Island* – as nowhere constitutes the whereness of self-awareness – while also pointing to shared themes and tropes. It is worth taking a moment here to mention a large number of novels that interrogate boundaries between realms and regions of fantasy and reality through the metaphysical remit of nowhere. *Tuck Everlasting* (1975) by Natalie Babbitt, *Fire and Hemlock* (1985) by Diana Wynne Jones, *The Seeing Stone* (2000) by Kevin Crossley-Holland or Lanagan's *Tender Morsels* are just a few examples of novels that are worth further attention on these grounds, but a full-blown discussion of the ontic relationships set up through recourse to nowhere in fantasy worlds is outside the scope of my investigation here.

Having mapped out conceptually the whereness of self-awareness, I now consider how this ontic structure works in relation to books that draw on nowhere topographies in their development of increasingly self-aware subjects. This apparent struggle to find a place in the world is mapped out in a number of novels wherein focal characters move to provincial or suburban areas that they identify as being *in the middle of nowhere*. This identification of a place as geographically insignificant typically reflects the subject's own sense of dislocation or ennui, but as I have started to establish, there is something deeper at work here than a figurative nod to developmental or liminal angst. For example, in Gillian Cross's *A Map of Nowhere* (1988) Nick's struggles with moral responsibility are intimately connected with the whereness of self-awareness. Searching for an address that will shape his encounter with nowhere, Nick describes the unfamiliar location as 'the end of everything' (9). Deep in the Fenlands that unsettle him, he will be forced to consider the conditions of his own humanity. A more recent example of nowhere topography is provided by *The Nowhere Girls* (2017), Amy Reed's challenge to a rape culture that can render girls invisible. Reed's polyphonic, political novel tells its story from a range of different perspectives, each mapped onto and realized through a shared space that 'doesn't know if it's a small town or a suburb' (15). Grace describes herself as being 'stuck in this purgatory between an unsatisfactory past and an unknown future' (15), while Rosina struggles to recognize herself in 'cookie-cutter houses' and streets that are not 'on the way to anywhere' (18). The novel works out its mighty challenge to the normalized practices of patriarchal abuse through its mapping of suburban nowhere, a space that eventually the girls locate, name and map for themselves as they come to terms with the whereness of self-awareness. Although nowhere is often dismissed as a site of insignificance at the outset of these novels, the embedded topography is such that it demands an encounter of ontological consequence – the characters come to understand what it might mean to be once they engage with an environment that does not look much like it matters.

The topographical expression of the whereness of self-awareness is poetically rendered in my final example, which floods its narrative with an oscillating expression of nowhere in relation to somewhere. I consider my reading of *Gaffer Samson's Luck* (1984) by Jill Paton Walsh as something of an intervention in a co-authored article by Gabrielle Cliff Hodges, Maria Nikolajeva and Liz Taylor: 'Three Walks Through Fictional Fens' (2010). Their paper is part of a wider research project on interdisciplinary approaches to place-related identities and I intervene in their discussion by offering a fourth 'walk through the fens', marking out the ontological trajectory between the opening and closing lines of the novel. My reading complements the attention they pay to the book's 'bundle' of space-time trajectories (2010: 191); James's ontological status as a character (198); and the parallels between the implied reader's and James's trajectory as he shifts from 'seeing the Fens as "nowhere" to seeing his attic room as "somewhere"' (201). My discussion focuses on the protagonist's journey to self-awareness, as he comes to terms with moving to the Fens and being nowhere as a result. From the first line, James is preoccupied with landscape and this concern soon develops into a heightened sensitivity to topography: '"We can't be nearly there", said James, from the back seat of the car. "Here isn't anywhere. It's been nowhere for miles!"' (Paton Walsh [1984] 1987: 7). Returning to Macfarlane's point about strong landscapes, it seems that James's refusal to recognize the whereness of the fen landscape renders it topographically weak. James does not see himself reflected in this place and so he refuses to recognize the whereness of the Fens, protesting that 'here isn't anywhere'. No matter that his parents quickly identify their location as Fenland between Peterborough and Cambridge (in the East of England), this place is empty of meaning for James and thus it must be nowhere in the Heideggerian terms of Da-sein: James *is not there*.

Although James considers his new 'maltings' home small in comparison with his old house in Yorkshire, he is immediately comfortable in the attic space his parents have chosen for him, identifying it as a familiar space of dwelling-within. He peers out at trees, 'tile and thatch and chimney-pots' and concedes that 'this looked like somewhere' (8). As soon as his gaze reaches beyond the vicinity of his home though, James is drawn back to 'nowhere again' (9). James's attempts to settle into himself and the local community are thwarted by his inability to map his location, or to understand the relationship between entities set within the vast flatness of the fenland vista. Watching a man and dog walking, he thinks that they are 'moving unnaturally slowly; then he realized that it just seemed slowly, with nothing anywhere near them to mark how far they had travelled' (17). The enormity of James's new horizon makes it difficult for him to conceptualize space and to plot himself in relation to it; James has lost touch with the instinctive sense of spatial awareness Schulman identifies as a primary cognitive function. His inability to measure his surroundings also has an impact on his sense of purpose and self-worth: 'He felt restless and pointless, as though he was somewhere he was just visiting, not somewhere he lived' (22). Consequently, even though James is able to recognize that his family home is somewhere, his own sense of whereness is depleted by the unmapped nowhere by which it is surrounded.

A number of Carroll's topoi are articulated through James's intense engagement with his local environment and the people he meets there, including the *sanctuary topos*, relating to domestic space and the *lapsed topos*, linked to archaeology and dilapidation in children's books. As established earlier, the sanctuary topos has echoes of Bachelard's dwelling-within, revealing the home as sanctified space. It is not surprising then that James finds an affinity between the comfort of his attic bedroom and Ely Cathedral,[25] which he visits with his parents soon after their arrival: 'someone had built something that would not shrink out of sight while still in your line of vision, even from far, far, across the shrinking and inhuman fen. James liked it, a lot' (31). James enjoys the fact that Ely 'answers flatness with height' (31) and thus the endless horizontal, which has been suffocating him, is lifted by the cathedral's verticality. As Carroll explains, 'The home shares in the physical and symbolic attributes of the sanctuary topos; it too is characterised by verticality, strict boundaries and an intense, interiorising central focus' ([2011] 2014: 19). Attic space and cathedral consequently reassure James that he will find a way of securing himself in these uncharted Fens; that it is possible to stand tall and be measured against a horizontal horizon. The sanctuary topos gives him hope, but it is in the lapsed topos that James eventually locates himself on ontic grounds.

James's efforts to build relationships with children at the local school are thwarted by extant playground factions, divided along fiat boundaries of 'village' and 'estate'. Although he lives within the boundaries of 'village' territory, James is denied access to the village gang on grounds of birthright. Subsequently, he is thrown into a friendship with Angie, another outsider due to her status as 'van dweller'. Part of James's journey to a fulfilling sense of whereness thus involves acceptance among the village children and his success in this is also dependent on bringing Angie with him into the village bounds. However, until James is able to map his environment in relation to whereness, he will not be able to claim identity as a villager – and self-awareness in the Fens will require a mapping of space in accordance with Carroll's lapsed topos.

The first and most successful friendship James forms in his new home is with Gaffer Samson, an elderly neighbour who (it can be inferred) is suffering from the final stages of cancer. Gaffer believes that he is being held to life by a talisman gifted him long ago and kept under the hearth of the cottage he occupied 'in time gone by' (Paton Walsh [1984] 1987: 44), so Gaffer sends James out to retrieve his 'luck'. Gaffer provides James with what seem to be simple directions, but when James struggles to locate the old cottage it becomes clear that he has misinterpreted Gaffer's map. James has failed to account for new developments in the village and realizes that he must reach into the past to bring whereness into focus. As it is, he searches fruitlessly for a cottage that no longer stands on the vertical plane it once occupied and pathetic fallacy reflects his mood: 'A vast sky overhead' and 'a vast land all around' make 'James dizzy' and 'the landscapes danced in space as he rode' (49). It is not until the Fenlands flood that the remains of Gaffer's cottage come into view, rising above the water on an island of lapsed sanctuary. Carroll's lapsed topos involves an archaeological recourse to the past, which opens up passages to 'those aspects of history that have been forgotten or overlooked' ([2011] 2014: 134). The past is denoted by the 'luck' which Jamie retrieves from the 'entangled edges' of forgotten floor tiles (Paton Walsh [1984] 1987: 83), preserved by a landscape that now gives itself up to Jamie.

The friendship between Gaffer and James reaches back into a forgotten history of place that will come to inform relationships with local children in the present. As Carroll goes on to explain, 'treasured objects carry a sense of heritage, that is, of social and symbolic value passed from one time into another through the medium of an object' ([2011] 2014: 135). Once James locates himself in the present via his tracking of Gaffer's luck (object) and his mapping of a historic sanctuary in a lapsed topos, he is finally accepted as a villager and comes to terms with the spatial vastness which has confounded him. James's narrative journey in the book is one of evolving self-awareness, forged through being in the Fens. If the opening sentence denies self and place, there is a telling shift in the closing lines as James is able to manage distance; he is able to locate himself and to see for himself a future in an embrace of childly might. James responds to his mother through a fog of satisfied exhaustion: 'And as though he were calling to her across a great distance, James answered … "It makes me think every minute will be my next!"' (Walsh [1984] 1987: 107). The negative structure of the opening lines now has the positive charge of a future in which James can 'be village' – a suitably vague fiat demarcation of ontological selfhood that brings James into Da-sein.

Characters find themselves in the middle of nowhere on a regular basis in children's literature – and to be nowhere frequently involves a degree of risk, caught up with the early ontic promise of dwelling-within. James puts himself at risk of drowning in a weir in order to come into being in the Fens, for else he is lost in a nowhere of unawareness. Close proximity to nowhere confirms that Da-sein encompasses death: '"Death" is encountered as a familiar event occurring within the world' (Heidegger [1927] 1996: 234), but the ontological manifestation of nowhere I have identified at work in children's literature is not an alternative way of thinking about death. Instead, nowhere has the ontological capacity to remind human being that to be is to encounter death. The metaphysical structure of nowhere in children's literature is as deep and broad as the regions I have traced in this chapter suggest. Via poetic reverie, nowhere provides ontic engagement with childhood dreams of dwelling-within, yet simultaneously invested in these nowhere encounters is the childly potential for being somewhere in the future. Nowhere conveys the ontological damage of belonging not where, while also opening up here-and-now visions of Erewhon. Nowhere extends its reach to the relatively inaccessible poles of being human, while taking seriously the mundane nowhere of an inward looking ontology that maps the whereness of self-awareness. Essentially, nowhere is an entity of ontological significance on its own terms, while also attesting to the conditions of being human.

5

Nothing Matters: Absent Imaginaries

I rolled and thumped and then I was just flying, feeling nothing above or below or to the sides of me and seeing nothing either, not even the square of light from the open trapdoor.

(Hartnett [2000] 2017: 191)

We set out upon our pursuit of being, and it seemed to us that the series of our questions had led us to the heart of being. But behold, at the moment when we thought we were arriving at the goal, a glance cast on the question itself has revealed to us suddenly that we were encompassed with nothingness.

(Sartre [1943] 2003: 29)

Ghosting

In *Thursday's Child* (2000) by Sonya Hartnett, Harper Flute discovers that nothing is all about her and that nothing has been beneath her always; or at least as far back as her 'eccentric' memory can reach (7). Subterranean tunnels have truly unearthed Harper and, in a similar moment of clarity, Sartre recognizes that nothing always hangs about being. Preparing to write this chapter, I reflected that each discussion in this book has edged a little closer to nothingness – but I was not quite right in this. Nothing has been here all along, for nothingness encompasses everything, as Hartnett and Sartre reveal. Nothing hangs in the ghostly otherness of ontological exchange; it lurks at the back of Puff's cave; it lingers in the absence of lost words in the wilderness; it ripples through the frozen thaw of a waterfall to nowhere. And yet, I have not dealt directly with nothing, just as Harper has not discovered the full extent of her brother's subterranean tunnels – and perhaps she never will: 'If Tin steps one day from the earth dusty, blinking his pale clear eyes, I will be the first thing he will see. His hand will be dirty when he places it in mine, and mine will not be clean' (219). Harper's account of existence on Australian farmland during the Great Depression is full of holes, which begin and end with Tin's burrowed network of tunnels.

Harper recounts that 'Tin's bound up in childhood forever, as far as my recollection goes, although the last time I saw him he was wizened and looking ancient as the hills' (7). Tin consequently becomes a cipher through which Harper can start to make sense of the nothingness that comprises her experience of being in the world and in order that she can relinquish the past and move into her future. There is something of the *puer aeternus* about Tin, though he only remains a boy from Harper's perspective – in real terms he has grown into his future ahead of time. Indeed, Tin represents a point of oscillation between *puer aeternus* and *puer existens*, concepts elucidated by Beauvais in *The Mighty Child*. Via a discussion of *The Little Prince*, Beauvais traces the shift from a Romantic *puer aeternus*, in which the child is immobilized by 'nostalgic recollections of the past', to *puer existens*, whereby the child of contemporary children's literature is 'ineluctably thrown forth, thrown into existence' (Beauvais 2015: 20). Tin is thrown into existence by the dirt that houses him and, in taking Tin's dirty hand in hers, Harper shares in the potential wrought by his actions. In the possibility of Tin continually foraging catacombs between being and nothing is also reflected Bachelard's 'antecedence of being', which he locates in childhood reverie: 'Thus we believe that one can know states which are ontologically below being and above nothingness' (Bachelard [1960] 1971: 111). Tin represents the ontic potential of childhood to which we have lifelong access through poetic reverie, a potential that is not trapped in *puer aeternus*. Furthermore, in Tin's incessant tunnelling – which spatially and temporally moves in all directions – can be found confirmation of Sartre's discovery that 'The permanent possibility of non-being, outside us and within, conditions our questions about being' (29). In the poetic power of its honeycomb structure, *Thursday's Child* provides childly images of the nothingness on which being is contingent.

Thursday's Child is a strong example of an entrenched nothingness at the core of children's literature. Hartnett's novel is strong in Macfarlane's sense of a *strong landscape* that knows something of us and we of it, so its unconventional approach to absence reveals something and nothing of human being as a result. In this chapter, I identify nothingness in the metaphysical groundwork of children's literature through the lens of two ubiquitous tropes: absent parents and imaginary friends. I suggest that conventional properties of the field can push beyond genre, indicating a fundamental metaphysical commitment to the nature of reality. It is true that missing parents of children's books can be incidental, with their withdrawal from narrative serving plot or character development – for example, a good number of Enid Blyton adventures hold parents in the margins in this way. However, absent parents frequently throw up a palpable absence with ontic value for the becoming-child. Drawing on a variant range of parental absence – as played out in Roald Dahl's *James and the Giant Peach* (1961), *Annelie in the Depths of the Night* (1987) by Imme Dros or Cynthia Voigt's *Homecoming* (1981) – I explore the metaphysical implications of this pervasive void. Imaginary friendships have a particular psycho-emotional function in children's books, but they also point to an ongoing concern with the ontological status of fictional objects and *qualia* in children's literature. Considering books that determine imaginary relationships in different ways – *Imaginary Fred* (2015) by Eoin Colfer and Oliver Jeffers, or *The Bone Sparrow* (2016) by Zana Fraillon – I uncover the metaphysical impact of the non-existent on human experiences of the external world.

Poverty of the Great Depression is all encompassing in *Thursday's Child* and this socio-historic context signals a Marxist concern with material deprivation; on (at least) one level this is a book about the consequences of having nothing. However, Hartnett's surreal tale of a boy born to dig reveals that *not having* is inextricably related to *not being* and these values can be seen in existential as well as ideological terms. As Sartre points out, ' "Having," "doing," and "being" are the cardinal categories of human reality. Under them are subsumed all types of human conduct' (Sartre [1943] 2003: 453). Indeed, the novel's political interests are embedded in ontological foundations that detail the conditions of being in the midst of nothing – and consequently it establishes a nothingness that is complex and multifaceted in its relation to human reality. Childness at work in *Thursday's Child* also associates parental absence with a Sartrean 'origin of nothingness,'[1] such that missing parents instigate questions about being in the world and can be understood as a figurative aspect of the book's ontological project. Beauvais's existentialist consideration of the 'questions of *time* and *otherness* which subsume the adult-child relationship' (Beauvais 2015: 5) reveals that such an approach puts pressure on ambiguities and gaps at work in this relationship. Beauvais points to acts of the imagination that reveal nothingness as a pervasive condition of being and observes that temporal tensions between adulthood and childhood stimulate this imaginative process:

> The imagination is one of the ways through which, in existentialist terms, we can detect that our consciousness is spangled with absences; or, more accurately, that anything present can be layered over with something absent, thereby demonstrating the presence of absence in existence.
>
> (88)

In this sense then, absent parents can be considered an imaginative act of children's literature, which is bound up in the child–adult exchange at the heart of its childness. As in the case of *Thursday's Child*, parents can be absent even while they are in the proximity of the child – they need not be dead or geographically remote in order for their absence to be imaginatively enacted. As Sartre would have it, 'Nothingness can be nihilated only on the foundation of being; if nothingness can be given, it is neither before nor after being, nor in the general way outside of being' (Sartre [1943] 2003: 45). For Sartre, nothingness digs away at being from within and yet its origin is not in being. This question of the origin of negation clings to being, while not being of it, and in the same way absent parents permeate childness (at work in children's literature), while not being of it. Sartre indulges in a simile that would not be out of place in *Thursday's Child*, given its figurative commitment to a subterranean excavation of being: 'Nothingness lies coiled in the heart of being – like a worm' (45).

Thursday's Child begins with a birth that is really a death and a death that is really a birth – hence existence and negation are entwined from the outset in the context of child–parent relations. On the day of Caffy's birth, 9-year-old Harper has been charged with taking care of her younger brother Tin and (in any case) Harper is keen to escape the 'dangerous' proximity of childbirth in the confines of their shanty: 'They either came and stayed, or came and didn't. Only a baby, but everything seemed dismaying somehow, everyone was so grim. I didn't want to be anywhere near the place' (Hartnett [2000] 2017: 10). As Harper's disquiet suggests, birth is as close to death as it is to life and there is no easy celebration to accompany Caffy's arrival. In an effort to escape the perceived grimness of birth, Harper takes 4-year-old Tin to the local creek, which 'was running high because of all the rain and the bank was soft and oozy' (11). Almost inevitably, given the figurative framing and narrative foreshadowing of the event, a landslide buries Tin and Harper runs home to her father and older brother Devon for help, expecting Tin to be suffocated after an hour in the 'freezing mire' (16). Much to Harper's astonishment though, a natural cave formed of tree roots has preserved Tin, allowing him to dig 'his own way out' (18). In this moment, Harper witnesses an act of coming into being that remains a lifelong puzzle to her.

Tin has excavated for himself a pocket of existence – a womb of sorts – and thereby he has (apparently) brought himself back into being. As Sartre points out, however, when grappling with the origins of being in a refusal of theological creationism: 'we need not conclude that being creates itself, which would suppose that it is prior to itself. Being can not be in *causa sui* in the manner of consciousness. Being *is itself*' (Sartre [1943] 2003: 20). Sartre deals with the paradox of a being that is neither uncreated (in its refusal of passive creation) nor self-generating. There is a tension here that renders Tin simultaneously the saved child (by tree roots) and the surviving child (by digging), a contradiction that upholds Sartre's observation that being 'is neither passivity nor activity' (20). The phenomenon of Tin's existence and his subsequent commitment to digging tunnels beneath (and beyond) the family home can thus be considered a surreal manifestation of existential being, to which parent–child relations add a further layer of metaphysical complexity.

Tin's struggle for survival in the mud is set against Caffy's entry into the world, which is also presented as a fight for survival in the milieu of material hardship. In a misguided attempt to take control of a situation that is beyond his means – materially and ontologically – Harper's father assumes responsibility for the parallel struggles of his offspring. As they strive to recover Tin from the mud, Da hisses out a plea: 'He was saying, "Take the new one instead. Take the new one instead"' (16). This soon to be forgotten pact has the ring of imprudent fairy-tale oaths and – in keeping with this surreal meditation on the privations of being – the exchange is revisited once the immediate threat to the children's life is averted. The aftershock of this desperate entreaty confirms that Court (Harper's father) has overreached paternal authority and taken responsibility for beings that are not his to claim. Notwithstanding, Harper's childly intuition recognizes that Caffy can be more easily dispensed with than Tin, as he is not yet a known entity and her father cannot bear to lose an already beloved child. Gazing on 'Caffy's frightful newborn' face, she reflects that 'It must be terrible … to be such a nothing that you could be bargained away' (19). As indicated by her meditative autodiegetic narration, Harper has internalized an aetonormative view of the world in which adults (and in this case her father) have the ability to dictate the conditions of a child's existence and to interfere in the process of becoming-child. Harper confides that 'it relieved me knowing he hadn't offered to exchange Devon or Audrey or myself, either' (Hartnett [2000] 2017: 19) – and it is a confidence designed to unsettle the parental authority on which it rests.

Just as Tin's excavations destabilize the material underpinning of the Flutes' timber shanty, so Court's misguided and desperate attempts to take care of his family result in existential crisis – and (quite literally) catastrophe opens the earth beneath them. Parental withdrawal is anticipated in the collapse of the family home, as it gives way to the network of tunnels beneath it: 'the roof of the house tore through the centre and the room where we slept and ate and did most of our living vanished – vanished as if the earth had eaten it and the planks that went flinging were like spitting out the bones' (87). The protective covering of Bachelard's dwelling-within is ripped away, and the roof becomes a force for ruin such that the metaphysical security of the house as a condition of being is overwhelmed by nothingness and it doubly vanishes; their home ceases to exist as material object and its destruction has implications for the circumstances of human being. Figuratively correlate with human bones, the broken timbers of the shanty emphasize the relationship between home and human being and hint at loss still to come. In a landscape saturated with insufficiency, Court was never in a position to protect his family and politically the narrative has sympathy for a man negated by his own father and a country that sent him to war. The existential thrust of this children's book demands his absence though, for Harper must realize the loneliness of her condition before she comes into being for herself. Indeed, Court's destructive inability to cope with the collapse of his home means that he can no longer care for his family. Harper marks her father's absence from this moment, as he succumbs to alcoholism and relies on others to rebuild his home: 'The shanty had fallen and Da was different; I still loved him, but he wasn't the Da from before' (135). Harper looks for her father where once he was and finds that he is no longer there and this absence of the looked for (expected) father colours Harper's experience of the Sartrean 'ground' on which Court once stood.

Harper's experience of non-being in respect of Court's absence – for after all her father still lives – can be explained by a Sartrean thought experiment around a failed meeting in a café and the conditions of expectation. Sartre runs late for a scheduled meeting with his friend Pierre, who is no longer at the café when Sartre arrives. Sartre looks around the café (the ground) searching for a figure he expects to see and everything else in the café – a person, a table, a chair – melts into the ground of nothingness (Sartre [1943] 2003: 34). These objects are negated by the fact that they are not the looked for figure – they are not Pierre – and thus they are part of a ground of Sartrean nihilation. A reflection on the conditions of Pierre's absence ensues, after which Sartre eventually concludes that Pierre's absence is not simply a thought, or a 'negative judgement' as Sartre puts it: 'non-being does not come to things by a negative judgement' (35). Harper's sense of her father's absence in this passage is quite different from observing that Tin is not to be found in this moment, for she was not specifically looking for Tin. Sartre explains that 'I myself expected to see Pierre, and my expectation has caused the absence of Pierre to *happen* as a real event' (34). Following this reasoning, Court's non-being is not the consequence of Harper's 'negative judgement' (something she thought) about her father; rather the negative judgement 'is supported and conditioned by non-being' (35). While searching for her absent father, Harper negates everything that is not the father she expected to see – including the newly diminished father she sees before her. Being is still an aspect of Court's existence, but the father Harper looks for slips away. This absent father haunts the father she sees before her – thus Harper's being-child emerges out of the absence that is nothingness, even as she moves beyond this moment.

Sartre actually expresses Pierre's absence from the café in terms of haunting, a concept Harper draws on to capture her mother's nihilation after Caffy's demise. The tragedy unfolds as an inexorable echo of previous events, as Harper is once again charged with the care of an infant and the conditions of Court's earlier bargain are replicated. While playing hide and seek with Harper, Caffy falls into a hole left by a well-sinker in their father's employ: 'Mam was going to murder me and all my trying was useless, just as it had been when Tin was smothered in the mud' (Hartnett [2000] 2017: 127). Tin is called upon to retrieve Caffy from the abortive well, but his efforts are in vain and he surfaces from underground, 'wanly luminous, cradling a dusk-blue bundle' (134). Tin is barely present, as if diminished by his father's unauthorized pact and his mother's retreat into an irretrievable absence. Almost suffocating herself with guilt, Harper craves her mother's reassurance, but the mother she expected is no longer there: 'Ghosting, she became ghostly: when I reached for her she could not take my hand because she was no longer able to touch' (129). In this moment then, Harper must confront an ontological truth – which performs as her mother's absence – as well as come to terms with the circumstances of her brother's death. She is left to take on a responsibility that her parents have relinquished: 'My mother and father had held up the sky, the sun, the stars and the moon, but they didn't any more' (135).

Just as Sartre wonders about the relations between 'being and that non-being that haunts it' (Sartre [1943] 2003: 36), it seems that Harper's narration is destined to take the weight of a reflection on existence burdened with nothingness – but she is only free to take this direction in the (effective) absence of her parents. Harper is left to coax life out of an endless landscape that bores her to the point of suffocation, so that she howls along with the dogs, 'doing all this just to get some commotion into my existence, some reaction to my being alive' (Hartnett [2000] 2017: 179). In action Harper comes into being, and yet it is only through the process of reflecting on her plane of activity – and we learn that she becomes a writer – that absence and presence are brought into a clear relationship with each other. Sartre establishes the temporal tensions implicit in writing a book, as follows:

> It is necessary that in the very constitution of the book as my possibility, I apprehend my freedom as being the possible destroyer in the present and in the future of what I am. That is, I must place myself on the plane of reflection. So long as I remain on the plane of action, the book to be written is only the distant and presupposed meaning of the act which reveals my possibilities to me.
>
> ([1943] 2003: 61)

Sartre's observations are well-attuned to the mighty potential of Harper's position as a child participant in the action of her story and her simultaneous role as a narrator who is able to reveal her possibilities to herself. Harper remains in possession of a childness that allows her to reflect and to call into being the parents whose absence allowed her to *apprehend her freedom*: 'It has been a long time since I've seen either of them, Mam or Da. It has been years. If not for the tiny brown pictures that I've closed inside my locket, I would have forgotten the look of their faces' (218).

Perceived through an existential lens it is clear that parental absence is an ontic condition of being-child. However, while I deploy an existential apparatus at work here, I am not suggesting that absent parents of children's literature necessarily function in existential terms, nor that the books in which they appear should be categorized as existential. It is more the case that a Sartrean reading of *Thursday's Child* underscores the ontic potential of absentee parents as metaphysical groundwork in children's literature, while also throwing up a theoretical framework for considering further examples of parents in absentia. Standing in distinction to Hartnett's *parental ghosting*, Roald Dahl delivers an efficient and darkly comic moment of *parental dispatch* in *James and the Giant Peach* (1961). Having established that James lives happily with his parents in the first paragraph, the second paragraph (almost) callously dispenses with mother and father: 'Both of them suddenly got eaten up (in full daylight, mind you, and on a crowded street) by an enormous angry rhinoceros which had escaped from the London Zoo' (Dahl [1961] 1973: 7). I point up the contrast here to stress that the process of ghosting in *Thursday's Child* is gradual, allowing for a poetic contemplation of the conditions of freedom. Sartre observes that 'Anguish … is the reflective apprehension of freedom by itself' ([1943] 2003: 63) and the extended duration of Hartnett's ghosting permits this sort of reflective anguish. In comparison, Dahl's passage is marked by the swift deployment of its parental dispatch, whereby James's parents are not allowed a sustained or active presence in the narrative. They are extinguished by an event that is as ludicrously improbable as it is sudden, thereby drawing ironic attention to its role in the conventional structure of children's literature. Indeed, a satiric tradition of such parental dispatch has developed in children's literature – perhaps the most protracted example being Lemony Snicket's *A Series of Unfortunate Events* (1999–2006). This does not mean, however, that there is no ontic potential in the hyperbole of Dahl's parental dispatch.

Convention has a role to play in this opening event that is not simply a function of plot or genre, for there is also ontic value in its iterative structure – and the heterodiegetic narration makes the most of this. Having dispatched James's parents, Dahl's obtrusive narrator doubles down on the event, making sure that the narratee has absorbed its implications:

> Now this, as you can well imagine, was a rather nasty experience for two such gentle parents. But in the long run it was far nastier for James than it was for them. *Their* troubles were all over in a jiffy. They were dead and gone in thirty-five seconds flat. Poor James, on the other hand, was still very much alive, and all at once he found himself alone and frightened in a vast unfriendly world.
>
> ([1961] 1973: 7)

The narrator asks the reader to reimagine the parents' death, because (evidently) this is an event that requires close attention. The event is short-lived at the level of narrative duration – and the brevity of death pangs, at thirty-five seconds flat, is also accounted for with comic precision – but the absence procured by parental demise has consequences that reach to the end of the book. Italicization of *their* troubles draws attention to the fact that parental troubles are of a different order from those still to be experienced by James. Mother and father are located in the past and the event of their death is time-limited – *they no longer are*. The temporal conditions of child experience are thereby brought into focus, since James has an immeasurable future before him in which *he found himself alone*. The absence so central to this passage is not related to the parents as beings who once were, since it is not for them to experience; their absence is thrown up in James as a result of their non-being. Parental absence is therefore a nihilation with which James is confronted as a facet of being very much alive. Moreover, it is an absence that endures into the future of a narrative still to unfold. The enduring nature of the absence with which James must contend thus takes on the ontic aloneness that Harper comes upon more gradually. Even though the agonies of James's being in the world are now and yet to come, he (and the narratee) is confronted with a long future in which to reflect on Sartrean anguish. As this focus on the temporal exchange of character experience and the duration of narrative structure confirms, the convention of absence with which Dahl plays has an ontological remit into which James is drawn.

Having dispensed with parents quickly, the narrative then endures James's miserable anguish at some length. He is 'overwhelmed by his own unhappiness' and 'great tears began oozing out of James's eyes' (12). This can be read at empathetic levels of identification and in terms of character development – plus the sentimentalization of James's distress could be considered manipulative in terms of reader positioning. However, the possessive stress on *his own* unhappiness is interesting in light of the (already established) ontic structure of absence. Given the oozing tears we can be in no doubt that it is James who is unhappy, so the possessive emphasis is not just a case of identification; something more is at work here at the level of existential anguish. The unhappiness belongs to James because it testifies to his condition of being human. The extended endurance of this unhappiness is once again treated with hyperbolic excess after James drops the magic bag of marvellous potential: 'All hope of a happier life had gone completely now. Today and tomorrow and the next day and all the other days as well would be nothing but punishment and pain, unhappiness and despair' (18). The thrownness of Beauvais's mighty child is stressed here as the futurity of nothingness threatens to overwhelm James (in his own unhappiness). I own to labouring this particular point, but it is important to establish that convention can work just as hard and deeply in popular, nimble fiction as it can in more poetic literature.

While James is not left in a state of abject misery for the duration of the book, absence marks his existence and readies him for the being with others he has longed for, a readiness that initiates his meeting with the old man in the green suit. When James asks what the green things are and where they come from, the man leans so close to James that 'the tip of his long nose was actually touching the skin on James's forehead' (14), implying that the answer lies within James. He might not have a scar on his forehead, but in common with Harry Potter,[2] parental absence identifies James as a being of significance. Consequently, the man insists that James must take the bag: ' "Here! You take it! It's yours!" ' (15). The bag is intended for James, but as consideration of ontological exchange has already confirmed, if it is for himself it is also for others. I still recall the horror I felt as a child when I read of James dropping that bag, for it seemed to me a calamitous moment of bad luck. Yet James had to drop the green things in order for them to dig down into the earth and open up the grounds of his existence to others – and though my child self could not have explained this at the time, I did come to recognize the necessity of that split bag. As Sartre points out, 'I need the

Other in order to realize fully all the structures of my being. The For-itself refers to the For-others' (Sartre [1943] 2003: 246) and this condition of being for self and others is going to be tested once James makes contact with the peach and its inhabitants. As James scrabbles in the earth for the burrowing green things he wonders what they were after, for 'there was nothing down *there*. Nothing except the roots of the old peach tree' (Dahl 1973: 17). In this moment, James glimpses the antecedence of being in Bachelard's terms – ontologically located between nothing and being. In the process of becoming child he identifies *nothing except something* in the earth beneath him and just as the green things dig down into the earth, so (like Tin) James will tunnel into the peach in order to reach a plane of being that allows him to move forward in his state of absence.

Parental absence presents in many ways in children's books and, although it is not the project of this chapter to identify each of these manifestations, it is the ontic structure that moves between different types of absence that interests me. In *Thursday's Child* and *James and the Giant Peach* absence is configured as an aspect of the child's ontological condition of being thrown forth. Although the parents in each case withdraw from their children's lives in different ways, their absence has an ontic value for becoming-child. These absent parents are no longer acting in accordance with being – they do not do parenting – and therefore they are not configured in the human reality of Sartre's cardinal categories. In their place is an absence to be taken forward in freedom by their children, in order that they can have, be and do in the future. This ontic structure of absence is true of all the examples I have considered. However, it is important to acknowledge that parental absence is not always marked by a precipitating event; and when no such event occurs, something else takes its place that has a bearing on child–adult relations, adding another aspect to the conditions of parental absence in children's literature.

Thursday's Child and *James and the Giant Peach* exhibit different modes of absence in their presentation of parental ghosting and parental dispatch, but each of these modes is demarcated by an event of some narrative significance. In *Annelie in the Depths of the Night* by Imme Dros, parents go missing in the elliptical region of aetonormative evasion. The novel relies on an aetonormative positioning of child and adult, whereby adults maintain control of the child through concealment; for Grandmother and parents know more than their young daughter about why she has been left with Grandma. Annelie is forced to glean information about her situation from *things not said* and thus she is surrounded by a nothingness triggered by the withdrawal of authoritative speech acts. It is evident that Annelie is a young child who has been sent away from her parents to stay with Grandma, but she does not know why: 'Grandma often doesn't answer when you ask her things. Or else she gives you an answer that is no use at all' (2). Immediately it is clear that something is being kept from Annelie and that she has become conditioned to the evasive practices of the adults in her life. When Annelie asks when her Daddy and Mummy will be coming, Grandma responds with: '"Oh, child, they may be quite a while"' (Dros [1987] 1991: 3). Annelie grapples with a *vague absence* that withdraws her parents from being-present, and positions them simultaneously in the past and a non-specific future – her parents used to be here and they might be again, but they are not here now. Memory confirms that Annelie's parents once existed: 'Daddy had brought her without any warning one day, in his green car full to bursting with toys and clothes' (3). *Without any warning* opens another negative space in the narrative, widening the gap between adult and child experience and inviting the child to act on it and make meaning from it. Annelie asks her father how long she is to stay with Grandma, but: 'Daddy didn't say. Daddy often doesn't answer either when you ask him things, or else he gives you an answer that is no use at all' (3). There is a rhythmic pattern to Annelie's request for information about her parents' whereabouts in the narrative, and in the iterative structure of vague absence, Annelie is confronted with the enormity of being alone.

Annelie in the Depths of the Night performs mostly as a dreamscape and Annelie's dreams – that soon drift into nightmares – seem to be precipitated by the vague absence of her parents. When Annelie becomes ill, her father arrives briefly to nurse her and when eventually she ends up in hospital, her missing mother appears and promises to visit her daughter periodically. Still no explanation is provided as to why Annelie cannot live with her parents and what keeps them from her. Of course, such an intensely symbolic narrative could be read in psychoanalytic terms, but the ontic value of the parents' vague absence is in danger of being obscured by such an interpretation. While engaging with Freudian and Jungian theory in *The Practice of Everyday Life*, Certeau also offers a way of moving past psychoanalysis into a cultural space of operation where everyday people act (through walking or speaking). He pauses (very briefly) to consider childhood culture and an observation he makes about 'voices of the body' allows me to build a related point about the ontological relevance of the withdrawal of authoritative speech acts in Dros's novel (and in other instances of vague absence).

Certeau establishes that bodies have a way of sounding out through cultural practices and draws on a range of examples from opera through to nursery rhymes, such as 'Hickory, dickory, dock' (Certeau [1980] 1988: 163). He argues that the social body 'speaks' in quotations and sentence fragments and in those fragments we can recognize (for example) parents' words and respond to the sounds things make. He goes on to observe: 'Through the legends and phantoms whose audible citations continue to haunt everyday life, one can maintain a tradition of the body, which is heard but not seen' (163). Annelie's everyday life is indeed haunted by the vague absence of her parents and the novel is full of songs and remembered phrases that *vocalize the parent body*. Combining this notion of a vocal, bodily haunting with an absence that Annelie takes on, I suggest that vague absence is marked aurally in the narrative by a vocalized body, rather than a precipitating event. In this way, Annelie's coming into being is manifest in her own responses to the *heard in absence* parent body. Authority is maintained in the aetonormative positioning of vague absence, yet Annelie's tendency to quote and respond to those voices represents a questioning of that authority. On these terms, a move is made into mighty childhood that has the potential to liberate itself from the authority that threatened to hold it back. Certeau also provides a relevant postscript to this, which threads back to written communications of children's literature: 'On the written page, there … appears a smudge – like the scribbling of a child on the book which is the local authority' (154). Thus, it seems that while vague absence manifests as a vocalized body of authority, the mighty child is positioned to answer back through retorts – equivalent to scribbles in the margins of authoritative texts – as it comes into being.

Although the context is quite different, a similar absence of information surrounds the disappearance of the Tillerman children's mother in Voigt's *Homecoming*. The novel opens just after Momma has left Dicey and her three younger siblings in a parking lot, vanishing without explanation; indeed, the children are not certain that they have been abandoned and wait overnight in the car for their mother to return. Dicey has been uneasy about her mother's behaviour leading up to the moment of abandonment:

> Sometimes she'd be gone for a couple of hours and then she wouldn't say where she had been, with her face blank as if she couldn't say. As if she didn't know. Momma didn't talk to them anymore, not even to scold, or sing, or make up games the way she used to.
>
> (Voigt 1981: 5)

Encoded in Dicey's attempts to piece together her mother's vague absence with which she must deal are the haunting, audible fragments of the Certeau's body *heard in absence*. Although their mother no longer sings to them, the children sing to each other and quote her into their own frame of reference. Throughout the Tillermans' long journey to find a home that functions as a dwelling-within, snippets of songs from their mother allow them to bring this vague absence into focus. In this way they shape a future in which they can come into being and the grandmother they never knew they had observes: '"I'll give you this much ... Your momma taught you how to sing"' (353). This vocalizing of the parent body can be seen at work in a number of books for young people that draw on aural bodies as they give ontic expression to vague absences. In *Crossover* (2014) by Kwame Alexander and *Another Brooklyn* (2016) by Woodson, parental absence is rendered vague by narrative structures that anticipate it long before it arrives. In both cases solid-body fragments of musical refrain weave through the temporal conditions of being human, as revealed in their opening lines: 'I'm not that big on jazz music, but Dad is' (Alexander [2014] 2015: 6); and 'For a long time, my mother wasn't dead yet. ... If we had had Jazz, would we have survived differently?' (Woodson [2016] 2017: 1).

So copious and profound are the absences left by parents in children's literature that I do not claim a comprehensive assessment of them in metaphysical terms. However, the instances of *parental ghosting*, *parental dispatch* and *vague absence* explored here provide an ontic structure through which to consider parental absence in the wider field of children's literature. Absence functions beyond the moment of loss and has an ontic function in the future-facing potential of becoming-child. In an exchange of authority for might, the child can also be seen to speak for itself, through a process in which bodies are mightily vocalized. As Auggie, Woodson's narrator, proclaims: 'I had wanted this – to step outside of Brooklyn on my own, no past, just the now and the future' ([2016] 2017: 159).

Oscillating ontologies

> The reverie which the writer leads in real life has all the oscillations of childhood reveries between the real and the unreal, between real life and imaginary life.
> (Bachelard [1960] 1971: 123)

Bachelard's investment in the poetics of childhood reverie allows for oscillation between real and imagined worlds in which oneiric houses and playmates come into being; through reverie such structures of being 'live again' (123). Oscillations reverberate through children's literature in a system of ontological connectivity between the real and unreal, so that plateaus of being materialize across the field. Rather than locating these oscillations in one book, genre or period they can be conceived in terms of Deleuze and Guattari's plateaus, whereby any multiplicity can be connected to other multiplicities by a rhizomorphic system of extension and correlation (Deleuze and Guattari [1980] 2013: 23). These metaphors of oscillation and rhizomorphic plateaus are useful as they suggest spatial and temporal movement in different directions. Thinking specifically about the relationship between the real and unreal in tales of imaginary beings or friendships, such oscillating movements across plateaus emphasize that no commitment need be made one way or the other to the real or unreal – spaces between the real and unreal can be opened up and explored. Indeed, although imaginary friendships manifest differently across children's books, in all cases I have come across the oscillating aspect of the real:unreal ratio is maintained. That is, the ontological status of the real and unreal remains open (to oscillation) and ontic questions remain unresolved. For example, there is no certainty surrounding the ontological status of Titus Oates in *The White Darkness*,[3] who (perhaps unexpectedly) speaks again to Sym on her journey home from Antarctica, when she seems to have come to terms with grief via her nowhere encounter: 'Oh, Titus! It's so good to see you. So unbelievably good. Thank you' (McCaughrean 2006: 258). I am not suggesting that Titus suddenly returns to a live human state in the same ontological position as Sym. Nonetheless, questions are raised as to Titus's status as a non-being arising in the world as a result of Sym's human intervention. Human being brings nothingness into being and thus Titus seems to exist. Furthermore, in the final sequence of *The Bear* (1994) by Raymond Briggs, the bear appears to swim out of Tilly's psychological landscape and into icy waters of a (potentially) real external world and it is no longer clear whether or not the little girl has imagined him. In both cases, a rupture between the real and unreal is opened by intense imaginary friendships that is not stitched up by the narrative. An obvious difference between these two examples is that one is taken from a prose novel for young adults and the other from a hybrid visual text for younger readers. Authors exploring the conditions of reality through imaginary friendships regularly exploit the formal complexity of children's literature, so – in order that I can consider the ontic play of these formal conditions – my discussion in this section focuses on a prose novel and a picturebook: Fraillon's *The Bone Sparrow* and *Imaginary Fred* by Colfer and Jeffers.

The Bone Sparrow is committed to an oscillation between the real and unreal and to a metaphysical groundwork that sends out rhizomes into several other areas of discussion in this book. Fraillon's poetically and politically complex novel about the (im)possibility of life in detention centres and refugee camps revisits the Quinean territory of fictional realism previously encountered in baby catalogues; swims aquatic life through the biotic communities of Coccia's immersion; and reverberates with an ontic absence that brings imaginary friendships into play. These metaphysical shoots are obviously interconnected, though in this section they grow up through my consideration of Subhi's relationship with an imaginary ocean and a Shakespeare duck. I draw on David Chalmers's exploration of consciousness in *The Conscious Mind* (1996) and Anthony Everett's challenge to fictional realism in *The Nonexistant* (2013), while demonstrating *The Bone Sparrow*'s openness to performing long-standing metaphysical disputes around the nature of mind and body and to exploring the ontology of fictional entities.

Born to life in a detention camp, which he has never left, Subhi relies on his imagination to move beyond the confines of Family Tent Three. From the opening line of the book it is clear that Subhi's response to his confinement is transformative: 'Sometimes, at night, the dirt outside turns into a beautiful ocean. As red as the sun and as deep as the sky' (Fraillon 2016: 3). Through this figurative resourcefulness, Subhi extends the boundaries of his reality; he has only ever seen pictures of the ocean, but because he has seen the sun and sky, he is able to bring the ocean into being through simile.[4] Of course what I am describing here are the literary tools used to create fictional worlds in general, but these imaginative tools serve as metaphysical apparatus through which Subhi brings the world into being in the process of becoming-child. My concern here is to establish some of the ontological possibilities and conditions of Subhi's relationship with the real and unreal and to explore the ontic conditions of the imaginary and real friendships he cultivates. Rather than engaging fully with psychological behaviourism or the political concerns of the narrative and its characters, my reading focuses on the phenomenological implications of Subhi's consciousness. Subhi's imaginative response to his world is constantly challenged by his sister Queeny who is sceptical about any level of reality beyond the concrete: 'Queeny says I'm stupid, saying that kind of stuff. But it's true. She just doesn't see it, is all' (3). Subhi contests Queeny's denial of his ocean on the phenomenological grounds of perception. In Subhi's view, Queeny cannot see the thing (in this case an ocean full of sea creatures) that he sees and, therefore, he concludes that her deductions about the nature of reality are wrong. I will return to the metaphysical conditions of Subhi's ocean and his view of it in due course. For now though, I want to establish that the oppositional stance of their sibling relationship serves as a narrative vehicle to consider different levels of reality in the novel. Therefore, I start by outlining the metaphysical remit of each of their responses to the conditions of reality.

Queeny refuses Subhi's ocean, full of 'animals that have swum all the way up to the tent, their faces pushing against the flaps, trying to get a look at us inside on our beds' (3), principally because incarceration has dispossessed her of access to the ocean and imagining it is not going to bring her any closer to it in real terms. Queeny's politics shape her view of reality and, furthermore, she uses her investment in the physical world to promote her ideological argument that the camp detainees have been deprived of things in the world to which they are entitled. Consequently, it is not only an imagined ocean that Queeny takes issue with: 'Queeny says they aren't real beds, but just old army cots and even older army blankets. Queeny says that a real bed is made with springs and cushions and feathers, and that real blankets don't itch' (3). Queeny challenges the surface logic of statements on material grounds, investing in a materialism that does not allow cots to be beds, or for Subhi's imagined ocean. Queeny wants to matter in the world and for this reason she searches out the material circumstances of her reality. This extends to taking photographs of conditions inside the camp so that 'the people out there will remember us. Soon they'll see that living in here isn't living at all' (106). The fact that Queeny's view is revealed as a politicization of reality – however valid in terms of the book's ethical remit – suggests that it is only one way of *viewing* the experiential world and (potentially) just as removed from reality as Subhi's imaginings. Queeny also dismisses Subhi's ocean on the grounds of his immaturity, asking him when he is going to grow up (4). Here Queeny invests in the idea that Subhi's recourse to a rich imaginative life can be explained and dismissed on developmental grounds. Queeny is able to reject Subhi's version of reality, because (in her view) he will grow out of it when he matures. However, the privileged position of Subhi's autodiegetic narration suggests that there is more to Subhi's version of reality than can be explained away by immaturity; that is, the narrative position immediately presents Queeny's stance as questionable.

The poetic resilience of Subhi's ocean throughout the novel indicates something more durable than the 'childish'[5] and time-limited psychological response to deprived circumstances attributed to his behaviour by Queeny. Indeed, Subhi's recourse to poetic images demonstrates openness to Bachelard's childhood reverie of the sort that extends beyond the physical conditions of childhood. These are the poetic images that seed worlds, taking their place in a phenomenological system of metaphysics, which allows Subhi to create a life-world for himself and those around him (at least those willing to accept his view of reality). When Eli, his best friend in the camp, is brutally killed by a 'Jacket' (a camp warden), Subhi draws on these imaginative resources and brings Eli's love of whales into the world he creates: 'And there he is, the whale, looking just the way Eli said. As big as a country and as beautiful as anything' (205). Certainly we are invited to consider this whale as a psychosomatic response to Subhi's feelings of loss and guilt, for this whale has access to Subhi's mind: 'Eli's whale sees inside my head and reads through my memories. A tear, deep and dark red like the Night Sea, swells in the whale's eye and rolls down his cheek and disappears into the water' (206). However, the manifestation of Eli's whale is not only a matter of psychological projection, for by this stage in the novel Fraillon has established ontic resonance for the phenomenological apparatus of Subhi's imagined ocean-world. Subhi's ocean is part of his ontological structure as a human being and thus poetic reverie feeds into becoming-child.

Subhi's willingness to invest in imagined entities lays the foundations for his relationship with a rubber duck, which he claims as his own after Harvey, one of the more caring Jackets, brings the inmates a paddling pool. Subhi has no frame of reference for this 'Shakespeare duck', a material fragment of history and popular culture to which he has no access: 'The rubber duck Harvey put in the pool has black hair and a moustache and a tiny triangly beard. It's wearing a blue jacket and under its wing is a bit of paper with writing on it that says *To quack or not to quack*' (16–17). Subhi might not understand Harvey's reference to 'a play', but he has learnt about ducks: 'I know that the feathers close to the duck's skin stay dry, even when they dive as deep down underwater as they can go.' (16). The concrete plastic toy thereby stands in for a concrete thing of the world external to the camp. The disjunction between the duck's ephemeral materiality on the one hand – involving a joke that Harvey laughs at, but which Subhi cannot comprehend – and its substantial significance for Subhi is key here. It opens up a gap between something and nothing that brings the duck into the remit of Brown's vitalized thingness: 'I look at the duck. For a second I think it gives me a little duck nod and a wink. "Well, hello there," it says' (17). This is the initiating moment of a conversation that continues throughout the book, lending (among other things) levity to a narrative that might otherwise be as bleak as the living conditions with which it grapples.

Subhi's relationship with a rubber duck involves the animation of a plastic object. The rubber duck is a physical thing that Subhi can hold and, as such, cannot be considered entirely a product of Subhi's imagination. In this respect, their bond resembles that between Calvin and Hobbes in Bill Watterson's comic strip,[6] in which a human child (Calvin) enjoys a complex relationship with

Figure 5.1 Ontological quandary (Watterson [1996] 1997: 83).

his stuffed tiger (Hobbes). However, in the case of *Calvin and Hobbes*, there is ambivalence as to whether Hobbes comes to life as a conscious being or whether he is purely the product of Calvin's (imaginative) consciousness, a point that Watterson makes succinctly in *It's a Magical World* (1997) (Figure 5.1).

To provide other examples from the wider conventions of Watterson's comic strip, sometimes Hobbes acts alone or seems to have knowledge about things that Calvin could not have recourse to, suggesting that Hobbes might have a degree of consciousness and ontological presence. Watterson also makes the most of the visual conditions of comic strip, depicting Hobbes variously as an inert toy in some strips and as an animated character in others. I am not suggesting that Hobbes ever has ontological status as a conscious entity outside of his fictional world, any more than Calvin does. Rather that, as per distinctions set out by Everett, it is conceivable that Hobbes has the same ontological status as Calvin (and other characters in Watterson's fictional world) inside the work of fiction 'with which we engage as a form of pretense' (Everett 2013: 4). Or to put it another way, within the 'pretense mandated by the fictional text' (34), Hobbes sometimes counts as a conscious being, alongside Calvin, and at other times he seems to be the product of Calvin's imagination. Within the '*as-if* conditions of make-believe' (2) in *Calvin and Hobbes*, the ontological status of Hobbes oscillates between the real and unreal, generating much of the comic strip's charm and humour. Returning to Subhi and his duck, evidently the situation is not quite the same. Within the conditions of Fraillon's fiction, the duck is a concrete object that is not accorded consciousness. The duck remains a rubber toy with which Subhi holds a one-sided conversation. Notwithstanding, there is an oscillation between the real and unreal in *The Bone Sparrow*, but the oscillation is of a different order from that at work in *Calvin and Hobbes*.

Within the fictional conditions of *The Bone Sparrow* it is clear that Subhi is hungry for any relationship that allows him temporary respite from the privations of the camp. Given this, the conversation Subhi strikes up with the Shakespeare duck can be considered a psychological response to his internment and the absence of his father, whom he hopes might be alive outside the camp. However, when considered alongside the ocean that Subhi imagines into being, it is possible that *something else* is coming into play here. Indeed, an argument can be made for the conscious and discursive duck as being a phenomenological aspect of Subhi's consciousness. I have already suggested that absence has ontic value and, in a related move, I suggest that Subhi's propensity for vitalizing the world around him (some of it propelled by vague absence) has ontological force in terms of Da-sein. *Being there* is an important theme of the book and consequently Fraillon's narrative throws up a number of different positions on the nature of human being and the ontological oscillation of the real and unreal. 'Inside' and 'Outside' are terms that hang heavily in an environment that denies the outside world, to such an extent that Outside takes on utopian values for Subhi. While Outside might be a place that Subhi can never be, he has been on the inside, which makes it worth him fighting to reach the outside world. The case I am building then is for conceiving Subhi's duck discourse as an ontic manifestation of Subhi's being on the inside, rather than viewing it only as a psychological behaviour.

Bringing Chalmers's exploration of consciousness into view, this move (of validating Subhi's being on the inside) entails considering consciousness as 'a natural phenomenon ... arising throughout the human species and very likely in many others' (Chalmers [1996] 1997: xiii). Moreover, consciousness has features – such as Subhi's experience of seeing, touching and talking to the duck – which can be considered as ontologically viable, just as the physicality of the duck's rubbery molecules makes it concretely real. The imaginative intensity of the ocean and duck in the novel gives rise to something like *qualia* and they take on ontological weight in relation to Subhi's being-human as a result. As Chalmers explains, 'We can say that a mental state is conscious if it has a *qualitative feel* – an associated quality of experience. These qualitative feels are also known as phenomenal qualities, or *qualia* for short' (4). Thus, Fraillon suggests that the things Subhi is conscious of, or makes conscious through his imagination, have qualitative value. Conceiving the speaking duck and animal-rich ocean as qualia helps Fraillon to express Subhi's Da-sein and to convey it in the sort of imaginatively rich terms that humanity has learnt to value through poetry and literature. Coming back to the contrasting ways in which Subhi and Queeny 'perform' reality, this investment in qualia allows for a joke at Queeny's expense: '"Pfft", the Shakespeare duck says from my pocket. "What does she know? I bet she doesn't even know that I talk"' (Fraillon 2016: 53).

When Subhi meets Jimmie, a lonely girl from the Outside who is mourning the death of her mother, qualia in combination with physical substance confirm Da-sein for each child and they are able to recognize each other through a process of ontological exchange. Subhi has been speaking to his duck when Jimmie first sneaks into the compound and initially he doubts her existence in verifiable reality: 'right in front of me, is a girl. Like that red dirt had up and whooshed her straight from the ground' (48). Subhi considers that Jimmie might be some sort of guardian angel sent to deliver him from captivity and he remains unsure of her until she 'hocks up the biggest ball of snot I've ever seen … That's when I know. Guardian angels don't hock up snot' (49). Bodily substance makes Jimmie real to Subhi and his instinct is to hide his duck from her: 'I shake my head and shove the duck in my pocket so that girl doesn't think I'm totally bonkers talking to a rubber duck' (48). This self-aware revelation pokes fun at behavioural readings of Subhi's relationship with the duck, while also confirming that we are not to read the duck's dialogue as proof of its consciousness. Just because Subhi can make the duck speak does not mean that it is conscious – and he knows it. The duck has *value in relation to Subhi* and not in terms of any ontological status that might be claimed for the duck at the level of consciousness.[7] That Subhi's duck discourse has palpable value in the world is confirmed by Jimmie's response. When the narrative perspective shifts to Jimmie in a subsequent chapter, we learn that 'she liked that he talked to a rubber duck' because 'Jimmie's mum used to talk to her garden gnome whenever she went outside' (62). Jimmie takes comfort from Subhi's expression of qualia, for his duck discourse provides evidence of something that is generally unavailable to anyone outside of the individual experiencing it. Subhi and Jimmie each represent life lived on the inside and outside, but they give each other a glimpse of an-other way of being.

Ontological oscillation is a dynamic that continues throughout the novel and has an important role to play in Fraillon's commitment to recovering and identifying different ways of being human. This happens on numerous levels that I do not have the space to explore here, but the ontological investment in imaginary relationships in *The Bone Sparrow* is important. Through its ontological commitment to qualia, expressed via Subhi's imaginative investment in the other (an other way of being), the novel echoes Levinas in its harnessing of ethical ontologies that validate life where it seems impossible. Even Queeny accepts that there might be an alternative to her version of reality: '"That girl.

The one you were making the pictures for. She's real, isn't she?" When I nod, I can see her eyes are watery and red. I turn away' (208).

While *The Bone Sparrow* is not typical of imaginary relationships in children's literature, it makes use of metaphysical groundwork put in place by various examples of imaginary friendships in the field. Frequently, such relationships are realized in picturebooks in order that ontological oscillation between the real and unreal can be played out in gaps between the visual and verbal. Some visual texts are more ambitious than others in terms of the tensions they play out, yet all recognize the formal potential for visualizing aspects of conscious experience that can be difficult to express – examples include: *Where the Wild Things Are* (1963) by Maurice Sendak; *The Snowman* (1978) by Raymond Briggs; *Jessica* (1989) by Kevin Henkes; *Aldo* (1991) by John Burningham; *I Love You Blue Kangaroo* (1998) by Emma Chichester Clark; or *Emma Kate* (2005) by Patricia Polacco. This is a rich area of experimentation for picturebook practitioners and other scholars have focused on the formal dynamics of imaginary relationships. For example, in *How Picturebooks Work* (2001), Nikolajeva and Carole Scott offer a detailed discussion of the ambiguities at work in books such as *Aldo* through the lens of mimesis and modality ([2001] 2006: 197–9). Therefore, my intention in exploring *Imaginary Fred* is not to focus primarily on the picturebook conditions of imaginary friendship. Rather, my emphasis is on the extent to which the picturebook exposes the metaphysical groundwork of such relationships – and where formal properties play a role in this exposure, I address them.

Imaginary Fred is a picturebook that pushes consideration of imaginary beings beyond a psychological expression of loneliness, which is a common approach to the genre (if it can be identified as such). For example, in their discussion of *Aldo*, Nikolajeva and Scott confirm that the 'pictures enhance the depiction of [the] complicated psychological process', whereby the nameless narrator starts to abandon her 'imaginary helper' (197–8). They also suggest that *Aldo* offers a 'visualization of the girl's fear and insecurity' (198). Twenty-five years on from *Aldo*, and *Imaginary Fred* plays with what are now established conventions of imaginary friendship in books for young children. Fred is conceived as an imaginary companion who comes into existence when 'a lonely little child' (Colfer and Jeffers [2015] 2016: 7)[8] wishes for him, but he 'would feel himself fade' when 'his friend would find a real friend in the real world' (10–11). The modal phrasing of the verbal text is iterative and anticipatory, implying that Fred's manifestation in the 'real world' responds to ongoing, familiar and universal childhood experiences. Jeffers's accompanying vignettes are dynamic and sketchily indicative of a recurrent situation, offering a symmetrical visualization of the conditions of Fred's existence. In common with earlier texts, imaginary friends are identified as a manifestation of human longing, isolation or loneliness. However, the focus here is not on the lonely child – it is more invested in the conditions of Fred's existence. Fred is visually represented in pixelated blue, while human characters are drawn with solid black outline – thus imaginary and human beings are visually distinguished from each other. Explanatory verbal phrasing also emphasizes ontological language through repetition: 'his friend would find a *real friend* in the *real world*' (my emphasis). This is a book interested in the conditions of reality and also in the nature of friendship – and I demonstrate that this involves an ontological move from the psychological domain of conscious experience to an expression of phenomenological qualia. *Imaginary Fred* also proposes that beings could exist solely in the phenomenological plane of being. These are beings who experience mental phenomena, but who do not take on the physical form associated with human being (an idea that I will come back to shortly).

The picturebook opens with a verbal articulation of conscious experiences of pain that can be difficult to verify, lending them weight from the outset: 'Headaches are a pain. A bee sting hurts even more. But there is one thing that's worse than getting stung on the head by a bee on a rainy day, and that is … loneliness. Being alone is no fun' (3). In that final sentence is an expression of existential isolation, whereby being is encompassed by Sartrean nothingness. However, this is not a state of being maintained or supported by Jeffers and Colfer's picturebook. *Imaginary Fred* confirms that loneliness is central to human experience, yet it also refuses the idea that it is a defining quality of human being. Instead, through a playful investment in ontological possibility, it envisages a generative process, whereby the qualia associated with friendship produce enough force to bring entities into being. Essentially, this is a thought experiment around the power of friendship and the propensity for mental phenomena to make things real. Fred soon tires of fading in and out of existence and 'wished he had a friend who would need him forever' (14). When Sam wishes for Fred, it turns out that Sam is the 'friend he had been dreaming of' (17), for they have a great deal in common. Fred anticipates that eventually Sam will move on without him, especially when he strikes up a friendship with a human girl called Sammi. This is the point at which convention breaks and *Imaginary Fred* makes its ontological move.

It turns out that Sammi can see Fred: 'Fred was surprised. He had never been visible to two people before' (30). Furthermore, Sammi has an invisible friend, Frieda, who can interact with Sam and Fred. The intimate pairings so common to tales of imaginary friendship have been supplanted with a four-way friendship. The book makes a joke of this, as the budding musicians form 'The Quarrelling Quartet'. The friends give a school recital to a bemused audience who can only see two performers on the stage and Jeffers's double-page spread makes the most of revealing that in some cases two makes four. Comic-strip conventions are employed in order that teachers can ask, '"Why are there only two of them?"', while the children play under a banner announcing them as a quartet (36–7). Something subversive is at work here and the school audience is evidently unsettled by it – and Fred is quite right to be surprised by all this. The idea of a group of imaginary and human friends contravenes the idea that imaginary friendships are behavioural products of an internal mental state to which nobody has access but the individual experiencing it.

Even more unusual is the development that Fred and Frieda (the imaginary pair of beings) are able to maintain a friendship independent of Sam and Sammi – and so 'they didn't see their human friends much any more' (42). By now it seems certain that these imaginary beings are not the product of someone else's psychological crisis. Given that this is the case, it seems that the conditions of their existence need to be reconsidered, while allowing for the picturebook's thematic investment in friendship. Once again, the phenomenal concept of mind proves useful in thinking this through. As Chalmers explains, 'This is the concept of mind as conscious experience, and of a mental state as a consciously experienced mental state' ([1996] 1997: 11). Unquestionably, *Imaginary Fred* invests in friendship as conscious experience – and I would add to this, it is a conscious experience to which qualia can be attached. All of the children are able to express themselves and to attest to their own feelings. Reflecting on his newfound friendship with Frieda, Fred reveals that 'He quite enjoyed being told what to do by Frieda and her dazzling smile' (Colfer and Jeffers [2015] 2016: 34). In this sense, Fred and Frieda can be understood as expressions of the ontic energy of conscious experience – they come into being because friendship makes people feel good. As Chalmers confirms, 'On the phenomenal concept, mind is characterized by the way it *feels*' (11). Fred and Frieda therefore have ontological force and can be seen as an expression of what it is like for people to experience friendship as a quantifiable phenomenon of lived experience. At the outset, it appeared that Fred (blue pixels) and Frieda (yellow pixels) were visually represented as pixelated beings in order to emphasize their ephemeral status as non-beings, as psychosomatic expressions of temporary behaviours in human children. However, it turns out that their pixilation is a visual expression of the condition of their being in the mental realms of human consciousness, just as the solid lines around Sam and Sammi attest to their physical status.[9]

This thought experiment could be considered a reversal of the philosophical 'zombie problem', which Chalmers rehearses in some detail ([1996] 1997: 93–9). Chalmers conceives of a *phenomenal zombie* version of himself, whereby his zombie twin maintains physical properties of human being, but has no conscious (mental) experience. For Chalmers, 'the question is not whether it is plausible that zombies could exist in our world', it is 'whether the notion of a zombie is conceptually coherent' (96). He finds that if we can conceive of a physical (live) being without consciousness, then we are in the realms of logical possibility: 'The mere intelligibility of the notion is enough to establish the conclusion' (96). Fred and Frieda are thrown up by a related experiment, which allows for beings with no physical state – and if we follow Chalmers's logic, the fact that we can conceive of them makes Fred and Frieda possible. Of course, I do not suggest that *Imaginary Fred* makes a case for imaginary friends as viable beings of the experiential world outside of its make-believe conditions. However, within the *as-if* conditions of the picturebook they acquire ontological validity. The picturebook even expresses the outcome in experimental terms: 'As this was the first case of its kind, imaginary scientists spent years trying to figure out how it had happened. Eventually they concluded that friendship is friendship. Imaginary or not, the same laws apply' (Colfer [2015] 2016: 44–5). I accept that this detailed discussion of ontological conditions might seem to weigh heavily on a light-hearted picturebook. However, it is important to establish the sophisticated capabilities of this literary form, alongside the commitment of children's literature to expressing metaphysical possibility through deceptively simple narrative structures and conceptual ideas.

The conventional apparatus of imaginary friendships in *Imaginary Fred* allows for an experiment in which nothing comes to be. The conventions of children's literature explored in this chapter demonstrate that nothing matters; that absence and imaginings *are something* and we come to this understanding through the play of familiar conventions. Conventional mechanisms of literary form and language might be broadly associated with the mundane and unimaginative, yet my exploration of absent parents and imaginary friendship suggests that convention can offer a starting point for grappling with the conditions of existence. I leave the final word on this to Lewis who argues in defence of linguistic convention that 'there must be *something* to our notion of conventions of language, even if we cannot say what. When we are exposed to the notion we *do* all manage to get the idea … So we must mean something' (Lewis [1969] 2002: 3). I take Lewis's plea for convention out of context in order to demonstrate that conventions really can make something – yes, we must *mean something* – out of nothing and bring new ways of being into view. Subterranean tunnels confirm the fundamental commitment to such a project in children's literature – tunnels that collapse worlds in order that they can be built anew and be understood better in the process.

Conclusion: Mountains of Metaphoric Refrain

> *Since I experience language as an intensely physical process, I cannot* not *think through metaphor. It isn't as though I make a choice to work with and through metaphor, it's that I experience myself inside these constantly swerving, intensely physical processes of semiosis.*
>
> (Haraway 2000: 86)

When reflecting on her propensity for using biological metaphors in *How Like a Leaf*, Haraway argues that 'biology is not merely a metaphor that illuminates something else, but an inexhaustible source of getting at the non-literalness of the world' (82). She argues that the biological world is full of 'real things' that *are* metaphors for exploring biological and ontological systems. Haraway locates metaphor in the experiential world, insisting that it is not something that stands in for the real at a distance. Words are intensely physical for Haraway and she finds 'words and language more closely related to flesh than to ideas' (85). This commitment to metaphor as a substantial entity of biological organisms has implications that this book corroborates in its engagement with metaphysical structures of children's literature. If metaphor has ontic presence it cannot be reduced to a substitute for that which is real; figurative language inheres in being and vice versa. Metaphor (and associated figurative articles) must be grounded, therefore, in the sort of metaphysical conditions attributed to it by philosophers and cultural theorists, such as Haraway, Bachelard, Heidegger, Coccia or Murdoch and by practitioners such as Jansson, Tan, Woodson, Hartnett, Garner, McCaughrean, Gulemetova or Fraillon – metaphor is not just about being, it is being.

There is a looping doubleness involved in this relationship between the biological world and language, which means that figurative literature understands what it means to be from inside itself and it can speak to the being of other things as a result. Haraway articulates this when she reveals that 'I have always read biology in a double way – as about the way the world works biologically, but also about the way the world works metaphorically' (24). Moreover, as Lewis ([1969] 2002) makes clear, language works through convention and there is *something* behind or within this commitment to convention. If we can only get at this something in linguistic and literary convention, the world starts to unfold in the purview of metaphysical systems. I hold that in the particular conditions and conventions of children's literature doubleness can be traced. Of course Haraway's double reading can be applied to all modes of cultural production in their involvement with biological function – this is not the preserve of books for young people – but my argument is that children's literature yields metaphysical structures relative to its own conditions. Children's books comprise metaphysical structures via figurative language – on one level they are of the external world – but their particular metaphysical structures are also generative and can bring worlds into being (as Bachelard insists of childhood reverie).

One aspect of Haraway's stance on biology and metaphor is of particular relevance to a literature that – by way of Bachelard or Woodson – can be considered seminal. Haraway explains that embryology and its commitment to the history of form and the genesis and shaping of form has led to her interest in tracing the sort of pattern formations that inhere in biological process (24). As is also evident in *A Manifesto for Cyborgs*, Haraway's investment in the shaping of form through process – via the sort of rhizomorphic shoots of *brown girl dreaming*, *The Lost Words* or *Strange Objects* – resists a static moment of origin that could be traceable through roots to a single point. Developmental theories can be entrenched in the stasis of origin and this is certainly true of approaches to and aspects of children's literature – the resilience of *puer aeturnus* and the pastoral reach of children's literature is a good example of commitment to retrospective beginnings in childhood studies. However, close attention to metaphysical structures of children's literature reveals that this is yielding ground. The seeded worlds of many books for young people overlap across plateaus in a dynamic process of becoming that resists a rooted centre. This dynamism can be traced variously through the fracturing ambivalence of ontological exchange, the vibrant thingness of baby books, the immersive connectivity of flora and fauna, the territorial indices of nowhere and the conventional absences of nothingness. Of course this is not the end of the story though – if beginnings are troubled by the metaphysical structures I have uncovered, so too are endings.

With endpoints in mind, let us imagine that 'A child in the dark, gripped with fear, comforts himself by singing under his breath. He walks and halts to his song. Lost, he takes shelter, or orients himself as best he can' (Deleuze and

Guattari [1980] 2013: 362). The lostness of the child presupposes a destination – an ending to a journey – but instead a sung refrain allows the child to be at home in a world where 'home does not preexist'; and the refrain 'opens the circle a crack, opens it all the way, lets someone in, calls someone, or else goes out oneself, launches forth' (362). The tune taken up by this child is the *Refrain* proffered in Deleuze and Guattari's *A Thousand Plateaus*, which is territorial in its assemblage – 'the bird sings to mark its territory' (363). In this way the refrain 'carries earth with it' (363) and allows for expression in and of the world that does not rely on linear pathways: 'In a general sense, *we call a refrain any aggregate of matters of expression that draws a territory and develops into territorial motifs and landscapes*' (376). There is an element of improvisation to the refrain that allows for spontaneous creativity, responding nonetheless to *territorial motifs and landscapes* – and to the conventions of children's literature that mark out its territory:

> One launches forth, hazards an improvisation. But to improvise is to join with the World, or meld with it. One ventures from home on the thread of a tune. Along sonorous, gestural, motor lines that mark the customary path of a child and graft themselves onto or begin to bud 'lines of drift' with different loops, knots, speeds, movements, gestures, and sonorities.
>
> (363)

In this venture, home is a resonance that refuses centrality – the interior space of home is not designed to keep being in place, rather it protects the germinal forces of action (362). Embedded in this is Haraway's embryonic shaping of form, so that refrain also recognizes the patterns of biological formation. There is generative potential in this embryonic process of improvisation, which can be traced through the mountainous landscapes of children's books and addresses metaphysical concerns around causation and being in the world.

Refrain resonates through Gertrude Stein's *The World Is Round* (1939) as Rose, the protagonist, attempts to go up a mountain with a blue garden chair. Stein's modernist circling of metaphysical questions draws ontological engagement with the vagueness of language into its repetitive structure. Rose's certainty about the reality of her mountain – 'When mountains are really true they are blue' ([1939] 2013: 31) – unravels as she attempts her ascent. It becomes clear that climbing mountains brings the whereness of self-awareness into play: 'And where was there. She almost said it she almost whispered it to herself and to the chair. Where oh where is there' (59). Rose herself is bound up in the mountain's dislocation at this point, so that ontic doubts about the mountain reflect on her being-there and the thingness of her blue chair. Notwithstanding, there is a territorial conviction that drives her on: 'Rose had courage everywhere she just went on going up there' (58). Refrain helps Rose to manage the disquiet she experiences about climbing fuzzy mountains until eventually she manages her climb and 'She was all alone on the top of everything and she was sitting there and she could sing' (61). In solitude Rose sings and her song reaches across the mountain tops to be picked up by a light on another hill, going 'round and round and it went all around Rose' (65). Rose's refrain reaches out and reflects back on her so that when she is really somewhere – on the mountain top – Da-sein is fulfilled in her being there.

When Rose sings she is heard. Her refrain flies from her blue chair on the summit to a yellow tent on the Lonely Mountains and a mouth-organ picks up the refrain. In *Comet in Moominland*, a tent is pitched just below the mountain peaks: 'From the tent came the sound of Snufkin's mouth-organ, but in this desolate place it was a strange sound indeed' (Jansson [1946] 1967: 63). The mouth-organ sets off the melancholic howling of a 'hyena some way off' and startles Sniff (63). While Snufkin's refrain wards against fear of thrownness in the world, its sonority is invested in the daunting chaos of the outside world. In *Harold and the Purple Crayon* (1955) by Crockett Johnson, an infant draws his world into existence in response to the sort of misty absence found in the Lonely Mountains. This sort of *generative visualization* – also seen in *Bear Hunt* (1979) by Anthony Browne or *Journey* (2013) by Aaron Becker – can be conceived as a visual refrain, marking out an embryonic process that brings phenomena of the world into being. It also expresses the improvisational hazards of venturing forth, for Harold's crayon anticipates a series of risks from getting lost to drowning in the ocean – and each of these risks is met by the crayon's purple refrain. When Harold draws a hill 'to see where he was' (Johnson [1955] 2012: 33), he finds that it is not high enough to see his bedroom and so the hill becomes a mountain – then Harold peers over the mountain top and slips into the nothingness on the other side. He finds himself 'falling, in thin air … But luckily, he kept his wits and his purple crayon' (38–9) in order to draw himself out of danger with a balloon. Harold knows that something comes of nothing when you are thrown into the world.

Notes

Introduction: Climbing Fuzzy Mountains

1 This point arises in Crane and Farkas's discussion of identifying entities. It relates in particular to Quine's notion of vague boundaries and to how we might establish the boundaries of entities in the world, such as mountains or desks. I will elaborate on this point in the forthcoming discussion, but for an introduction to these ideas see Crane and Farkas (2004: 146–9).
2 'Childly' is a widely used adjective in children's literature scholarship. It is the adjectival companion to 'childness', which Hollindale proposes in *Signs of Childless in Children's Books* (1997) as a positive solution to 'linguistic poverty' (1997: 45) in articulations of childhood. I go on to discuss my commitment to Hollindale's concept of childness, but for a full discussion, see Hollindale (1997: 44–61).
3 For further discussion of philosophical vagueness, see Chapter 4.
4 In his discussion of the importance of maps in the *Moomin* series, Böjrn Sundmark remarks on the illustrative (as opposed to cartographic) qualities of Jansson's map for *Moominvalley in November* (1970) and he observes that it is a map 'characterized by absence' (Sundmark 2014: 170). He goes on to suggest that this absence is served by an illustrative vagueness, of the sort I identify in Jansson's verbal language in *Comet in Moominland*. Sundmark reflects further that 'The Moomintrolls are gone from the valley, so they cannot be represented in the picture, and the others, the creatures who have gone to Moominvalley in search of the happy family, are oddly vague in the contours themselves. They are not completely there. In fact, all of Moominvalley is under erasure, it seems' (170) – and he demonstrates that this visual vagueness is borne out in central themes of absence and loss in the book. I would add to Sundmark's analysis a suggestion that Jansson's ability to engage with metaphysical concerns is thrown up in this visual and verbal imagery.
5 I should stress that in this context 'poetry' refers to literary expression in the widest sense, particularly given the framing of discussion via Bachelard's poetics. I include writers of fiction, illustrators and so on in the designation 'poet'.
6 For an extended discussion of birch tree poem, see Chapter 3.
7 For a full discussion of fictional realism and a rebuttal of this position, see *The Nonexistent*, by Anthony Everett (2013) – ideas which I discuss further in Chapter 5.

1 Ontological Exchange

1. The sequence involving Mary is taken from Garner's *The Stone Book* (1976). Initially *The Stone Book* was part of a sequence of four separate novellas, also including: *Granny Reardun* (1977); *The Aimer Gate* (1978); *Tom Fobble's Day* (1977). Later they were published together – in the order listed here – as part of *The Stone Book Quartet* (1983).
2. Woodson was born in 1963 and so the memoir deals in part with the consequences and impact of the 1964 Civil Rights Act for those living in the American South. Woodson spent part of her childhood living with her grandparents in Greenville, South Carolina, and this is the site of the ghostly apparition experienced by the persona here.
3. See the introduction for a full discussion of etymological links between metaphysics, transfer and metaphor.
4. Given that it functions as a metaphysical structure of children's literature, ontological exchange can be found at work earlier than 1945. For example, Lewis Carroll's *Alice's Adventures in Wonderland* (1865) includes several examples of ontological exchange.
5. For more extensive discussion of animals at large in the metaphysics of children's literature, see 'Animal Messes' in Chapter 3.
6. Metaphysical conditions of imaginary friendships in children's books are considered at length in Chapter 5.
7. *The Way Home* is not paginated – numbering commences from and is inclusive of the title page.
8. I was not able to secure permission to reproduce this image, so please refer to a print copy of *The Way Back Home* to view the double-page spread under discussion (Jeffers 2007: 14–15). I would have captioned this moment: 'A sunrise awakening'.
9. The metaphysical importance of utopian nowhere in children's literature is explored fully in Chapter 4.
10. 'Oh, at that time, / While on the perilous ridge I hung alone' (Wordsworth [1850] 1986: Book First, lines 335–6).
11. I use Waller's definition of domestic fantasy here, in which she draws generic parallels with fantastic realism in *Constructing Adolescence in Fantastic Realism* (2009). The distinguishing factor is that domestic fantasy often involves the familial domains of home and domestic space (Waller [2009] 2010: 21).
12. Other titles in the series include *The Borrowers Afield* (1955), *The Borrowers Afloat* (1959), *The Borrowers Aloft* (1961), *Poor Stainless* (1966) *The Borrowers Avenged* (1982).
13. For example, Maria Nikolajeva's (2006) entry on Mary Norton in *The Oxford Encyclopedia of Children's Literature*.

14 Definition of 'possible' traced back to the fourteenth century from Onions (1966: 699).
15 *Anochronies* is Gerard Genette's term for 'the various types of discordance between the two orderings of story and narrative' ([1972] 1983: 36).
16 For an extended discussion of material things and thingness in children's books, see Chapter 2.
17 Care is central to Heidegger's notion of Da-sein (being there) and although Levinas does not attribute the reference here, there is no doubt that Levinas directly alludes to Heidegger's concept. He takes issue with the centrality of self in Heidegger's ontology later in this chapter ('Humanism and An-Archy' in [1972] 2006) and he does identify Heidegger's ideas then.
18 For Philippa Pearce's own reflections on time at work in *Tom's Midnight Garden* see *Travellers in Time: Past, Present, and to Come*: proceedings of the summer institute at Newnham College, Cambridge University, England, presented 6–12 August 1989, by Childrens' Literature New England.
19 I have known students to reject the book on their account.
20 Stephens (1992) argues that the humanist project renders the child subject of children's literature open to manipulation. For a sense of Heidegger's challenge to French existentialism – through the lens of humanism on his terms – see Heidegger's 'Letter on "Humanism"' ([1946] 1998).
21 I was not able to secure permission to reproduce this image, so please refer to a print copy of *The Way Back Home* to view the double-page spread under discussion (Jeffers 2007: 14–15). I would have captioned this moment: 'A sunrise awakening'.
22 For further discussion of imaginative acts of parental absence, see Chapter 5.
23 Sartre discusses 'bad faith' at length in a dedicated section in *Being and Nothingness* ([1943] 2003: 70–94).
24 I am aware of the gender binaries at work here, in which Moomintroll is the active counterpart to the Snork maiden's passivity, but I do not have the space to unpack this further.
25 For more extensive discussion of animals at large in the metaphysics of children's literature, see 'Animal Messes' in Chapter 3.
26 The radical feminist agenda in this book, in which Lanagan sets up a sort of Kristevan 'Women's Time', makes enemies of men (for the most part) and demonizes sex, an issue that Lydia Kokkola addresses in *Fictions of Adolescent Carnality* (2013: 189–93). Via Lanagan's portrayal, Dought is embittered by a callous and prejudiced society that renders him a deviant outcast. Lanagan never really tackles the relentlessly negative and somewhat archaic feminism of her intriguing character/novel and Dought is effectively murdered as a consequence of his interaction with the sisters in their alternate reality, mirroring the dwarf's punishment in the Grimms's tale.

27 I am aware that gender-neutral pronouns are part of a discourse gaining momentum in the twentieth century and I am not arguing that 'it' only refers to non-human beings. Rather, I am observing that etymological development points to an association between 'it' and non-human beings – an association that Lanagan deploys in a knowing way here to diminish Dought.

28 When making this particular observation about the tyranny of things, Brown is using the writing of Henry James to explore the decorative role and function of objects.

29 See Chapter 3 for a full discussion of metaphysical immersion in the natural world.

2 Something Matters: Things about Nappies

1 Pegasus is Quine's example, Puff is mine. I discuss the fancy stuff at work in Puff, the Magic Dragon later in this chapter.

2 Philosophers such as Anthony Everett refuse Quine's commitment to Pegasus in terms of possibility and surface grammar. In *The Nonexistent* (2013), Everett argues that there are no such things as fictional characters, for they are only realized within the *as-if* conditions of pretence. I discuss this position at some length in Chapter 5.

3 For an introduction to Aristotle's categories of 'things' see Teichman and Evans (1999). They provide a useful list of his ten categories: Substances; Qualities; Quantities; Relations; Places; Times; Positions; States; Actions; Affections (1999: 11).

4 Mothercare is a British retailer, specializing in goods for parents, babies and young children. Its first store opened in 1961, followed by mail order business in 1962.

5 *The Baby's Catalogue* is not paginated – numbering commences from and is inclusive of the title page.

6 Carroll's 'Objects and Toys' is forthcoming in *The Cambridge Companion to Children's Literature in English, Volume 2*. No pagination is currently available.

7 As Heidegger notes in the 1962 edition, 'This work presents the text of a lecture which was held in the winter semester, 1935–6, at the University of Freiburg.' The lecture was entitled 'Basic Questions of Metaphysics.'

8 Carroll confirms such explanations in her discussion of the distinctive approaches to toys provided by Roland Barthes and Lois Kuznets: 'The distinction here is not so much about the material properties of the object, *but rather the agency of the child*' (my emphasis – Carroll forthcoming: n.p.).

9 It is fitting that a female photographer should inadvertently challenge the gendered implications of Heidegger's protracted illustration. Heidegger's housemaid is only able to recognize the methodological shortcomings of a male metaphysician who

ignores the round-about-us, whereas Hoban uses her camera to achieve ontic vision.

10 *Look Again!* is not paginated – numbering commences from and is inclusive of the title page.
11 Italicized words are etymological variations of 'again' in: Onions (1996: 18).
12 See Chapter 1 for discussion of the ontological exchange.
13 It should be noted that Mitchell goes on to demonstrate contradictions in Gombrich's stance in the nature-convention debate and his discussion of Gombrich's sometimes puzzling commitment to contour can be followed here: Mitchell ([1986] 1987: 85–90).
14 Allison's mistake stems from the fact that she wants to support Hoban's own claims for universalism, apparently conflating 'fundamental' with 'universal.' Hoban explains that she tries not to localize her images:

> They're universal because even when I shoot in Paris or wherever I shoot, I try not to localize it. Once in a while it has to be changed, like a fire hydrant – they don't have that in Europe. So in one book that was printed in German, I had to change two pictures. I always try to make it so it can be everybody. It can be a boy or a girl; it can be dark or light because it is concepts, you know, shapes or curves. (Hoban in Allison 2000: 148)

Her revelation about cultural translation alerts us to the cultural specificity of objects though and there is naivety in her claim to universalism here.

15 *Black White* is not paginated – numbering commences from and is inclusive of the first image in the book.
16 The 'Rubber Duckie' song has appeared multiple times on *Sesame Street*. It was first screened in 1970 and was sung by Ernie (puppet voiced by Jim Henson) in his bath. It was written by Jeff Moss and released by Columbia Records, New York (1970).
17 'Puff, the Magic Dragon' was written by Peter Yarrow and Lenny Lipton and recorded by Peter, Paul and Mary in 1963 on the album, *Moving*. For copyright reasons I have cited lines from the 2015 picturebook – also penned by Lipton and Yarrow – but it should be noted that the picturebook text differs slightly from the original lyrics (published by Cherry Lane Music Publishing). In the lines I quote here, 'giant rings' have become giant's rings, emphasizing the theme of imaginative fantasy, but I find that it troubles the ontic resonance of the more ambiguous 'giant rings' of the original recording. In my own experience of childhood listening, giant rings took amorphous shape in my childly mind and I welcomed them as an acceptable and viable offering from child to dragon. For this reason, my analysis of the song's ontology considers the original wording. The possessive formation of 'giant's' introduces another fantasy character into a song that (for me) is very much focused on an intimate relationship; that Puff is alone in Honah Lee without

Jacky is crucial. I should point out that the picturebook is not alone in making this particular change, as a rendition of the song by Bonnie 'prince' Billie and Red on *Songs for the Young at Heart* (2006) also refers to 'giant's rings'. Such changes to scansion and wording are typical in folk music of course, but there are further alterations to the picturebook narrative that make use of the illustrative potential picturebook form and reflect ideological concerns of the twenty-first century.

18 *Not a Box* is not paginated – numbering commences from and is inclusive of the title page.

19 I was not able to secure permission to reproduce an image from *Not a Box*, but I thank Antoinette Portis for assistance in this matter. Please refer to a print copy to view the illustrations under discussion. I would have used the racing car as an example (Portis [2006] 2008: 7), using the caption: 'A racing car is a matter of childly thingness'.

20 Blurb cited from the Penguin UK online catalogue https://www.penguin.co.uk/books/60553/brown-bear--brown-bear--what-do-you-see-/9780241137291.html (accessed 13 May 2019).

21 Johnson ([1955] 2012).

22 It is commonplace in many ontological systems that shape can be a property of a thing. For example, in 'The Shape of Shapes: An Ontological Exploration', Robert J. Rovetto establishes that irregular or uneven shapes can be properties of 'mind-external objects or things in the world', such as planets or trees (2011: n.p.).

23 *Triangle* is not paginated – numbering commences from and is inclusive of the title page.

24 I was not able to secure permission to reproduce an image from *Triangle*. Please refer to a print copy to view the illustrations of Triangle under discussion. Under an image of Triangle I would have used the caption: Triangle is a *rigid* designator in a triangular world (Barnett and Klassen [2017] 2018: 10–11).

25 *Transcendental idealism* is an important aspect of Kant's philosophy, which he expounds in *Critique of Pure Reason* (1781). Kant merges empirical realism – allowing for the independent and reality of objects in the world – with transcendental idealism, which suggests that the properties of objects inhere in our mental structures, structures that we then impose on the experiential world.

26 I discuss Lewis's identity theory in more detail in Chapter 1.

27 *Naming and Necessity* first appeared as a series of three lectures given by Kripke in 1970 and was first published in a 1972 collection edited by Donald Davidson and Gilbert Harman: *Semantics of Natural Language*. The edition to which I refer is the 1980 transcript of the lectures with a preface by Kripke.

28 In a challenge to Kant's epistemological take on truth, Kripke reveals that the question of whether truths are necessary or contingent is actually metaphysical in remit. Kant makes synonymous use of necessary and *a priori* truths and designates

them epistemological – either we know things necessarily *a priori* or based on tested experience *a posteriori*.
29 See Chapter 3 for a more extensive discussion of the metaphysical implications of anthropomorphism in children's literature.
30 For a discussion of exhibition ethics relevant to Cole's didactic imperative, see Gazi (2014).
31 I am aware of the homogenizing and xenophobic practice of aligning Aboriginal peoples with indigenous flora and fauna, and Crew challenges such racist perspectives in his novel. I also discuss this issue in reference to *Walkabout* ([1959] 2015) by James Vance Marshall in Chapter 3. Furthermore, I go on to discuss the wider significance of flora and fauna in children's books in Chapter 3 and 'nowhere' is considered in detail as an area of central metaphysical concern to children's literature in Chapter 4.

3 Something Else Matters: Rhizomes and Animal Messes

1 The actual 1969 translation of Bachelard's line reads: 'A world takes form in our reverie, and this world is ours' ([1960] 1971: 8).
2 For further discussion of the ontological value of images and representations of things, see my discussion of Gombrich and contour and Barthes's metaphysical consideration of photographs in Chapter 1.
3 'Birches' first appeared in *Atlantic Monthly* in 1915 and was subsequently collected in Frost's *Mountain Interval* in 1916. I refer to Frost (1989: 1100–1).
4 In referring to 'nerve fibres' I borrow from Deleuze and Guattari ([1980] 2013: 7). They refer to 'a multiplicity of nerve fibers' that connect the limbs of a puppet, while also connecting that puppet to other puppets in other dimensions.
5 *The Lost Words* is not paginated – numbering commences from and is inclusive of the title page.
6 For information on the root systems of heather, see: A. J. MacDonald et al. (1995).
7 During an email exchange (2 December 2019) about the Heather image, Jackie Morris revealed: 'I wanted to paint the heather, ling, tormentil and all the other things that heather shares its measure with. But sometimes it's not possible.' In my estimation, the image and words combine to suggest much more than is present in the final illustration – the suggestive expanse of this image reaches beyond what we actually see.
8 As Macfarlane explains in 'How the Lost Words became songs to save the countryside' (*The Guardian*, 16 January 2019), *The Lost Words* has been read and deployed by adults and children from a wide range of different communities: https://www.theguardian.com/music/2019/jan/16/

spell-songs-robert-macfarlane-the-lost-words-vanishing-nature-folk-musicians (accessed 8 August 2019).

9. On his website, Tan explains: 'The central image of this story came from footage of a nuclear explosion, and wondering what the opposite of such an horrific event might look like. An explosion of flowers?' (Tan n.d. a.). Tan's website includes a number of commentaries on his works of literature and illustration. These commentaries are undated, but are referenced and linked, so can easily be located. His commentary on 'Bee' can be found here: https://www.shauntan.net/tfic-notes (accessed 12 October 2020).

10. In the author's note, Barker also reveals that she is indebted to many different sources for information about flowers, but especially to '*Wild Flowers as They Grow*', by G. Clarke Nuttall (Cassell); and am grateful also for the help I have been given at Kew Gardens' (Barker [1948] 1974: 52).

11. The Cottingley Fairies were the subject of a 'hoax' photograph taken by two cousins, Elsie Wright (16) and Frances Griffiths (9), in 1917.

12. *Flotsam* is not paginated – numbering commences from and is inclusive of the title page.

13. *The Fox and the Star* is not paginated – numbering commences from and is inclusive of the title page.

14. *Adrian Simcox Does NOT Have a Horse* is not paginated – numbering commences from and is inclusive of the title page.

15. Coleridge imagines for his sleeping babe a childhood situated in pastoral mountainscapes, in contrast to his own boyhood: 'For I was reared / In the great city, pent 'mid cloisters dim, / And saw nought lovely but the sky and stars' (Coleridge [1798]1997: 232, 52–4). For a reading of 'Frost at Midnight' in terms of environmental ethics and constructions of childhood, see Sainsbury (2013: 99–102).

16. Originally entitled *The Children* in its first edition of 1959, *Walkabout* combines the efforts of Donald Gordon Payne and James Vance Marshall. A British author, Payne used the Australian Marshall's studies of flora and fauna in the Australian outback as inspiration for his book. Payne also took Marshall's name as a pseudonym for several other works of fiction (not all written for children), of which *Walkabout* is probably the best-known example. I should also mention that Nicolas Roeg's intriguing 1971 film drew attention to the book, but it departs significantly from Marshall's novel and I do not deal with the film here.

17. Marshall engages in a drawn-out satiric comparison of the 'civilized' human child, 'coddled in babyhood, psychoanalysed in childhood' with the 'Aboriginal', who 'knew what reality was' (28).

18. For more information on the 1967 Referendum in Australia, see the 'Right Wrongs' page on the Western Australian Museum website http://museum.wa.gov.au/referendum-1967/dispelling-myths (accessed 26 August 2019).

19 The Aboriginal boy's death is one of the most problematic aspects of this novel, since it is framed by a patronizing account of indigenous culture and beliefs. I do not have the space to discuss it here, but I am aware that the discriminatory treatment of this character, and in particular the depiction of his death, is somewhat at odds with and cannot be separated from Peter and Mary's journey into immersion.
20 In 1997, Derrida delivered a paper, 'The Autobiographical Animal', which was later published in French as *L'animal que donc je suis* (2006) and then in English as *The Animal That Therefore I Am* (2008).
21 'Butterfly' first appeared as a short story entitled 'The Butterflies' in a collection edited by Susan La Marca and Pam MacIntyre, *Where the Shoreline Used to Be: Stories from Australia and Beyond* (Penguin Books, 2016).
22 Tan's commentary on 'Butterfly' can be found here: https://www.shauntan.net/tfic-notes (accessed 12 October 2020).
23 *Beyond the Fence* is not paginated – numbering commences from and is inclusive of the title page.
24 Although originally published in English, such has been the success of *The Lost Words* that a Welsh language version, *Geiriau Diflanedig*, was published by Graffeg in October 2019, translated and adapted by Mererid Hopwood.
25 See Macfarlane (2017) and Balmford et al. (2002) for further details of this research project.
26 See an interview for Time (1999), for further details of Tajiri's childhood interest in insects and the depletion of their natural environment, which led to the game's development.
27 For further discussion of the extent to which young people are positioned as environmental saviours in children's literature, see Sainsbury (2013: 118–22) and Beauvais (2015: 169–78).

4 Mapping the Nowhere

1 *The Ice Palace* does not appear on publisher's lists for children, yet this is a book that is absolutely committed to childhood and which understands the natural, physical, emotional and symbolic landscapes of being a child and forging intense childly friendships. It recognizes what it means to be a child and becoming-child in the world. On these grounds, *The Ice Palace* is a book entirely relevant to my discussion of the metaphysics of children's literature.
2 Samuel Butler's *Erewhon or, Over the Range* (1872) was first published anonymously and could be said to explore the conditions of utopia as it edges into dystopia.

3 Etymological details pertaining to 'edifice' can be found under the entry for 'edification' in: Onions (1966: 301).
4 As Grenby (2016) recounts, Thomas Spence (1750–1815) was born in poverty in Newcastle. He was a revolutionary and pamphleteer of the late eighteenth and early nineteenth century, publishing numerous pamphlets in his lifetime, including *The Rights of Infants* (1797). He revealed himself as a utopian visionary of sorts in *A Supplement to the History of Robinson Crusoe, Being the History of Crusonia, or Robinson Crusoe's Island, Down to the Present Time* (1782) and *Description of Spensonia* (1795).
5 The 'texts' under discussion here are the 'subtitle' of Newbery's *Lilliputian Magazine* and Spence's *The Rights of Infants*.
6 Grenby is cautious about the extent of Spence's influence in this respect, but ambition for practicable social reform is evident in *The Rights of Infants*.
7 I allow whereness (as a concept) to travel in an ontic direction throughout this chapter, before resting on a definition of 'whereness' as a spatial concept in its own right from Arthur Schulman (1983). See the final section of this chapter for further discussion.
8 *Fox* is not paginated – numbering commences from and is inclusive of the title page.
9 *The Arrival* is not paginated – numbering commences from and is inclusive of the title page.
10 See Chapter 3 for further discussion of Derrida's view of fables.
11 In a 1948 article, George Orwell challenges Wilde's position on machinery:

> Wilde assumes that it is a simple matter to arrange that all the unpleasant kinds of work shall be done by machinery. The machines, he says, are our new race of slaves: a tempting metaphor, but a misleading, one, since there is a vast range of jobs – roughly speaking, any job needing great flexibility – that no machine is able to do. (Orwell 2013: n.p.)

However, I am not alone in thinking that Orwell misinterprets Wilde's point on machines, missing his apparent dig at such science fictions via his utopian aside. Several comments on the *Guardian*'s (2013) reprinting of Orwell's opinion piece also question his reading of Wilde's utopian 'vision of Socialism' (2013: n.p.).

12 As confirmed by Edward Brook-Hitching in *The Phantom Atlas*, the Mountains of the Moon is a much-contested mountain range, first identified as a possible source of the Nile in fifth century BC (Brooke-Hitching 2016: 162). By the early nineteenth century 'the myth of the Mountains of the Moon being the source of the Nile was much in doubt', although it appears on John Carey's 'A New Map of Africa' (1805), whereon he 'links the Mountains of Kong with the Mountains of the Moon to form one giant range going across the entire continent' (164). Grahame's reference to the

Mountains of the Moon indicates his awareness of its contentious status, drawing on its mythical whereness to emphasize the extreme reach of the Rat's restlessness. Once a marker of his 'simple horizon', 'the great ring of Downs' has become something more ambivalent, complex and unsettling – just as the Mountains of the Moon has moved from being somewhere marked on a map to being nowhere at all (Grahame [1908] 2010: 96).

13 By 'insular utopian vision' I do not mean 'limited' or 'parochial' – I am thinking here of a vision that looks to the here-and-now of the local and every day, thus satisfying Wilde's demand that we stop sailing on and on to ever more distant utopian islands.

14 Althusser defines Ideological State Apparatuses as 'a certain number of realities which present themselves to the immediate observer in the form of distinct and specialized institutions' ([1971] 2008: 17).

15 For a contextual overview of Stefansson's position on polar exploration, see Bravo (2019: 196–204).

16 For further discussion of Leopold, see Chapter 3. I also discuss the ethical implications of Leopold's work in Sainsbury (2013).

17 Moriarty has recently published a book for Routledge: *Antarctica in British Children's Literature* (2020).

18 The origin of the Ocean Chart, which appears in the 1876 edition of *The Hunting of the Snark*, is a matter of some controversy. The image is commonly attributed to Henry Holiday – illustrator of the first edition – but as Doug Howick explains (2011), it is unlikely that this is the case. The map is not listed among the nine illustrations supplied by Holiday and he makes no mention of it in his own reminiscences of the illustrative process. More likely, suggests Howick, Carroll created the map himself (2011: 7), and this view is supported by a German blog dedicated to illustration of *Snark*: https://snrk.de/page_the-ocean-chart (accessed 1 June 2020), suggesting that Carroll produced it in collaboration with a typesetter. I would like to think that this obfuscation of the chart's origin is a calculated manoeuvre to nowhere on Carroll's part.

19 Stefansson measures previous Arctic expeditions in terms of relative success, as new approaches to polar exploration are developed. He sees the 'fourth stage', allowing for his notion of the Pole of Inaccessibility, as an advance on the sort of 'third stage' expedition carried out by Robert Edwin Peary (which failed – according to Stefansson – due to its ignorance of local terrain).

20 Reported by Bettina Kümmerling-Meibauer in her entry on Norman Lindsay in *The Oxford Encyclopedia of Children's Literature* (Kümmerling-Meibauer 2006: 448).

21 See Moriarty (2017) for further discussion of 'heroic era' expeditions to the Antarctic in the context of children's literature.

22 The maiden (and final) voyage of the Batavia reportedly came into trouble during its stopover at the Cape of Good Hope. Pelsaert, the ship's commander, fell ill and his indisposition allowed tensions and poor discipline to arise on board. For more information on events leading to the Batavia wreck and massacre see details at the Western Australian Museum: http://museum.wa.gov.au/research/research-areas/maritime-archaeology/batavia-cape-inscription/batavia (accessed 15 October 2019). The aftermath of the shipwreck is also dealt with in Crew's *Stanger Things*, which I discuss in Chapter 1.

23 Etymological details pertaining to 'orientation' can be found under the entry for 'orient' in: Onions (1966: 632).

24 For further discussion of 'Wayfarer's All' see Chapter 4 and endnote 4.12.

25 Ely cathedral is also the site of Peter's encounter with Tom and Hatty in *Tom's Midnight Garden*, marking the point at which Tom must let go his commitment to the garden topos.

5 Nothing Matters: Absent Imaginaries

1 Sartre reflects at length on 'the origin of nothingness' in *Being and Nothingness* [1943] 2003: 45–69.

2 In J. K. Rowling's *Harry Potter and the Philosopher's Stone* (1997), Harry's lightening scar is the only thing he likes 'about his own appearance' and it elicits 'the first question he could ever remember asking his Aunt Petunia' (Rowling 1997: 20). Harry asks how he got the scar – and of course it turns out to be a mark of his parents' death and absence (although Aunt Petunia does not provide him with a full and honest answer).

3 For discussion of *The White Darkness* in the context of nowhere, see Chapter 4.

4 For further discussion of representing real entities, see my discussion of the artistic representation of things in Chapter 2 and also see my discussion of Jacqueline's response to an image of birch trees in Chapter 3.

5 See Chapter 3, 'Childness and Youth' in Hollindale (1997) for an account of problematic adjectival renditions of child experience (44–61).

6 *Calvin and Hobbes* was first published in the United States and syndicated from 18 November 1985 to 31 December 1995. https://publishing.andrewsmcmeel.com/books/comics-and-humor/calvinandhobbes/index.html (accessed 1 October 2019).

7 Such a claim could be made through recourse to the 'zombie problem', which finds that if we can conceive of a physical (live) being without consciousness then we are in the realms of logical possibility. For a full discussion of *phenomenal zombies* and *psychological zombies*, see Chalmers ([1996] 1997: 93–9) and my discussion in relation to *Imaginary Fred* on p. 211.

8 *Imaginary Fred* is not paginated – numbering commences from and is inclusive of the title page.
9 I was not able to secure permission to reproduce illustrations from *Imaginary Fred*, so please refer to a print copy to view the variation in style under discussion. I would have captioned the visual distinction between human and imaginary being as follows: 'Pixilation and solid lines signal an ontic investment in qualia.'

References

Primary sources

Ahlberg, Janet and Ahlberg, Allan. 1984. *The Baby's Catalogue*. London: Penguin. First published 1982.

Alexander, Kwame. 2015. *Crossover*. London: Andersen Press. First published 2014.

Anderson, Matthew Tobin and Hawkes, Kevin. 2007. *Me, All Alone, at the End of the World*. London: Walker Books. First published 2005.

Barker, Cicely Mary. 1974. *Flower Fairies of the Garden*. Glasgow: Blackie & Sons. First published 1944.

Barker, Cicely Mary. 1974. *Flower Fairies of the Wayside*. Glasgow: Blackie & Sons. First published 1948.

Barnett, Mac and Klassen, Jon. 2018. *Triangle*. London: Walker Books. First published 2017.

Bickford-Smith, Coralie. 2016. *The Fox and the Star*. London: Penguin. First published 2015.

Briggs, Raymond. 1994. *The Bear*. London: Julia MacRae.

Brown, Peter. 2018. *The Wild Robot*. London: Piccadilly Press. First published 2016.

Campbell, Marcy and Luyken, Corinna. 2018. *Adrian Simcox Does NOT Have a Horse*. New York: Dial Books.

Carroll, Lewis. 2000. *The Hunting of the Snark*. Illus. Mervyn Peake. London: Methuen. Illustrated edition first published 1941. First published 1876.

Carroll, Lewis. 2006. *The Annotated Hunting of the Snark*. Ed. Martin Gardner. New York: W. W. Norton. Annotated edition first published 1962. First published 1876.

Coleridge, Samuel Taylor. 1997. 'Frost at Midnight'. *The Complete Poems*. Ed. William Keach. London: Penguin. 231–2. Poem first published 1798.

Colfer, Eoin and Jeffers, Oliver. 2016. *Imaginary Fred*. London: HarperCollins. First Published 2015.

Coppo, Marianna. 2018. *Petra*. London: Thames and Hudson. First published in Italian 2016.

Cottrell Boyce, Frank. 2012. *The Unforgotten Coat*. Illus. Carl Hunter and Clare Heney. London: Walker Books. First published 2011.

Crew, Gary. 1991. *Strange Objects*. Port Melbourne, Victoria: Mammoth Australia. First published 1990.

Cross, Gillian. 2001. *A Map of Nowhere*. Oxford: Oxford University Press. First published 1988.
Dahl, Roald. 1973. *James and the Giant Peach*. Illus. Nancy Ekholm Burkert. Harmondsworth: Puffin. First published 1961.
Davies, Nicola and Carlin, Laura. 2018. *King of the Sky*. London: Walker Books. First published 2017.
Deneux, Xavier. 2018. *Jungle Animals*. Paris: Twil/Tourbillon. First published in French 2017.
Doyle, Roddy. 2012. *A Greyhound of a Girl*. London: Marion Lloyd. First published 2011.
Dros, Imme. 1991. *Annelie in the Depths of the Night*. Illus. Margriet Heymans. Trans. Arno and Erica Pomerans. London: Faber and Faber. First published in Dutch 1987.
Ellis, Carson. 2017. *Du Iz Tak?* London: Walker Books. First published 2016.
Ellis, Sarah. 2016. *Outside In*. Toronto: Groundwood Books. First published 2014.
Fox, Mem and Horacek, Judy. 2004. *Where Is the Green Sheep?* Boston, MA: Houghton Mifflin Harcourt.
Fraillon, Zana. 2016. *The Bone Sparrow*. London: Orion Books.
Frost. Robert. 1989. 'Birches'. *The Norton Anthology of American Literature*. New York and London: W.W. Norton. Poem first published 1915.
Gaarder, Jostein. 1996. *Sophie's World*. Trans. Paulette Moller. London: Phoenix. Print. First published in Norwegian 1991.
Garner, Alan. 1976. *The Stone Book*. London: HarperCollins.
Gleeson, Libby and Greder, Armin. 2011. *I Am Thomas*. Crows Nest, NSW: Allen & Unwin.
Grahame, Kenneth. 2010. *The Wind in the Willows*. Ed. Peter Hunt. Oxford: Oxford University Press. First published 1908.
Gulemetova, Maria. 2017. *Beyond the Fence*. Swindon: Child's Play.
Hartnett, Sonya. 2017. *Thursday's Child*. London: Walker Books. First Published 2000.
Hoban, Tana. 1971. *Look Again!* New York: Macmillan.
Hoban, Tana. 1986. *Shapes, Shapes, Shapes*. New York: Greenwillow.
Hoban, Tana. 2017. *Black White*. New York: Greenwillow. First published 1993.
Hopgood, Tim. 2017. *Walter's Wonderful Web*. London: Macmillan. First published 2015.
Jansson, Tove. 1967. *Comet in Moominland*. Trans. Elizabeth Portch. Harmondsworth: Puffin. First published in Swedish 1946.
Jeffers, Oliver. 2007. *The Way Back Home*. London: HarperCollins.
Johnson, Crockett. 2012. *Harold and the Purple Crayon*. London: HarperCollins. First published 1955.
Konigsburg, Elaine Lobl. 2015. *From the Mixed-Up Files of Mrs. Basil E. Frankweiler*. London: Pushkin Children's Books. First published 1967.
Lanagan, Margot. 2010. *Tender Morsels*. London: Vintage. First published 2008.

Lear, Edward. 1992. *A Book of Nonsense*. London: Everyman Library. *A Book of Nonsense* first published 1846 and *Nonsense Songs, Stories, Botany, and Alphabets* first published 1871.

Lindsay, Norman. 1995. *The Magic Pudding: Being the Adventures of Bunyip Bluegum and His Friends Bill Barnacle & Sam Sawnoff*. Sydney: Angus & Robertson. First published 1918.

Lipton, Lenny and Yarrow, Peter. 2008. *Puff, the Magic Dragon*. Illus. Eric Puybaret. London: MacMillan. First published 2007.

McCaughrean, Geraldine. 2006. *The White Darkness*. Oxford: Oxford University Press. First published 2005.

McCaughrean, Geraldine. 2007. *Stop the Train*. Oxford: Oxford University Press. First published 2001.

McCaughrean, Geraldine. 2014. *The Middle of Nowhere*. London: Usborne. First published 2013.

McCaughrean, Geraldine. 2018. *Where the World Ends*. London: Usborne. First published 2017.

Macfarlane, Robert and Morris, Jackie. 2017. *The Lost Words*. London: Hamish Hamilton.

Marshall, James Vance. 2015. *Walkabout*. London: Puffin. First published as *The Children* in 1959.

Martin, Bill, Jr. and Carle, Eric. 1995. *Brown Bear, Brown Bear, What Do You See?* London: Puffin. First published 1984.

Martin, Marc. 2016. *A River*. London: Templar. First published 2015.

Mowat, Farley. 1982. *Lost in the Barrens*. New York: Bantam. First published 1956.

Negrescolor, Joan. 2018. *Animal City*. San Francisco: Chronicle. First published in Portuguese 2017.

Nesbit, Edith. 1996. *The Story of the Amulet*. London: Penguin. First published 1906.

Norton, Mary. 2003. *The Borrowers*. London: Puffin. First published 1952.

Oxenbury, Helen. 1971. *Helen Oxenbury's ABC of Things*. London: Heinemann.

Pearce, Philippa. 2008. *Tom's Midnight Garden*. Oxford: Oxford University Press. First published 1958.

Portis, Antoinette. 2008. *Not a Box*. London: HarperCollins. First published 2006.

Pratchett, Terry. 2001. *The Amazing Maurice and His Educated Rodents*. London: Doubleday.

Reed, Amy. 2017. *The Nowhere Girls*. London: Atom.

Robinson, Joan G. 2014. *When Marnie Was There*. London: HarperCollins. First published 1967.

Rowling, Joanne. 1997. *Harry Potter and the Philosopher's Stone*. London: Bloomsbury.

de Saint-Exupéry, Antoine. 1991. *The Little Prince*. Trans. Katherine Woods. London: Mammoth. First published in French 1943.

Southall, Ivan. 1973. *Josh*. London: Heinemann Educational Books. First published 1971.

Steig, William. 1977. *Abel's Island*. London: Hamish Hamilton. First published 1976.
Stein, Gertrude. 2013. *The World Is Round*. Illus. Clement Hurd. London: HarperCollins. First Published 1939.
Stevenson, Robert Louis. 1953. *Treasure Island*. London: HarperCollins. First published 1883.
Stevenson, Robert Louis. 2014. *Kidnapped*. Ed. Ian Duncan. Oxford: Oxford University Press. First published 1886.
Tan, Shaun. 2007. *The Arrival*. London: Hodder. First published 2006.
Tan, Shaun. 2018. *Tales from the Inner City*. London: Walker Studio.
Tolkien, J. R. R. (1994) *The Lord of the Rings*. London: BCA with HarperCollins. First published in one volume 1968, including: *The Fellowship of the Ring*, 1954; *The Two Towers*, 1954; *The Return of the King*, 1955.
Tomlinson, Jill. 1992. *The Owl Who Was Afraid of the Dark*. London: Mammoth. First published 1968.
Twain, Mark. 2003. *The Adventures of Huckleberry Finn*. Ed. Peter Coveney. London: Penguin. First published 1884.
Vesaas, Tarjei. 2009. *The Ice Palace*. Trans. Peter Owen and Elizabeth Rokkan. London: Peter Owen. First published in Norwegian 1966.
Voigt, Cynthia. 1981. *Homecoming*. New York: Atheneum.
Walsh, Jill Paton. 1987. *Gaffer Samson's Luck*. London: Puffin. First published 1984.
Watterson, Bill. 1997. *It's a Magical World*. London: Warner Books. First published 1996.
Wein, Elizabeth. 2012. *Code Name Verity*. London: Electric Monkey.
White, Elwyn Brooks. 1963. *Charlotte's Web*. Harmonsworth: Penguin. First published 1952.
Wiesner, David. 2012. *Flotsam*. London: Andersen Press. First published 2006.
Wiesner, David. 2015. *David Wiesner's Spot*. Boston, MA: Houghton Mifflin Harcourt.
Wild, Margaret and Brooks, Ron. 2000. *Fox*. Sydney: Allen and Unwin.
Woodson, Jacqueline. 2014. *brown girl dreaming*. New York: Nancy Paulsen Books.
Woodson, Jacqueline. 2017. *Another Brooklyn*. London: Oneworld. First published 2016.
Wordsworth, William. 1986. 'The Prelude or The Growth of a Poet's Mind'. *The Norton Anthology of English Literature, Fifth Edition, Volume 2*. Ed. M. H. Abrams. Anthology first published 1962 and poem first published 1805.

Secondary sources

Allison, Alida. 2000. '"I" of the Beholder: An Interview with Tana Hoban'. *Lion and the Unicorn* 24: 143–9.
Althusser, Louis. 2008. *On Ideology*. London: Verso. First published 1971.

Bachelard, Gaston. 1971. *The Poetics of Reverie: Childhood, Language, and the Cosmos.* Trans. Daniel Russell. Boston: Beacon Press. Translation first published 1969. First published in French 1960.

Bachelard, Gaston. 1994. *The Poetics of Space.* Trans. Maria Jolas. Boston. Beacon Press. Translation first published 1964. First published in French 1958.

Baggini, Julian. 2002. *Philosophy: Key Themes.* Basingstoke: Palgrave Macmillan.

Balmford et al. 2002. 'Why Conservationists Should Heed Pokémon'. *Science.* https://www.researchgate.net/publication/11440003_Why_Conservationists_Should_Heed_Pokemon (accessed 9 August 2019).

Barthes, Roland. 2010. *Camera Lucida: Reflections on Photography.* Trans. Richard Howard. New York: Hill and Wang. First published in French 1980.

Baudrillard, Jean. 2005. *The System of Objects.* Trans. James Benedict. London: Verso. First published in French 1968.

Bazin, André. 2005. 'The Ontology of the Photographic Image'. *What Is Cinema? Vol. 1.* Trans. Hugh Gray. Berkeley: University of California Press, 36–45. First published in French 1945.

Beauvais, Clémentine. 2015. *The Mighty Child: Time and Power in Children's Literature.* Amsterdam: John Benjamins.

de Beauvoir, Simone. 2015. *The Ethics of Ambiguity.* Trans. Bernard Frechtman. New York: Open Road. First published in French 1948.

Berger, John. 2009. 'Why Look at Animals?' *About Looking.* London: Bloomsbury. First published 1980.

Berkeley, George. 2004. 'Selection from Three Dialogues between Hylas and Philonous'. Ed. Tim Crane and Katalin Farkas. *Metaphysics: A Guide and Anthology.* Oxford: Oxford University Press, 77–100.

Bettelheim, Bruno. 1991. *The Uses of Enchantment: The Meaning and Uses of Fairy Tales.* London: Penguin. First published 1976.

Bradford, Clare, Mallan, Kerry, Stephens, John and McCallum, Robyn. 2008. *New World Orders in Contemporary Children's Literature: Utopian Transformations.* Basingstoke: Palgrave MacMillan.

Bravo, Michael. 2019. *North Pole: Nature and Culture.* London: Reaktion Books.

Brooke-Hitching, Edward. 2016. *The Phantom Atlas: The Greatest Myths, Lies and Blunders on Maps.* London: Simon and Schuster.

Brower, Jeffrey. 2010. 'Aristotelian Endurantism: A New Solution to the Problem of Temporary Intrinsics'. *Mind* 119 (476): 883–905. https://doi.org/10.1093/mind/fzq072 (accessed 16 March 2019).

Brown, Bill. 2003. *A Sense of Things.* Chicago: University of Chicago Press.

Brown, Bill. 2015. *Other Things.* Chicago: University of Chicago Press.

Bursztynski, Sue. 2004. 'When a Picture Is Worth a Lot of Words'. *January Magazine.* November 2004. https://www.januarymagazine.com/kidsbooks/whereisgreensheep.html (accessed 14 May 2019).

Carroll, Jane Suzanne. 2014. *Landscape in Children's Literature*. Abingdon: Routledge. First published 2011.

Carroll, Jane Suzanne. Forthcoming. 'Objects and Toys'. *The Cambridge Companion to Children's Literature in English, Volume 2: 1830–1914*. Ed. Eugene Giddens, Zoe Jaques and Louise Joy. Cambridge: Cambridge University Press, n.p.

de Certeau, Michel. 1988. *The Practice of Everyday Life*. Trans. Steven Rendall. Berkeley: University of California Press. Translation first published 1984. First published in French 1980.

Chalmers, David J. 1997. *The Conscious Mind: In Search of a Fundamental Theory*. Oxford. Oxford University Press. First published 1996.

Church, Ellen Booth. 2018. 'Why Colors and Shapes Matter'. New York: Little Scholastic. http://www.scholastic.com/browse/article.jsp?id=3746476 (accessed 19 November 2018).

Cliff Hodges, Gabrielle, Nikolajeva, Maria and Taylor, Liz. 2010. 'Three Walks through the Fictional Fens: Multidisciplinary Perspectives on *Gaffer Samson's Luck*'. *Children's Literature in Education* 41: 189–206.

Close, Frank. 2009. *Nothing: A Very Short Introduction*. Oxford: Oxford University Press. First published as *The Void* in 2007.

Coccia, Emanuele. 2019. *The Life of Plants: A Metaphysics of Mixture*. Trans. Dylan J. Montanari. Cambridge: Polity Press. First published in French 2017.

Crane, Tim and Farkas, Katalin. eds. 2004. *Metaphysics: A Guide and Anthology*. Oxford: Oxford University Press.

Deleuze, Gilles. 2014. *Difference and Repetition*. Trans. Paul Patton. London: Bloomsbury. First published in French 1968.

Deleuze, Gilles and Guattari, Félix. 2013. *A Thousand Plateaus: Capitalism and Schizophrenia*. Trans. Brian Massumi. London: Bloomsbury. First published in French 1980.

Derrida, Jacques. 1984. *Margins of Philosophy*. Trans. Alan Bass. Chicago: University of Chicago Press. First published in French 1972.

Derrida, Jacques. 2008. *The Animal That Therefore I Am*. Trans. David Wills. New York: Fordham University Press. First published in French 2006.

Descartes, René. 2017. *Meditations on First Philosophy with Selections from Objections and Replies*, 2nd edn. Trans. John Cottingham. Cambridge: Cambridge University Press. Translation first published 1986. First published in Latin 1641.

Dobrin, Sidney I. and Kidd, Kenneth B. 2004. *Wild Things: Children's Culture and Ecocriticism*. Detroit: Wayne State University Press.

Duschinsky, Robert. 2012. '*Tabula Rasa* and Human Nature'. *Philosophy* 87 (342): 509–29.

Eagleton, Terry. 2015. 'Utopias, Past and Present: Why Thomas More's Remains Astonishingly Radical'. *Guardian*, 16 October 2015. https://www.theguardian.com/books/2015/oct/16/utopias-past-present-thomas-more-terry-eagleton (accessed 20 October 2019).

Effingham, Nikk. 2013. *An Introduction to Ontology*. Cambridge: Polity Press.
Evans, Gareth. 2004. 'Can There Be Vague Objects?' Ed. Tim Crane and Katalin Farkas, Katalin. *Metaphysics: A Guide and Anthology*. Oxford: Oxford University Press, 209.
Everett, Anthony. 2013. *The Nonexistent*. Oxford: Oxford University Press.
Frank, Priscilla. 2017. 'Meet the Queer, Anti-Fascist Author Behind the Freakishly Lovable "Moomins"'. *Huffpost*, 14 September 2017. https://www.huffingtonpost.co.uk/entry/tove-jansson-moomins-cartoon_us_59b94115e4b086432b0361c3?guccounter=1 (accessed 15 March 2018).
Fuller, Benjamin Apthorp Gould. 1949. 'The Messes Animals Make in Metaphysics'. *Journal of Philosophy* 46 (26): 829–38.
Gadamer, Hans-Georg. 2004. *Truth and Method, Second Revised Edition*. Trans. Joel Weinsheimer and Donald G. Marshall. New York: Continuum. First published in German in 1960.
Gazi, Andromache. 2014. 'Exhibition Ethics – An Overview of Major Issues'. *Journal of Conservation and Museum Studies* 12 (1): 4. https://www.jcms-journal.com/articles/10.5334/jcms.177/ (accessed 1 December 2018).
Genette, Gérard. 1983. *Narrative Discourse: An Essay in Method*. Trans. Jane E. Lewin. Ithaca, NY: Cornell University Press. Translation first published 1980. First published in French 1972.
Gombrich, Ernst H. 1981. 'Image and Code: Scope and Limits of Conventionalism in Pictorial Representation'. *Image and Code*. Ed. Wendy Steiner. Ann Arbor: Michigan Slavic, 11–42.
Graham, Judith. 2014. 'Reading Contemporary Picturebooks'. *Modern Children's Literature: An Introduction*, 2nd edn. Ed. Catherine Butler and Kimberley Reynolds. Basingstoke: Palgrave Macmillan, 54–69. First edition published 2005.
Grenby, Matthew. 2016. 'Thomas Spence, Children's Literature and "Learning … Debauched by Tradition"'. *Liberty, Property and Popular Politics: England and Scotland, 1688–1815. Essays in Honour of H. T. Dickinson*. Ed. Gordon Pentland and Michael T. Davis. Edinburgh: Edinburgh University Press, 131–46.
Gruen, Lori, ed. 2018. *Critical Terms for Animal Studies*. Chicago: University of Chicago Press.
Haraway, Donna J. 2000. *How Like a Leaf: An Interview with Thyrza Nichols Goodeve*. London: Routledge.
Haraway, Donna J. 2004. *A Manifesto for Cyborgs: Science, Technology, and Socialist Feminism in the 1980s*. London: Routledge. First published 1985.
Haraway, Donna J. 2006. 'When We Have Never Been Human, What Is To Be Done?' *Theory, Culture, and Society* 23 (7–8): 135–58.
Haraway, Donna J. 2016. *Staying with the Trouble: Making Kin in the Chthulucene*. Durham, NC: Duke University Press.
Harju, Maija-Lissa and Rouse, Dawn. 2018. '"Keeping Some Wildness Always Alive": Posthumanism and the Animality of Children's Literature and Play'. *Children's Literature in Education* 49: 447–66.

Hegel, Georg Wilhelm Friedrich. 2008. *Outlines of the Philosophy of Right*. Trans. T. M. Knox. Ed. Stephen Houlgate. Oxford: Oxford University Press. Translation first published 1952. First published in German 1821.

Heidegger, Martin. 1967. *What Is a Thing?* Trans. W. B. Barton Jr. and Vera Deutsch. South Bend, IN: Regnery/Gateway. First presented as a lecture in German 1935–6.

Heidegger, Martin. 1975. 'The Origin of the Work of Art'. *Poetry, Language, Thought*. Trans. Albert Hofstadter. London: Harper and Row, 15–87. First presented as a lecture in1935 and published in German 1950.

Heidegger, Martin. 1996. *Being and Time*. Trans. Joan Stambaugh. Albany: University of New York Press. First published in German 1927.

Heidegger, Martin. 1998. 'Letter on "Humanism"'. Trans. Frank A. Capuzzi. *Pathworks*. Ed. William McNeill. Cambridge: Cambridge University Press. Collection first published in German 1967 and essay first published in German 1946.

Hirsch, Julia. 1983–4. 'Photography in Children's Books: A Generic Approach'. *Lion and the Unicorn* 7–8: 140–55.

Hollindale, Peter. 1997. *Signs of Childness in Children's Books*. Stroud: Thimble Press.

Howick, Doug. 2011. 'A Perfect and Absolute Mystery'. *Knight Letter*. Winter 2011. Vol. II, Issue 17. No. 87: 5–13.

Hunt, Peter. 2018. *The Making of the Wind in the Willows*. Oxford: Bodleian Library.

Jackson, Rosemary. 1988. *Fantasy: The Literature of Subversion*. London: Routledge. First published 1981.

Jaques, Zoe. 2018. *Children's Literature and the Posthuman: Animal, Environment, Cyborg*. Abingdon: Routledge. First published 2015.

Kant, Immanuel. 2007. *Critique of Pure Reason*. ed. and trans. Marcus Weigelt. London: Penguin. First published in German 1781, 1787.

Kokkola, Lydia. 2013. *Fictions of Adolescent Carnality: Sexy Sinners and Delinquent Deviants*. Amsterdam: John Benjamins.

Kripke, Saul A. 1980. *Naming and Necessity*. Cambridge, MA: Harvard University Press. First published 1972.

Kristeva, Julia. 1982. *Powers of Horror: An Essay in Abjection*. Trans. Leon S. Roudiez. New York: Columbia University Press. First published 1980.

Kümmerling-Meibauer, Bettina. 2006. 'Norman Lindsay'. *The Oxford Encyclopedia of Children's Literature*. Ed. Jack Zipes et al. Oxford: Oxford University Press, 448.

Lees, Stella and Macintyre, Pam. 2006. 'Gary Crew'. *The Oxford Encyclopedia of Children's Literature: Volume 1*. Ed. Jack Zipes. Oxford: Oxford University Press, 363.

Leopold, Aldo. 1968. *A Sand County Almanac: And Sketches Here and There*. Oxford: Oxford University Press. First Published 1949.

Levinas, Emmanuel. 2006. *Humanism of the Other*. Trans. Nidra Poller. Urbana: University of Illinois Press. Translation first published 2003. First published in French 1972.

Lewis, David. 1986. *On the Plurality of Worlds*. Oxford: Blackwell.

Lewis, David. 2002. *Convention: A Philosophical Study*. Oxford: Blackwell. First published 1969.

Liebregts, Peter. 2010. 'Forward'. *The Literary Utopias of Cultural Communities 1790–1910*. Ed. Marguérite Corporaal and Evert Jan Van Leewen. Amsterdam: Rodopi, 1–8.

Locke, John. 2004. *An Essay Concerning Human Understanding*. London: Penguin. Print. This edition first published 1997. First published 1690.

Lycan, William. 2014. 'The Intentionality of Smell'. *Frontiers in Psychology* 5: 436. https://www.ncbi.nlm.nih.gov/pmc/articles/PMC4034408/ (accessed 10 February 2018).

MacDonald, A. J. et al. (1995). 'Regeneration by natural layering of heather (*Calluna vulgaris*): frequency and characteristics in upland Britain'. *Journal of Applied Ecology*. 32, 85–99.

Macfarlane, Robert. 2013. *The Old Ways: A Journey on Foot*. London: Penguin. First published 2012.

Macfarlane, Robert. 2015. *Landmarks*. London: Hamish Hamilton.

Macfarlane, Robert. 2017. 'Badger or Bulbasaur – Have Children Lost Touch with Nature?' *Guardian*. https://www.theguardian.com/books/2017/sep/30/robert-macfarlane-lost-words-children-nature (accessed 1 August 2019).

Macfarlane, Robert. 2019. 'How the Lost Words Became Songs to Save the Countryside'. *Guardian*. https://www.theguardian.com/music/2019/jan/16/spell-songs-robert-macfarlane-the-lost-words-vanishing-nature-folk-musicians (accessed 8 August 2019).

MacLachlan, Christopher. n.d. 'A Teller of Tales: Further Thoughts on Robert Louis Stevenson's *Kidnapped*'. *The Association of Scottish Literary Studies*. https://asls.arts.gla.ac.uk/Kidnapped.html (accessed 27 October 2019).

Merleau-Ponty, Maurice. 2012. *Phenomenology of Perception*. Trans. Donald A. Landes. Abongdon: Routledge. First published in French 1945.

Midgley, Mary. 1983. *Animals and Why They Matter: A Journey around the Species Barrier*. Harmondsworth: Penguin.

Mitchell, William, J. T. 1987. *Iconology: Image, Text, Ideology*. Chicago: University of Chicago Press. First published 1986.

Moriarty, Sinéad. 2017. 'Unstable Space: Mapping the Antarctic for Children in "Heroic Era" Antarctic Literature'. *Children's Literature in Education* 46: 56–72.

Murdoch, Iris. 2001. *The Sovereignty of Good*. London: Routledge. First published 1970.

Nikolajeva, Maria. 2006. 'Mary Norton'. *The Oxford Encyclopedia of Children's Literature: Volume 3*. Ed. Jack Zipes. Oxford: Oxford University Press, 175–7.

Nikolajeva, Maria and Scott, Carole. 2006. *How Picturebooks Work*. London: Routledge. First published 2001.

Nikolajeva, Maria. 2010. *Power, Voice and Subjectivity in Literature for Young Readers*. New York: Routledge.

Nodelman, Perry. 2008. *The Hidden Adult: Defining Children's Literature*. Baltimore: Johns Hopkins University Press.

Onions, Charles Talbut, ed. 1966. *The Oxford Dictionary of English Etymology*. Oxford: Oxford University Press.

Orwell, George. 2013. 'Opinion'. *Guardian*. 27 January 2013. First published 1948. https://www.theguardian.com/commentisfree/2013/jan/27/george-orwell-assesses-oscar-wilde-socialism (accessed 29 September 2019).

Pauli, Michelle. 2011. 'Allan Ahlberg – a Life in Writing'. *Guardian*. 30 April 2011. https://www.theguardian.com/culture/2011/apr/30/allan-ahlberg-life-in-writing (accessed 11 March 2019).

Piaget, Jean. 1954. *The Construction of Reality in the Child*. Abingdon: Routledge.

Plato. 1987. *The Republic*, rev. edn. Trans. Desmond Lee. London: Penguin. Translation first published 1955; first written *c*.375 BC.

Plumwood, Val. 2002. *Environmental Culture: The Ecological Crisis of Reason*. Abingdon: Routledge.

Probyn-Rapsey, Fiona. 2018. 'Anthropocentrism'. *Critical Terms for Animal Studies*. Ed. Lori Gruen. Chicago: University of Chicago Press, 81–109.

Quine, Willard Van Orman. 1980. 'On What There Is'. *From a Logical Point of View: Nine Logico-Philosophical Essays*. Harvard: Harvard University Press. Anthology first published 1953 and essay first published 1948.

Rahn, Suzanne. 1985. 'News from E. Nesbit: The Story of the Amulet and the Socialist Utopia'. *English Literature in Transition, 1880–1920*, 28(2): 124–44.

Rovetto, Robert J. 2011. 'The Shape of Shapes: An Ontological Exploration'. *CEUR Workshop Proceedings*. Ed. Janna Hastings, Oliver Kutz, Mehul Bhatt and Stefano Borgo. Volume 812, n.p.

Rustin, Margaret and Rustin, Michael. 2001. *Narratives of Love and Loss: Studies in Modern Children's Fiction – Revised Edition*. London: Karnac Books. First published 1987.

Sainsbury, Lisa. 2013. *Ethics in British Children's Literature: Unexamined Life*. London: Bloomsbury.

Sartre, Jean-Paul. 2003. *Being and Nothingness: An Essay on Phenomenological Ontology*. Trans. Mary Warnock. London: Routledge. First published in French 1943.

Sartre, Jean-Paul. 2008. 'Existentialism is a Humanism'. *The Study of Philosophy, 6th Edition*. Ed. S. Morris Engel and Angelika Soldan. Lanham: Rowman & Littlefield. First published 1946.

Schulman, Arthur. 1983. 'Maps and Memorability'. *The Acquisition of Symbolic Skills*. Ed. Don R. Rogers and John A. Sloboda. New York: Plenum Press. First published 1982.

Soper, Kate. 1995. *What Is Nature?* Oxford: Blackwell.

Spence, Thomas. 1982. 'The Rights of Infants'. *Pigs' Meat: Selected Writings of Thomas Spence*. Ed. G. I. Gallop. Nottingham: Spokesman, 114–26. First published 1797.

Stefansson, Vilhjalmur. 1921. *The Friendly Arctic*. Tronoto: Macmillan.

Stephens, John. 1992. *Language and Ideology in Children's Fiction*. Harlow: Longman.
Sudjic, Deyan. 2009. *The Language of Things*. London: Penguin. First published 2008.
Sundmark, Böjrn. 2014. '"A Serious Game": Mapping Moominland'. *Lion and the Unicorn* 38 (2): 162–81.
Suojanen, Mika. 2015. 'A Direct Object of Perception'. *Electronic Journal for Philosophy* 22 (1): 28–36.
Tan, Shaun. n.d. a. 'Commentary on Tales from the Inner City: Bee'. https://www.shauntan.net/tfic-notes (accessed 12 October 2020).
Tan, Shaun. n.d. b. 'Commentary on Tales from the Inner City: Butterflies'. https://www.shauntan.net/tfic-notes (accessed 12 October 2020).
Tan, Shaun. n.d. c. 'The Arrival'. https://www.shauntan.net/arrival-book (accessed 17 October 2020).
Teichman, Jenny and Evans, Katherine C. 1999. *Philosophy: A Beginner's Guide*, 3rd edn. Oxford: Blackwell. First published 1991.
Time. 1999. 'The Ultimate Game Freak'. *Time*. http://content.time.com/time/magazine/article/0,9171,2040095,00.html (accessed 4 August 2019).
Tolkien, J. R. R. 1947. 'On Fairy-Stories'. *Essays Presented to Charles Williams*. Ed. C. S. Lewis. London: Oxford University Press.
V&A 2019. 'Building the Museum'. https://www.vam.ac.uk/articles/building-the-museum (accessed 30 June 2019).
Varzi, Achille. 2001. 'Philosophical Issues in Geography – An Introduction'. *Topoi* 20: 119–30.
Waller, Alison. 2010. *Constructing Adolescence in Fantastic Realism*. London: Routledge. First published 2009.
Waller, Alison. 2019. *Rereading Children's Books: A Poetics*. London: Bloomsbury.
Weil, Kari. 2018. 'Difference'. *Critical Terms for Animal Studies*. Ed. Lori Gruen. Chicago: University of Chicago Press, 188–207.
Wilde, Oscar. 1909. *The Soul of Man under Socialism*. London: Arthur L. Humphreys. First published 1891.

Index

absent parents 187–200
    parental dispatch 195–7
    parental ghosting 187–94
    vague absence 197–200
aetonormativity 8–9, 76, 89, 97, 191, 197, 199 (*see also* Nikolajeva)
again-ness 65–8
Ahlberg, Janet and Allan
    The Baby's Catalogue 56–64, 83, 89
Alexander, Kwame
    Crossover 200
Althusser, Louis
    On Ideology 157
Anderson, M. T. and Kevin Hawkes
    Me, All Alone, at the End of the World 22–3
Antarctic and Arctic Exploration 160–2, 164–9, 172–5, 178
anthropomorphism 18, 45, 82, 88, 101, 107, 124, 12–19, 133, 156, 169
astonishment of being 1–7
authority (adult) 3, 89–91, 109, 133, 191, 200–1

baby books 12, 56–7, 59–61, 64, 69–73, 77–80, 83–4, 86, 89, 202, 214
Bachelard, Gaston
    The Poetics of Reverie 2, 7–8, 11, 19–23, 25, 34, 49, 93–6, 103, 109–10, 135, 138–41, 143–8, 151, 156, 163, 167, 169, 172, 184, 188, 192, 197, 200, 203, 213–14
    The Poetics of Space 27, 68, 170
Barker, Cicely Mary
    Flower Fairies of the Garden 105
    Flower Fairies of the Wayside 104–5, 224 n.10
Barnett, Mac and Jon Klassen
    Triangle 80–3
Barthes, Roland
    Camera Lucida 69

Baudrillard, Jean
    The System of Objects 72–3
Bazin, André
    'The Ontology of the Photographic Image' 69
Beauvais, Clémentine
    The Mighty Child 3, 8, 19, 76, 97, 100, 142, 188–9, 196
de Beauvoir, Simone
    The Ethics of Ambiguity 44
becoming 12, 27, 91, 93, 95, 97, 100, 102, 109, 115–16, 120, 122–3, 128–32
being
    animal 58, 94, 97, 102, 114–15, 117–23, 128, 131–3, 145, 147, 153, 161
    for 22–3, 29, 33, 35–6, 40–3, 49, 51–3, 146, 148, 192, 197
    with 19–20, 22–3, 25, 35–6, 41–5, 51–3, 58, 97, 99, 118–20, 132, 146, 148, 196
    within 138–9, 141, 145–6, 148–51, 156–7, 160, 163, 169–70, 172, 183, 186
Berger, John
    'Why Look at Animals?' 121–2
Berkeley, George 10, 117
Bettelheim, Bruno
    The Uses of Enchantment 48
Bickford-Smith, Coralie
    The Fox and the Star 107–8
biosphere 91, 107, 112–13, 123, 143, 161
    biotic community/teamwork 100–2, 106–7, 109–14, 116, 120–1, 125, 129–31, 202 (*see also* Leopold)
Bradford, Clare et al.
    New World Orders 101, 143, 162, 164, 167
Bravo, Michael
    North Pole: Nature and Culture 161–2
Briggs, Raymond
    The Bear 201

The Snowman 208
Brooke-Hitching, Edward
  The Phantom Atlas 177, 226 n.12
Brown, Bill (*see also* thingness)
  A Sense of Things 50
  Other Things 53, 57–9, 63–5, 68, 71, 73, 75, 82–4, 87–90, 204
Brown, Peter
  The Wild Robot 126–33

Campbell, Marcy and Corinna Luyken
  Adrian Simcox Does NOT Have a Horse 109–11
Carroll, Jane Suzanne
  Landscape in Children's Literature 139, 184–5
  'Objects and Toys' 58–9, 220 n.8
Carroll, Lewis 162
  The Annotated Hunting of the Snark (ed. Martin Gardner) 164–5
  The Hunting of the Snark 163–8, 177
de Certeau, Michel
  The Practice of Everyday Life 157–60, 198–200
Chalmers, David
  The Conscious Mind 202, 206, 210–11, 228 n.7
child/childhood
  becoming 12, 97–8, 100, 109, 111, 113–14, 189, 191, 197, 200, 202, 204, 214
  might 3, 5, 7–11, 25, 76, 89, 97, 100, 133, 137, 142–3, 151–2, 155, 162–3, 167, 182, 185, 188, 194, 196, 199–200 (*see also* Beauvais)
  potential 1–3, 11, 45, 51, 60–1, 64, 76, 83, 93, 97, 100, 142–3, 152, 155, 162–3, 173, 186, 188, 201
  reverie 1–3, 7, 21–3, 25–6, 49, 93–6, 107, 109–11, 116, 134, 139–41, 151–2, 156–7, 167, 186, 188, 200, 203–4, 214
  solitude 8, 20–6, 32, 34–6, 40, 42–3, 45, 49, 67, 216
childness 2–3, 5, 7, 11, 16, 27, 73, 75–6, 100, 137, 160, 189, 190, 194 (*see also* Hollindale)
Close, Frank
  Nothing 45

Coccia
  The Life of Plants 102–7, 110–11, 113, 116, 202, 213
Coleridge, Samuel Taylor
  'Frost at Midnight' 109, 224 n.15
Colfer, Eoin and Oliver Jeffers
  Imaginary Fred 189, 201, 208–11
convention 7, 12, 28, 30, 56, 70, 81–2, 84, 114, 128, 188, 195–6, 205, 208–11, 214–15
Coppo, Marianna
  Petra 83
Cottrell Boyce, Frank
  The Unforgotten Coat 149, 151
Crane, Tim and Katalin Farkas
  Metaphysics 4–5, 9, 38, 55
Crew, Gary
  Strange Objects 89–91, 223 n.31
Cross, Gillian
  A Map of Nowhere 182

Dahl, Roald
  James and the Giant Peach 189, 194–7
Da-sein 3, 16, 122–3, 155, 160, 163, 171, 174–5, 183, 186, 206–7, 216, 219 n.17 (*see also* Heidegger)
Davies, Nicola and Laura Carlin
  King of the Sky 149, 151
Deleuze, Gilles
  Difference and Repetition 136–7, 142
  and Félix Guattari
    assemblage 64, 97–100, 102–3, 110, 112–13, 116, 172, 215
    rhizome 12, 91, 96–9, 102, 111–12, 125, 127–9, 136, 152, 201, 214
    roots 93–9, 101, 109, 111–12, 123, 129, 131, 214
    A Thousand Plateaus 64, 96–8, 100–2, 105, 111–13, 116, 128, 145, 149, 163, 169, 201, 214–15
Deneux, Xavier
  Jungle Animals 71
Derrida, Jacques
  The Animal That Therefore I Am 94, 114–15, 117–23, 128, 132, 152–3
  Margins of Philosophy 37–41
Descartes, René
  Meditations 32
différance 37–41, 44 (*see also* Derrida)

Doyle, Roddy
   A Greyhound of a Girl 36–9, 41, 44
Dros, Imme
   Annelie in the Depths of the Night 189, 197–9

eco-criticism 28, 71, 101–2, 121, 125–7, 143, 160–1, 171
Effingham, Nikk
   An Introduction to Ontology 18, 78–9, 81, 95, 138
Ellis, Carson
   Du Iz Tak? 124
Ellis, Sarah
   Outside In 138, 157–60
endurantism 31
   perduration 31
epistemology 9, 12, 56, 71, 77, 84, 86–9, 94, 107, 113, 116, 128
equivalence 61–2, 70–1
Everett, Anthony
   The Nonexistent 78, 202, 205, 211
existentialism 19, 23, 30, 34–5, 39, 41, 44, 49, 51–3, 151, 189, 191–2, 194, 196, 209, 219 n.20

fable 62, 107–8, 128–9, 145, 149, 152–3
fancy stuff 73–6, 85
flora and fauna 12, 9–91, 94, 97–100, 102, 108–9, 112, 114, 120, 126, 130, 133, 161, 214, 223 n.31
Fox, Mem and Judy Horacek
   Where is the Green Sheep? 77–80
Fraillon, Zana
   The Bone Sparrow 189, 201–8, 213
Frost, Robert
   'Birches' 94–5, 98
Fuller, Benjamin
   'The Messes Animals Make in Metaphysics' 12, 94, 117–18, 124, 126, 128
fuzzy mountains 1, 4–7, 9, 179–80, 216
   (*see also* ontological vagueness)

Gaarder, Jostein
   Sophie's World 7, 9–11
Gadamer, Hans-Georg
   Truth and Method 66–7, 73, 91
gallery of false principles 83–4, 88, 91
   (*see also* museology)

Garner, Alan
   The Stone Book 15–17, 19, 36, 38, 91, 213
generative 209, 214–15
   visualization 216
Gleeson, Libby and Armin Greder
   I Am Thomas 149, 151–2
Gombrich, Ernst
   'Image and Code' 70–1
Graham, Judith 56
Grahame, Kenneth
   The Wind in the Willows 155–7, 169, 177, 226 n.12
Grenby, Matthew 142–4, 226 nn.4, 6
Gulemetova, Maria
   Beyond the Fence 118–20, 213

handiness 61–2, 64–6, 68, 73, 88, 90–1
   (*see also* Heidegger)
Haraway, Donna
   How Like a Leaf 11, 213–15
   A Manifesto for Cyborgs 94, 111, 115, 117–18, 126–7, 129–31
   'When We Have Never Been Human, What Is to Be Done?' 115, 127–8
Hartnett, Sonya
   Thursday's Child 187–94, 213
Hegel, Georg Wilhelm Friedrich
   Outlines of the Philosophy of Right 49
Heidegger, Martin
   Being and Time 2, 20, 29, 31, 38, 61, 85–6, 123, 155, 163, 183, 186
   'Letter on "Humanism"' 52
   'The origin of the work of art' 41, 58, 63–4
   What Is a Thing? 61–2, 65, 68, 73–8, 81, 88, 90
Hoban, Tana
   Black White 69–72
   Look Again! 65–9
   Shapes, Shapes, Shapes 71
Hollindale, Peter
   Signs of Childness in Children's Books 2–3, 16, 20, 75
Hopgood, Tim
   Walter's Wonderful Web 77
humanism 1, 19, 22, 29, 35, 46–7, 51–2, 117
Hunt, Peter 156

imaginary friends 12–13, 21,
    188–9, 200–12
immersion 52, 97, 102–3, 105–7, 109,
    111–17, 120, 126, 130–2, 202
    (*see also* Coccia)

Jackson, Rosemary
    Fantasy: The Literature of
        Subversion 27, 29
Jaques, Zoe
    Children's Literature and the Posthuman
        94, 98, 118, 126
Jansson, Tove
    Comet in Moominland 1–7, 43–5, 213,
        216, 217 n.4
Jeffers, Oliver (*see also* Colfer)
    The Way Back Home 21–3, 36, 39–42
Johnson, Crockett
    Harold and the Purple Crayon 77, 216

Kant, Immanuel 121, 222 n.28
    Critique of Pure Reason 222 n.25
    Ding an sich 74
    Ding für uns 74
    transcendental idealism 80, 222 n.25
Kokkola, Lydia
    Fictions of Adolescent Carnality 97–8,
        219 n.26
Konigsburg, E. L.
    From the Mixed-Up Files of Mrs. Basil
        E. Frankweiler 84–9
Kripke, Saul
    Naming and Necessity 81–3
Kristeva, Julia
    Powers of Horror 46–7, 219 n.26

Lanagan, Margot
    Tender Morsels 43, 46–9, 182, 219 n.26,
        220 n.27
Lear, Edward
    A Book of Nonsense 162–3, 168–9
Leopold, Aldo
    A Sand County Almanac 100–1, 107,
        113, 121, 161
Levinas, Emmanuel
    Humanism of the Other 15, 17–19, 22–3,
        25, 27, 29–30, 33, 35, 37, 40–1,
        43–4, 46–7, 51–2, 146–9, 207
Lewis, David

On the Plurality of Worlds 5, 31, 38, 81
Convention: A Philosophical Study
    211, 214
limitrophy 94, 118–20, 122 (*see also*
    Derrida)
Lindsay, Norman
    The Magic Pudding 138, 162, 168–9
line of flight 145–7, 163, 172 (*see also*
    Deleuze and Guattari)
Locke, John
    An Essay Concerning Human
        Understanding 10, 67–70

McCaughrean, Geraldine
    The Middle of Nowhere 141, 175
    Where the World Ends 175
    The White Darkness 162, 172–4, 201
    Stop the Train 171–2
Macfarlane, Robert
    and Jackie Morris
        The Lost Words 99–101, 103, 120–6,
            223 n.8, 225 n.24 (*see also* Morris)
    Landmarks 120, 122
    The Old Ways 176–7, 183, 188
mapping 12, 135–6, 152–3, 155–8, 160,
    164–7, 171, 174, 176–86, 217 n.4,
    226 n.12, 227 n.18
Marshall, James Vance
    Walkabout 111–16, 223 n.31, 224 nn.16,
        17, 225 n.19
Martin, Bill, Jr. and Eric Carle
    Brown Bear, Brown Bear, What Do
        You See? 77
Martin, Marc
    A River 102, 108
Merleau-Ponty, Maurice
    Phenomenology of Perception 26–7,
        46–8, 52
metaphor 5, 7, 11, 18, 22, 34, 41, 87, 95,
    106, 158, 160, 172, 201, 213–14
metaphoric transfer 10–11, 17, 174
Midgley, Mary
    Animals and Why They Matter 117,
        121
might (*see* child/childhood might)
miniature 24, 27–8, 30, 111, 117, 170–1
Mitchell, William, J. T.
    Iconology 70, 221 n.13
Moriarty, Sinéad 164, 167, 227 nn.17, 21

Morris, Jackie
  The Lost Words 99–101, 103, 120–6, 223 n.7 (*see also* Macfarlane)
Mowat, Farley
  Lost in the Barrens 101
Murdoch, Iris
  The Sovereignty of Good 11, 213
Museology 83–91

Negrescolor, Joan
  Animal City 102, 108–9
Nesbit, Edith
  The Story of the Amulet 154–5
nihilation 46, 48, 190, 192–3, 195
Nikolajeva, Maria 183
  and Carole Scott
    How Picturebooks Work 208
    Power, Voice and Subjectivity 8–9, 76, 89, 97, 191, 197, 199
Nodelman, Perry
  The Hidden Adult 8, 98
Norton, Mary
  The Borrowers 8, 24–30, 35, 111
nothing 11–12, 25, 34, 38–9, 41–2, 45–6, 74–5, 88, 90, 136, 148, 156, 159, 161, 165, 167, 174, 176–7, 184, 187–93, 196–7, 201, 204, 209, 211–12, 214, 216
nowhere 8, 11–12, 135–86
  belonging not where 138, 141–53
  here and now 153–60
  in extremis 160–75, 201
  in the middle of 90, 175–86

object 5, 10–13, 30–2, 38, 50, 56–61, 63–76, 78–9, 81–91, 94, 102, 105–6, 120, 125, 141, 143, 149–50, 152, 159, 185, 189, 192, 204–5
ontological
  commitment 56–7, 68, 71, 77–84, 94, 108, 207
  edification 138, 141, 146, 156, 172
  exchange 8, 11, 15–53, 56, 67, 86, 91, 102, 160, 187, 196, 207, 214
    abusive 46
    epiphanic 19, 36, 43, 52–3, 111, 171
    genial 36–7, 39, 43
    negatively charged 21, 43, 46, 50

oscillation 16, 28, 58, 68, 87, 140, 164, 183, 188, 200–12
  positively charged 36, 41–2
  reciprocal 18, 24, 26, 33, 36, 40–1
  satiric 44–5
  vagueness 1, 4–5, 7, 63, 165, 167, 170, 177, 179–81, 186, 198–200, 206, 215, 217 n.4
Oxenbury, Helen
  Helen Oxenbury's ABC of Things 56

pastoral 94, 97–9, 109, 111, 214
Pearce, Philippa
  Tom's Midnight Garden 24, 30–6
Piaget, Jean
  The Construction of Reality in the Child 57–9, 68
plant-life 94, 99, 102–5, 107, 109–11, 124, 128, 133, 161, 171
Plumwood, Val
  Environmental Culture 121
Pokémon 125–6, 225 n.26
pole(s) of inaccessibility 12, 136, 160–75
Portis, Antoinette
  Not a Box 75–6
posthumanism 94, 97, 118, 126–33
Pratchett, Terry
  The Amazing Maurice and his Educated Rodents 133
Puff, the Magic Dragon 55, 73–5, 221 n.17

qualia 13, 189, 206–7, 209–10
Quine, Willard Van Orman
  'On What There Is' 5, 55–7, 59, 61, 72, 77, 79, 85, 95, 104, 106, 202

Reed, Amy
  The Nowhere Girls 141, 182–3
representation
  contour 69–71, 81
  photography 65–6, 68–9, 71, 107, 149, 151, 203
  poetry 11, 93–6
rigid designator 81–3 (*see also* Kripke)
Robinson, Joan G.
  When Marnie Was There 36, 41–3
Rustin, Margaret and Michael
  Narratives of Love and Loss 24

de Saint-Exupéry, Antoine
  The Little Prince 7, 21–2, 188
Sartre, Jean-Paul
  Being and Nothingness 16, 18–20, 29, 33–5, 39, 41–2, 46, 51, 187–94, 196–7, 209
  'Existentialism is a Humanism' 51
Schulman, Arthur
  'Maps and Memorability' 176–7, 184
solidity 67–8, 70, 80
solitude (*see* child/childhood)
somewhere 84, 135–41, 144–53, 156–67, 169–72, 174, 176–8, 180–1, 183–4, 186, 216
Soper, Kate
  What Is Nature? 131
Southall, Ivan
  Josh 23, 43, 49–53
Spence, Thomas
  'The Rights of Infants' 142–4, 152, 226 nn.4, 6
Stefansson, Vilhjalmur
  The Friendly Arctic 160–3, 165, 167, 169–70, 172, 174
Steig, William
  Abel's Island 156, 162, 169–71
Stein, Gertrude
  The World Is Round 215–16
Stephens, John
  Language and Ideology in Children's Fiction 19, 36, 40
Stevenson, Robert Louis
  Kidnapped 180–1
  Treasure Island 59, 180–1
Sudjic, Deyan
  The Language of Things 70, 72
surface grammer 18, 55, 78–9, 81, 95, 138

Tan, Shaun
  The Arrival 149–51
  Tales from the Inner City 103–4, 107, 115–17, 124, 133–4
territory 145, 147, 156, 163, 167–9, 172, 178, 184, 202, 214–16
thingness 12, 58–61, 63, 65–6, 68, 71–6, 82–91, 94, 102, 150, 157, 204, 214–15 (*see also* Brown; Heidegger)
thrownness 20, 45, 65, 69, 76, 86, 98, 135, 139, 163, 173, 188, 196–7, 216
Tolkien, J. R. R.
  'On Fairy-Stories' 169

Tomlinson, Jill
  The Owl Who Was Afraid of the Dark 18–19
Twain, Mark
  The Adventures of Huckleberry Finn 176

utopia 8, 12, 22, 136–7, 141–4, 149, 152–60, 162, 171, 175, 206

Varzi, Achille 4, 178–9, 181
Vesaas, Tarjei
  The Ice Palace 135–41, 148, 167
Voigt, Cynthia
  Homecoming 189, 199–200

wait 60, 83
Waller, Alison
  Constructing Adolescence in Fantastic Realism 218 n.11
  Rereading Children's Books 115
Walsh, Jill Paton
  Gaffer Samson's Luck 183–6
Watterson, Bill
  Calvin and Hobbes 204–5
Wein, Elizabeth
  Code Name Verity 178–9
whereness 144, 158, 170, 176–7, 179–85
  awareness of whereness 12, 136, 174, 175
  whereness of self-awareness 177–8, 180–3, 186
White, E. B.
  Charlotte's Web 43, 45–6
Wiesner, David
  Flotsam 106–7
  Spot 125–6
Wild, Margaret and Ron Brooks
  Fox 138, 144–9
Wilde, Oscar
  The Soul of Man Under Socialism 153–4, 162, 226 n.11, 227 n.13
Woodson, Jacqueline
  Another Brooklyn 200
  brown girl dreaming 8–10, 17–18, 43, 93–8, 213–14, 218 n.2
Wordsworth, William
  'The Prelude' 23, 218 n.10

zombie problem 211, 228 n.7 (*see also* Chalmers)

www.ingramcontent.com/pod-product-compliance
Lightning Source LLC
Chambersburg PA
CBHW050324020526
44117CB00031B/1767